Becoming

THE ONE

ONE WITH GOD, ONE IN MARRIAGE

Dear Claire,
   May your future marriage
glorify God. He loves you
with an infinite, everlasting love.

   Abundant blessings,

   Salomé Roat

   Js. 1:17

A Guide for Becoming Healthy and Whole
for Your Future Spouse

SALOMÉ ROAT

Cover Design: © Cristian Canelos/Trace Chiodo
Interior Design: © Cristian Canelos
Cover and Interior Photography: © Natalie McMullin

ISBN-13: 978-0692972113 ISBN-10: 0692972110

Printed in the United States of America.

For additional information on this topic and others,
please visit our website:
www.btomovement.org

I dedicate this book to my loving parents, José Canelos and Zayda Martínez de Canelos. You may not have started marriage the way God intended, but you have taught me to search for the only One who could help me do it the right way. You have persevered, and God's mercy has always been over you.

I dedicate this book to the love of my life, my honey Leon, who shines and has demonstrated to me what the love of Jesus means on a daily basis. You became the one for me.

I dedicate this book to my children: Christian, Amy, Jessica, and my two babies in Heaven.

And finally, I dedicate this book to the many young people who will read it. Remember, with God's help, you will become the one. With His help, He will lead you to your future spouse. And with His help, you and your spouse will transform this world into a better place.

What People Are Saying About Becoming the One (Readers and Group Members)

Over the years I've read scores of good books on this subject. This one by my friend Salomé ranks right up there with the best. I encourage you to read it and get a copy or two for couples who are struggling. This book is not only a tremendous resource for married couples but also a wonderful tool for singles who are planning on one day finding their soul mate for life.
— *Pastor Dick Bernal*
Jubilee Christian Center

Salomé Roat has done a wonderful job researching and carefully articulating what it takes to "become the one" for that special person God has destined to be your life partner. She inspires the reader not to just look for the right person, but to become the right person. And she does that with a thoroughly biblical foundation that comes alive in a beautiful way as she demonstrates each principle with her own story and the stories of others. I encourage all single people, parents of single people, and even married people to read this book to gain a wealth of insights into what it takes to make a great marriage that impacts the world.
— *Chuck Starnes*
Relationship Coach
www.chuckstarnes.com

I want to congratulate Salomé on what is perhaps the best book on marriage I've ever read! I highly recommend it to you, the reader, for the following reasons: Salomé's book is one of great substance, with outstanding biblical principles to apply. Secondly, she brilliantly and creatively augments what she writes with stories that are fascinating, real, personal, and relevant. As a pastor, I want to see marriages that are healthy; Salomé's desire is the same for you, and you'll see that come through greatly in this book. Finally, I've known Salomé and her husband, Leon, and their three wonderful children for many years now. This family bears much fruit! Read this book, apply it, and share it with others—it is destined to be a great book and will bless many!

— *Pastor Brad Matthew Abley, MDiv*
Author, A Heart After God Bible Study Series: 1 Thessalonians: A Church with a Powerful Legacy for Today's Christian
Vice President of ELIM Bible Institute in Siaya, Kenya
www.empowered-living.org

I was lucky enough to read this book at a point in my life where lots of things didn't make sense. It helped me understand that marriage is not a solution or a way to fix a relationship that is hurting. On the contrary, it is a goal that we accomplish once we have healed ourselves and become someone that has something to offer to the person we love. Chapter by chapter I realized that marriage is not the end of a phase in our lives but the beginning of what is probably the most important and challenging adventure we will ever have to face. The good news is that if we do things the right way, we won't be alone. We will have God on our side and the reassurance that the person we picked to be our companion is indeed the one.

— *Esteban Vasco*
Pilot
26 years old

We love this book. Becoming the One is a much-needed resource for those desiring a rich and fulfilling marriage. Salomé captivates her audience with testimonies from real-life experiences. Her experience with singles and married couples is evident as she releases truths and wisdom needed in this generation for a successful marriage. Her book is biblical, practical, and an easy read. Her questions and blessing prayer at the end of each chapter make this a great resource for individual and group study. We highly recommend your using this book as a discussion guide with singles and married couples, to awaken the soul and spirit to our Creator's involvement and purpose of the highest covenant possible. Her chapters on spirit and soul connection are a must-read for all who want a successful marriage. This book can become a catalyst to launch our nation into stability and adventure with God through covenantal marriages. She reveals keys of wisdom and breakthrough for your personal life and marriage.

Through the use of biblical truth, modern-day statistics, and real-life stories, readers become open to discussion of their experience and restoration through the healing power of Father God's covenantal love for us. Truly "the journey to becoming one is about something greater . . . it's about a life of loving God, loving others with pure love only God can give us."

— *Fred and Sonya Haley*
Bethel Associate Ministers at Bethel Church (Redding, California)
Retired Pastors with Christian and Missionary Alliance
Married 51 years

Most believers desire a godly, life-giving marriage but just don't know how to navigate all the questions, obstacles, and emotions that arise on the journey. Salomé has successfully created a spiritual road map that has already helped guide many young ladies into healthy marriages tooled with wisdom and resources for maintaining godly intimacy once the wonder of the wedding and honeymoon is over. Her own marriage is a genuine example of this, and anyone questioning whether it is possible to have a marriage of your dreams will be greatly encouraged as well as equipped by this book. I certainly have been!

— *Jill Robson*
Project Manager
www.transformourworld.org

When Sue and I celebrated our fiftieth anniversary, we were overwhelmed to the point of tears at the reality of this particular milestone. Overwhelmed at the goodness of God in matching us up. Overwhelmed by His faithfulness to us. Overwhelmed that we were passing a milestone that most couples never see. Overwhelmed at ourselves, as if we had run a 1000-mile marathon and made it! We have always tried to give our children and grandchildren the best that we could. It suddenly dawned on us that this particular anniversary was one of the greatest gifts of all: the heritage of a vibrant marriage that has only gotten stronger through the challenges of life because we chose no other option than to face them together.

Peter called Christ-followers "a chosen generation" (1 Peter 2:9). A more accurate translation, which appears in the Spanish Bible, is that we are "a chosen lineage." Fifty years of marriage gives one a perspective on "lineage." Our marriage is not just about us; it's about all the generations of Thompsons that are coming after us and the reality that the "ceiling" we will be putting on our life together in the next fifty years (we signed up for fifty more!) will become the "floorboards" for the households of our generations to come. That's why we salute our good friend, Salomé Roat, for this foundational, transformational book. It comes from her heart to you, and if you receive it as such, it will prepare you for a romance today that will engender a love pattern for the generations that will follow you.

— *Dave Thompson*
Senior Vice President of Harvest Evangelism
Transform Our World Network
www.transformourworld.org

Overall this book left me with hope and also inspiration. I loved the last two chapters because this is the first time that someone clearly mentioned the dreams God has for marriage are way bigger than just to be married and have kids. I loved to see all the examples of how God used and is using marriage to change the world. I almost feel this book is like a reference guide, and it is absolutely something for a number of newlyweds I know. I will definitely read it again and again.

— *Clarette du Plooy*
Zurich, Switzerland

When my friend Karina first invited me to Becoming the One, I thought it was just an ordinary women's group, but I was pleasantly mistaken. There's a special anointing on this group of women. Becoming the One is more than just preparing for an earthly husband, but it is growing in who we are as women created by a Divine God. We are "becoming the one" whom He can call to lead others to Christ. We are "becoming the one" who will stand in the gap and fight for His holy name. We are "becoming the one" who will operate in the fullness of God's Spirit here on earth. My time spent with this group of women has strengthened my faith in God, has created an environment to nurture my prophetic gifting, and it has helped build my self-confidence. Without Becoming the One, I don't think I would have had the courage to leave my parents' home and move to Miami to pursue one of my dreams to become a professional body builder. To me, Becoming the One will be a lifelong pursuit, but I am thankful that my first steps were taken with these women, and I look forward to the unfolding of who I become.

— *Asaya Azah*
BS Biology, MPH
30 years old

I am so blessed to know Salomé and be part of this ministry group. To me, "becoming the one" means to surround myself with a community of people who are pursuing God, encouraging each other in this journey, and not to be only a listener of the Word but a do-er. After all, it's all about becoming more like Christ. This group has become my safe place where I can rest from the burdens and worries of life. I can be transparent with all you ladies and know I am not alone. Whenever we pray, worship, or share what God is saying over each other, it changes my whole outlook.

— *Joyce*
MA CF-SLP
23 years old

I joined this group during a time when I really needed spiritual guidance. This group felt like a covering from God while the Lord was healing me. Through this group, I have felt my heart get closer to God in ways that it had not before. I don't see this group as a ticket out of singleness, but rather as an opportunity to get closer to God and be open and ready for whatever God has in store for my life. Whether God is leading you to go on a missions trip or you are looking for guidance in your relationships, this group is a safe place. The women of this group encouraged me in my relationship with God. This group feeds my soul and reminds me of the richness that comes from having a genuine, intimate relationship with God. "Becoming the one" isn't only about finding your spouse. Really, it's about finding yourself and discovering who you are in Christ. Once you establish this, you are on the road to having a successful marriage.

— *Brittany*
BA Global Studies, MS Environmental Studies
29 years old (married April 30, 2017)

Words may not be sufficient to let you know how much the Becoming the One teachings have impacted my life. I cherish every night we meet and the things I've learned.

— *Sheetal*
Aerospace Engineer
30 years old

Acknowledgements

From the bottom of my heart, I would like to thank the beautiful young lady who listened to God's voice six years ago as she prayed for me at Bethel Church in Redding, California. She courageously told me God had inspired me to write a book for young people like her. She thanked me ahead of time for doing so because she saw the book already written. Thank you, whoever you are, for your words because the book has now become a reality. Words spoken have power. I hope you are abundantly blessed!

Thanks to my wonderful husband for all his love, support, and patience through this season of writing, especially these last couple of years. Thank you for never complaining about the many hours spent on this project, the many late nights I felt inspired to write, the meals not made, and the times you picked up food on the way home to give me more time to write. Thank you for being an inspiration to me. Thank you for loving God and cherishing me with such sweet, unconditional love. Thanks for being the one God blessed me with. I get to spend the rest of my life with you, my best friend, the one I will always love. This book would have been impossible without you.

Thank you to my three children: Christian, Amy, and Jessica. To Christian, for being prompt to listen from the beginning and wanting to learn from this material. Thank you for your suggestions, your desire to help, your advice, and your sweet words. "Train up a child in the way he should go, and when he grows old, he won't depart from it." To Amy, for your encouragement at all times, your interest in learning, and your honesty when we discussed the many topics of this book. Thanks to your friends for listening and wanting to learn from me. To Jessica— thank you, sweetheart, for your great patience. You are the one who got to see this project coming to life before your eyes. Thank you for taking this message to others and mentoring younger girls on this topic of becoming the one. Thank you, my children, for your willingness to become the one.

Thank you to a very special man, a great friend and brother in Christ, who was my editor, researcher, and encourager through this whole process. When I had my first manuscript and didn't know how to continue, you came and offered to assist me, not realizing I had been asking the Lord to send someone to help me with my organization. You have been an angel to me, and I am forever grateful to you, Rick Crawford.

Thank you to my mom, my biggest encourager, for praying for me and the many people who will be touched by this book. Thank you especially for letting me share some of your own experiences that were painful, as God will use them to bless many.

Thank you to my girlfriends and prayer warriors. There are so many, but I would like to give a special thanks to Kim Vase, Marcia Crawford, Sarah Constable, Carolyn Mitchell and Dana Reginato. Each of you has blessed me with wise counsel, prayers, time, and wonderful insights.

Thanks to my amazing brother, Cristian Canelos, for your biblical knowledge and support. Thanks for your graphic design skills, prayers, and love.

Thank you to every couple and single person I was able to interview and to the hundreds of people who took the time to fill out my survey at the beginning of this journey. Thanks to the many friends who sent me great suggestions, comments, and insights through phone calls and emails, as well as my blog and Facebook page. You were all so open and vulnerable, and I appreciate your willingness to use your testimonies to help others.

Special thanks to Carl and Susan Orthlieb, Sheila and Armand Wong, Chris Hogan, Relate 20/20, Dick Bernal, Ed and Ruth Silvoso, Karina Jaramillo, Dave and Sue Thompson, Simon and Brittney Kumar, Monique Zolezzi, McKenna Giordano, Sharon Philip, Dave Shaw, Tracy Falcocchia, María José Calisto, Chuck Starnes, Clarette Du Plooy, and Vinicio and Mela García for your support, prayers, and encouragement.

Thanks to my BTO (Becoming the One) groups, mentors, coaches in training, and guys and girls willing to learn. You have proven that what the Holy Spirit is doing through this material is working, and each of you is becoming the one. Thanks for your constant prayers, encouragement, and support.

Thanks to my Spanish translator and best friend, Anita Arellano, for your prayers and encouragement.

Many thanks to my last and final editor, Lauren Stinton. You heard God's voice and finished this book well.

And finally, my greatest thanks to the One who makes it all possible when it's in His will. Thank You to my first and greatest love, Jesus; my heavenly Father; and the Holy Spirit for trusting me with this project and for encouraging and comforting me at all times. To God be all the glory.

Contents

Foreword

I can't wait for you to read this book! No matter what your marital status is, or what season of life you find yourself in, prepare to be encouraged. You'll find hope and biblically based wisdom that is applicable whether you are single, engaged, newly married, divorced, or remarried.

I first met Salomé when I started as the women's pastor at the church she was attending. We instantly hit it off, not only because we are both fluent in Spanish (the official language of Heaven) but because of her pure and precious heart. I immediately saw her sincere love for the Lord and His people. Salomé is a powerful intercessor, and I was so thankful to have her praying for and with me as I served on staff. So many things bless me about my dear sister. Salomé fears and loves the Lord above all else. She is a devoted and loyal wife and a loving and nurturing mom. Not to mention the most amazing cook and hostess! Salomé's smile and laugh are truly contagious.

As I was reading this book, I envisioned myself sitting down in Salomé's living room, listening to her recount stories, share insights, and give practical advice. I could visualize her loving smile and open arms ready to give the reader a big hug, especially when describing some of the tough issues of life and relationships and sharing how to navigate through them. This book resounds with a powerful and beautiful message: God has an amazing plan for your life that is infused with hope and full of His goodness and grace.

More than thoughtfully written words on a page, this book is an invitation to catch a glimpse of Salomé's passion, heart, and soul. Her warm and welcoming personality shine through in her writing, and I join her in her prayer that this book will encourage, equip, and propel you forward in your relationship with the Lord. Marriage is God's idea. No one ever gets married thinking, I sure hope this makes me miserable! On the contrary, in Becoming the One Salomé leads the reader into the discovery of God's design, purpose, and roadmap for a healthy, thriving marriage relationship that puts Him at the very center. This book so beautifully reflects the wonderful woman that Salomé is. I'm so proud to call her my friend, and I pray that you will enjoy getting to know her as well as you read this book.

Let me encourage you to open your heart to the Lord and this timely message and prepare to BECOME THE ONE.

— Jesica Silvoso MacNaughton
Marriage & Family Ministry
Transform Our World
www.transformourworld.org

Introduction

Just a few days ago, I sat down with one of the ladies in my Becoming the One group to chat about her new relationship. Karina started coming to the group last year. In her late thirties, she had long ago lost hope about getting married, but God had other plans. Over the last two years, she's gone through a time of preparation, during which she truly found the love of God and started looking into personal growth and how to take her relationship with Jesus to a deeper level. As she attended the group, her story began to change. Her life was already in a process of transformation in that she learned to pray fervently and to wait and trust. In the group she found people she could talk to, who would pray for her about the broken place she found herself in. She also invited many other ladies to the group and revealed to us a passion and revival that were refreshingly new for her. Slowly she started having hope that God could have an amazing man for her as she became the one for him, finding spiritual health and wholeness.

As we sat together, she told me how my story impacted her and helped her ask God for His will in her love life. She'd met a nice gentleman through a good friend of hers but never felt anything romantic for him, so they remained just friends. But he didn't give up and pursued her until last month, when he decided he'd done enough and had to let go. During this time Karina realized she had to put this man in God's hands, so she prayed a simple and very sincere prayer that came from the deepest place in her heart. It was a prayer very similar to what I prayed when I was just starting to date my husband.

She prayed, "Lord, this man has remained in my life and doesn't leave. Even though he has let me know of his feelings many times and I have rejected him, he is not going away. If this man is not going to play with my heart or my feelings, give me a special love that will make me know it is from You."

The day after she prayed this prayer, everything changed.

She woke up to a new awareness of this man and felt a special kind of love for him. She started to miss him for the first time, and she had peace that this revelation was from God. Because Karina hadn't been interested in him, at first the man couldn't believe she suddenly was. They talked and prayed and realized God orchestrated their meeting, wanting them to be friends and grow in their walk with Him so they could have what He was showing to them: a beautiful relationship based in His love and assurance. They've decided to pursue a serious relationship and get to know each other. Karina told me she is so in awe of God's goodness and she has so much peace.

We live in a world where singles have more questions than answers. As I've mentored and counseled young people in the area of relationships, a few key points have stood out to me. First of all, the Christian community needs to be more aware of the purpose of dating. Dating is fun, not stressful. There should be no pressure in dating whatsoever.

Second, you can prepare for marriage now, even if you're single. Then when you meet that right person, you will be emotionally and spiritually ready for them. Wouldn't it be nice to meet someone, get to know them, fall in love with ease, and be able to step into a lifelong relationship with them that is free of pressure and strife? Isn't that what all of us want?

Third, it is possible to be successful at relationships and stay married forever. In this book we'll talk about how.

No matter where you are in your life—single, dating, engaged, or even married—you can start becoming the one right now. It involves getting healthy, knowing what you want, and knowing how much God means to you. That last point is one of the key steps in becoming the one. Understanding how much God means to you and how much you mean to Him will keep you from settling for less than what He has for you—and what He has for you is a godly, loving spouse. Personally, I believe God has marriage in mind for nearly every person. The Bible talks about how the man who finds a wife finds favor from the Lord (Proverbs 18:22). We are in need of more of His favor, aren't we?

Through the love of God and really encountering His love, you will start to experience true growth; you can be healed and find your true identity. You have been rescued from darkness and birthed into the light—His light. When

I see couples living in God's love, His healing, and the identity He has given them, I see His power witnessing to many. I see a good, solid marriage because the couple walks in their identity and the purpose God has for them, and they go on to transform others.

If you let God do an inward work in you, you will naturally want to find the person He has for you, the one you get to love and spend the rest of your life with. You will be astounded by what God does for you and in you as you pursue becoming the one.

I'm glad you've decided to join me on this journey. Let the adventure begin!

I

WHY MARRIAGE IS IMPORTANT

The beginning of wisdom is this: Get wisdom.
Though it cost all you have, get understanding.
— Proverbs 4:7

We live in a time when many people don't know what marriage really means or how to become the one for their future spouse. Over and over again, I've heard, "I didn't know anything about marriage and how to be a good spouse before my wedding—or even after my wedding." But that doesn't have to be the case. You can start preparing for your marriage right now. Understanding the foundation and practical truths of marriage will help you make a great decision for your future.

Chapter

I

AN ECUADORIAN LOVE STORY

Most of us are suckers for a good love story. It doesn't even have to be all that unique or creative—we want to hear how all these spinning pieces that seem random and unconnected were brought together by God to form a solid, strong, healthy match between two people. A match He wanted to happen.

Whether they met at school, work, church, while travelling, on the internet, through friends, or even on a blind date, each couple's love story is special and tinged with hints of divine guidance. From dating to engagement to the wedding day and honeymoon, love stories are narratives we enjoy hearing and are willing to share again and again. When times grow difficult, these stories of newness and hope are the glue that helps us stay together, reminding us of why we fell in love in the first place.

Marriage, however, is not just about dating, the betrothal, or the honeymoon. Marriage is really what happens when the honeymoon is over. Becoming the one for your spouse is far more than the physical act of making love. You are forming an emotional and spiritual bond with your marriage partner that, if cultivated, will last a lifetime. Marriage is a covenant made between not two but three entities: the husband, the wife, and God. In its broadest scope, that is what marriage means and looks like—a divine covenant.

Making the commitment to marry and live together for the rest of your years is a deep and profound decision. How can you be certain you are choosing the right marriage partner? That is the central question of this book.

The day I married my husband, I was not anxious about the future. I knew with certainty that God had confirmed His perfect will for us, and because He had done so, Leon and I knew our marriage was going to be a forever deal, no looking back, no hesitation. From the very beginning, God was a part of our relationship, and His involvement made it that much easier for us to commit to one another and not be afraid, even though we had plenty of things we could have been nervous about. For instance, we weren't just trying to blend two lives, but we were meshing together two countries, two cultures, and two languages. He was from the United States and had been living in Ecuador for only four months, while I had grown up there. We were both still working on our language skills. We decided to stay in my country until I finished my degree in law and could adjust to being married in my own culture, which would hopefully make the transition easier. I was marrying more than just a man that day; I was marrying the promise of a new country. That by itself was fairly intense, but I also found it exciting, knowing that I would follow my husband anywhere because I loved him and was committed to him with all my heart.

In addition to these things, I also had something more serious on my mind. I was molested when I was a young child, and as I prepared myself as a bride, I wondered, Am I still a virgin? I had told Leon what happened, everything I remembered, but I wasn't fully certain what to expect when he and I made love for the first time. I supposed I would find out that night.

The ceremony was set to take place outside my parents' ranch house in the small town of Puembo, a few miles away from Quito, Ecuador. This was the wedding location I'd been dreaming of for years, and though the day was hot, a light breeze stirred the trees and everything—finally—seemed to be in place. Swans hand painted by my mother's friends floated in the pool, and the flowers and decorations were carefully displayed. The quartet of musicians was waiting, and the food was prepared and arranged the way my mom and I had been imagining and planning for many months. I was ready to become Mrs. Salomé Roat—or in Ecuador, María Salomé Canelos de Roat.

Leon arrived at the ranch house early, and he later told me he found the house in a bit of disarray. And the guests startled him. People weren't just late—they were really late. An hour after the wedding was supposed to start, which is right on time for us in Ecuador, guests began to arrive and find their seats. Some moved toward the shade in the makeshift seating area to avoid the heat, while others ignored the temperature and socialized. Leon and I waited in separate rooms, alone with our thoughts. I knew without a single doubt that God's delight, love, and favor over Leon and me were never going to leave. We had made Him a part of our relationship, and so we knew what He was thinking for us. I was a little nervous, but it was not about any of the important things. I just had never liked being the center of attention, and in a short while, every eye was going to be on me. Also, I wanted to be amazingly beautiful for my husband.

A few minutes later, I walked down the aisle with my father, who presented me to my husband. Seeing Leon wipe his eyes as he looked at me filled me with a deeper love for him. I could feel it in my chest tangibly. This was the moment I'd been waiting for, the moment God had led us to. We held hands and the presence of the Lord knit our hearts together. My nervousness about looking beautiful and being the center of attention was replaced with peace, because I knew our marriage was blessed. When you know you are following God's will, a sense of God's delight and presence in what you are doing fills your whole being. That was exactly what Leon and I experienced on our wedding day. God was not just a spectator. He was invited to be part of our covenant. We were fearless.

We sat down and the pastor began the ceremony. Thirty minutes later, Leon started pulling at his collar, signaling his readiness to get to the rest of the ceremony, but the first pastor was just getting warmed up. The Ecuadorian sun intensified over the next hour, and the pastor finally concluded his sermon on marriage and the good news of Jesus, which allowed the traditional ceremony to begin. We said our vows, participated in communion, and had an amazing time in worship. We sealed the moment with prayer and more blessings from our pastors. Then finally came a beautiful kiss—a couple of kisses, actually, as our photographer didn't catch the first one.

During the reception we talked and laughed, took pictures, and ate amazing food. One of our Ecuadorian traditions caught Leon completely unaware. I had neglected to tell him that men and other relatives sign the groom's shirt with markers as part of the celebration. Leon was a great sport about it, but he was never able to wear that shirt again.

Although the day had a few minor glitches, it was perfect for Leon and me. We were married in the Creator's presence and in front of loved ones—two souls from two very different countries united in holy matrimony. I can laugh about the surprises of the wedding day now, but they were small compared to the beauty I felt in the ceremony.

As the years have passed, my marriage to Leon has been a lot like our wedding day as we've worked through some unforeseen circumstances and a few difficult times, keeping our minds on the Lord's will. This is one of the main points I want to communicate in this book: He who sees the beginning from the end can certainly guide us in our relationships. After all, marriage was God's idea, and we evoke His name during the ceremony. No one else could have thought of the union of a man and a woman in such an incredible way.

The Big Picture of Marriage

Looking back, I've often wondered how I knew Leon was the perfect choice for me. I've never questioned the choice I made, and it has made me wonder how couples come together. How do men and women find the right marriage partner? Does God have a perfect marriage match for every person? How do we find the one?

I met Leon Roat in January 1987 when I was eighteen years old. Leon, who was from California, had been invited on a mission trip to Ecuador by his good friend Bill. We both happened to be participating in a missions conference in Quito, and on three or four different evenings, we managed to make eye contact and smile at each other from across the room. On the last night of the conference, he approached me, and my heart pounded as our conversation began.

After a short talk, I gave him an Ecuadorian kiss on the cheek, a hug, and at his request my address and phone number so we could keep in touch. When I thought about it later, I realized a connection began when we first exchanged glances. I knew in my heart that this was something wonderful. In the months that followed, Leon wrote to me in English and broken Spanish. We told each other about our everyday-life activities: work for him, college for me, church for both of us, and our desire to see each other again. Our friendship grew closer through letters and phone calls.

In August 1988, a year and a half after our first meeting, Leon came to visit me in Ecuador. This time he wasn't on a mission trip. He specifically came to pursue a deeper relationship with me. As you may imagine, I felt nervous, knowing he was ready for a more serious friendship and had come all the way to Ecuador to get to know me. Talk about pressure! Before he arrived, I asked myself several times, "What if I don't feel anything for him?" He was coming all the way to my country with serious intentions. What if he wasn't the man I'd been praying for? Yet in my heart I was hoping this was what God had for me. Our long-distance relationship was helping me understand what "true love" meant. One day I got down on my knees and cried out to God to give me a special kind of love for Leon—but only if he was the one I should marry.

That is exactly what He did. That Saturday morning while we were on a boat ride with my family, love happened. I will never forget the way my stomach fluttered while I sat next to Leon. I felt a tingle up and down my spine when he touched me, and all at once, I became aware that I didn't want to live without him. Deep in my heart, I knew my prayers were answered and I'd found the man I'd been waiting for. Leon asked me to be his girlfriend hours later. He had to use a Spanish dictionary, and I helped him say some of the words.

How can a person be certain they are choosing the right marriage partner? Before my husband and I started dating, that question plagued me. It's the question every couple ponders as the relationship gets serious. Marriage is one of the most important decisions a person can make, and yet most young couples are unprepared and understand little about the marriage commitment.

As I asked that question, I began to realize how complex the marriage relationship really is. When we marry someone, we tend to think we are marrying only one person, but we're actually joining a pre-established family structure. This causes the marriage to take on new meaning, and we begin to realize there is more risk. My "pre-established family structure" came with hurting pieces. Although my father was very successful in business, he struggled in relationships. He married my mother after a failed marriage, and as a result, I grew up with two half-brothers and a half-sister who stayed with us on the weekends. Both my mom and I dearly loved my siblings, but six years after my parents married, they divorced and left behind a wake of heartache and emotional trauma. I loved my parents and wanted them to be together, so I begged my mother to remarry my father. My mother clearly remembers the words I spoke on Christmas Eve when I was nearly four years old. "All I want for Christmas is to have my daddy back home," I told her.

She listened to me. About a year after their divorce, my parents married again and had a beautiful son, Cristian, who made me the happiest big sister in the world. But sadly, our parents' relationship never recovered from the trust issues and lack of communication. From that point on, my brothers, sister, and I lived in a tug of war between two factors: believing that our home was normal and acknowledging the obvious signs that my parents couldn't communicate well with each other.

Deep down I knew my parents were unhappy, and like many children from dysfunctional families, I grew up thinking it was my fault. I carried this guilt for years until the day Jesus took it from me. My parents showered love and affection on their children—just not each other. There were plenty of good times in my home but a lot of tension between my parents. They always thought the best of me and helped me to believe I could do great things, and I'm so thankful for their trust and unconditional love toward me, but the true love I wanted to see between them was not there.

Naturally this had a profound impact on my life and spiritual development. As I matured into a teenager, I became determined in my search for intimacy. The Lord put a desire in my heart to have success in the one area where my parents had failed. Instead of dating for the sake of dating, I began to understand the Lord had prepared one man to be my husband. This was the start of my personal journey toward becoming the one—maturing into a woman of God who was emotionally and spiritually healthy, prepared by the Holy Spirit for her future husband.

Twenty-seven years after saying, "I do," my husband and I are still happy and committed, and we love each other more now than when we started. We have found success in marriage, and God has placed a longing in our hearts to help others find success in marriage, too. We feel the Christian community needs to be more aware of the purpose of dating, how to have successful relationships, preparing for marriage, and how to stay married forever. In broad strokes, those are the central goals of this book. This book will also explore:

- Unexpected reasons people want to get married
- Dating and healthy relationships
- God's role in the marriage commitment
- Covenant
- The purpose of marriage
- Preparing for marriage
- Determining compatibility during dating
- The value of building your marriage
- Avoiding divorce
- Talking about marriage with partners, friends, and family
- Christian living
- Effective communication

- Understanding God's favor
- Building a legacy
- Becoming a transformational couple

Becoming the one is more than just a time of preparation. It is coming to the humble realization you need to work on yourself and pay attention to the many factors that will lead you into having a blessed marriage. Many people lose hope for their future and settle for something that is less than God's will. If you can learn to trust Him even in this area of marriage, He will give you the necessary foundation so you can be a man or woman who is secure in knowing His will for you. Marriage is certainly not the easiest relationship, but it is rewarding, adventurous, intimate, and completely worth it. Loving your spouse the way you are supposed to love them is the greatest call and the finest gift you can give.

> *Becoming the one is more than just a time of preparation. It is coming to the humble realization that you need to work on yourself and pay attention to the many factors that will lead you into having a blessed marriage.*

The best way to start this process is by having an open and learning heart. I invite you to do it His way. You will never regret it.

Discussion Questions:

1. Did your parents discuss the topic of dating and marriage with you during your youth? If so, what did they say? What was the experience like? If not, how did you learn about dating and marriage?

2. What is your definition of marriage? Do you believe most marriages have a chance? Why or why not?

3. In your opinion, what's the purpose of dating?

4. What qualities do you look for in the person you want to date?

5. Do you think it is important to involve God in your decision to get married? Why or why not?

Prayer:

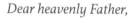

Dear heavenly Father,

I come to You in the name of Jesus and ask You to guide my thoughts toward a deeper understanding of the purposes of marriage and dating as I read this book. I want to make You my first priority. Grow me into the person You want me to be. Help me to become the one for the person You want me to marry.

Chapter

2

WHAT IS INTIMACY?

How God Designed Your Relationship with Your Spouse

Zayda was a beautiful, innocent young lady from a small town a few hours away from Quito, the capital of Ecuador. The fifth of seven children, she was filled with dreams and an adventurous spirit. She attended an all-boys high school—she was the only girl in the entire school—because she wanted to pursue the same career as her father, who was an agronomist.

When she was in her early twenties, her siblings started to get married. Even her younger sister got married before her, and Zayda began feeling some pressure. But then at her other sister's wedding, she met a man named José. He was the groom's boss and appeared to be a gentleman; he was a very charming and successful man. Zayda felt captivated by his ways, and when she found out he was divorced and a father, she thought how precious it would be to already have little children in her life. José soon declared his love for her and proposed.

Being an affectionate daughter, Zayda went to her parents and asked for their approval. They adamantly refused. They actually got on their knees and begged her not to marry this man, but Zayda thought she was completely in love and decided to accept his marriage proposal anyway. She packed, left home, and two and a half short months after she met José, they married in a very lonely civil ceremony.

That is the story of how my parents met. Neither of them had a personal relationship with Jesus, any understanding of the true meaning of marriage, or why they really wanted to be together for the rest of their lives. It has taken many years for my mom to let go of the guilt of disobeying her parents and to begin to understand God was going to use all of this for good. She's been a strong believer for the last thirty-two years, and she has told me there is nothing worse in life than going against the loving will of your parents. Many times she has regretted her decision, but she never regretted having her two most precious treasures: her children. What she regrets the most is that she didn't know Jesus personally during this time. "How different it would have been if I would have known Him early in my life," she told me. "How different it would have been if I had learned to hear His voice and obey Him." God has ministered with so much love to both my parents, but it has been a long, difficult, painful recovery process for them after so much loss.

My mom is an honored, beloved counselor at her church, which has used her story to help others not make the same mistake. Her love for Jesus is inspiring, and her love for others is beyond doubt. She now faithfully takes care of my dad, who has some health issues, and because of her great love for God, she has not given up.

My parents represent just two of many young couples who marry for the wrong reasons. Why did my parents have such urgency to get married? Why do people really want to get married in the first place?

In a survey I recently conducted, four hundred people of varying ages rated love, commitment, and companionship as the top reasons they wanted to get married. Some couples stated that peer pressure caused them to rush toward marriage. "All my friends are getting married and it felt right," they said.

Others get married because they want to escape a painful family situation. Some young people marry because they think marriage will solve a personal problem, while others marry during the infatuation stage of a relationship. They believe in the "power of love," and without much thought of the future, and without even knowing each other very well, these couples believe marriage will be an exciting ride with no conflicts.

Many people, however, get married for the right reason: They are seeking a deeper connection with a soul mate.

Research shows that, whether married or not, Americans are more inclined to choose love as a reason for marriage than any other factor. In a 2010 Pew Research Center survey, love was more important to Americans than companionship, making a lifelong commitment, having children, and financial stability[1]. In my opinion, this information just highlights a bigger need in the human experience. I believe the central reason people want to get married is the desire for intimacy

---

1 D'vera Cohn, "Love and Marriage," Pew Research Center, February 13, 2013, http://www.pewsocialtrends. org/2013/02/13/love-and-marriage.

and connection. Love, commitment, and companionship all lead to deeper levels of intimacy, and the goal in marriage is the formation of a deeper connection with one person. We were created for a relationship that meets our desires for emotional and spiritual connection. We all have the need to be loved, valued, and to belong, and true intimacy meets all these needs.

Searching for Intimacy

My search for intimacy started in my teens, when I first began to think about marriage. Like many girls my age, I hoped to find a man who would learn to meet my emotional, physical, and spiritual needs. I wanted to grow old with someone who would cherish me all the days of my life, and I wanted to love someone deeply. A romantic and a dreamer, I imagined that one day I would meet my prince. Through much prayer and waiting for God's will, I finally met this special man. Leon and I dated, fell in love, and married. This filled a void in my heart, but I soon realized the need for intimacy is never completely satisfied. This emotional and spiritual connection is like a hunger that must be fed now and in the future.

What Is Intimacy?

Intimacy is taking a deep look into your partner's soul. It's the experience of emotional closeness that lights up the human spirit, and it occurs when two people are able to be emotionally open with one another and reveal their true feelings, thoughts, fears, and desires. Only when you can see the deepest parts of your spouse and accept them unconditionally, with an extreme delight, can you be fully intimate with them. In his book *Keep Your Love On*, Danny Silk describes how the experience of intimacy is the most satisfying experience a human being can have. He says intimacy or "into-me-see" is created between two people who can say, "We can be ourselves together because you can see into me and I can see into you."[2] Vulnerability, total acceptance, and delight are essential in creating an intimate relationship. This is why Proverbs 5:18 says, *"May your fountain be blessed, and may you rejoice in the wife of your youth."*

Many people think of intimacy in terms of lovemaking. Although one type of intimacy involves sex, that is just a portion of what intimacy can mean. Intimacy is intellectual, too. When two friends exchange thoughts, share ideas, and enjoy similarities and differences of opinion, their friendship becomes stronger and more

---

2 Danny Silk, *Keep Your Love On* (Redding, CA: Red Arrow Publishing), 2013.

intimate. In the same way, when feelings are shared between two people, the result is more understanding of self and the other person. This also helps form an emotional and spiritual connection. Another way to deepen a relationship is through experiences. When a couple participates in activities together, the result is a more complete view of one another. Shared experiences develop connection. In addition, when a couple prays together and listens to the Lord for answers, spiritual intimacy occurs.

Think of it this way: We achieve intimacy when we connect with our mates on a deep spiritual level, so that our very souls are exposed before one another. This happens when we connect with our partners on three planes: spirit, soul, and body. When we feel united emotionally and there is vulnerability, intimacy happens. In a very real way, our souls become intertwined, which is why sharing ideas, emotions, and even areas of struggle can take relationships to new levels of satisfaction. Both men and women should strive to listen to their mates' hopes and dreams.

Physical intimacy or sexual relations are an activity married couples share in their search for an emotional and spiritual connection. Making love gives us a one-of-a-kind orgasmic feeling, which causes us to blend our souls emotionally and spiritually. Although a healthy sex life is crucial for success in a marriage, lovemaking is, again, only one aspect of this connection. As a marriage matures, deeper intimacy develops because partners learn to care for one another's spirit, soul, and body.

God's Love and Intimacy

Looking for a deeper level of intimacy in a mate is a normal part of healthy relationship building, but there is an even deeper connection that the human spirit cries out for: We need God's love. For us to experience a close relationship with our partners, we first need to experience the unconditional love of our heavenly Father.

Practically speaking, how do we build intimacy with God? How do we feel loved by God in a way that draws us to love Him back, understanding that an intimate relationship with Him will help us have true intimacy in marriage? In my pursuit of a more intimate relationship with God, I have learned to be intentional. To get to know someone well, I have to spend time with them and find out more about them. The more I care about them, the more I want to know and the more I want them to know I am interested in their heart and desires. All healthy relationships start, grow, and continue in a similar way, including our relationship with God. The more we get to know Him, the deeper and more intimate our relationship with Him will be. The more questions we ask, the more we seek Him; the more we are interested in Him, the more intimate we become with Him. His heart for us is that we would delight in Him, and to delight in Him, we need to get to know Him. Many people don't have a good view of God; they believe He is angry, absent, punishing, boring, legalistic, etc. But these negative beliefs will change as we get to know Him for who He truly is. He really is good. I love how Pastor Bill Johnson says, "God is always in a good mood." That is certainly a healthy way of seeing Him. He is all loving, all merciful, all understanding. He is full of grace and compassion and forgiveness. He is fun and funny—and, yes, worthy of all our reverence. He cherishes those times when we worship Him with everything we are. He is a good Abba Father, a wonderful Savior, and a powerful Holy Spirit. He pursues us with all His heart and wants us to know Him more; He wants us to know and feel His love and pursuit of us. That is why Jeremiah 29:13 says, *"You will seek me and find me when you seek me with all your heart."* Intentionality is key. When our hearts are set to pursue Him, we will find Him. There is no doubt of it.

We can't consistently demonstrate deep affection toward someone if we've never experienced being loved by God. The Lord knows us well and loves us perfectly. That connection changes us and allows us to love and experience intimacy in relationships more freely.

Getting to know another person sexually, emotionally, spiritually, and intellectually can be exciting; however, this needs to be pursed in a healthy manner. Many pre-marrieds are looking to fulfill an unmet need, deal with loneliness, or escape an abusive family life, or they believe that marriage will help them heal a deep emotional wound. What I've learned is that marriage can certainly help a person deal with life's traumas—but it's dangerous to rely only on your partner to save you. Expecting a spouse to solve your deepest problems is a formula for disaster. God has put a marriage partner in your life to offer help. Your partner knows you more deeply than anyone and can help you weather storms; however, it is through a relationship with God that you and your spouse can muster the strength to handle life's challenges. In a healthy marriage, partners accept each other the way they are, see each other in their moments of greatest vulnerability, and accept each other no matter what.

A Test of Intimacy

The first real test of my relationship with Leon came after five years of marriage. Leon and I were thrilled with the birth of our first child, Christian, but sorrow waited around the corner in the form of two miscarriages. This was the hardest and most painful time in my life. Coming from a different country and being away from my family gave me an intense desire to have more children. I wanted to have a big family, but I started to think it wasn't meant to be.

After a long season of heartache, I couldn't take it anymore and began to want the desire for children to leave me. One afternoon I made the decision to stop trying to have more children. It was during this time that Leon showed me a level of love and intimacy that still astounds me. He listened and empathized with me at my lowest point. I remember one evening in particular when I was depressed and praying. My menstrual cycle had started that morning, and I was devastated, thinking I might never get pregnant again. That evening as I wept, Leon touched my shoulder, prayed for me, and said that being barren wasn't God's will for us. He told me the Lord was going to give us more children, and his confidence helped me to be brave. Moreover, his prayer showed me I was cherished. Sensing Leon's complete commitment helped me feel connected and able to be more vulnerable with him. I could trust my husband, which helped me trust the Lord more.

That same evening, Leon stayed with me as I cried out to the Lord for peace. He kept on quietly interceding for me. An amazing sense of peace and contentment overcame my heart, and the next morning when I woke up, my period had stopped. After a few days, I took another pregnancy test, and guess what? I was pregnant. We had a beautiful baby girl seven months later and another wonderful daughter three years after that. God is so good and faithful!

As a woman and a wife, I feel the most connected in my marriage when my husband listens to me and tries to understand the part of my heart that God is still touching and healing. When Leon is compassionate enough to show empathy and to love me through the tough times, that is when I feel the most connected to him. To me, that is true intimacy.

It's amazing to think about where we started so many years ago, when he and I first began dating. I have been on a journey of developing intimacy and understanding, and Leon has met my needs in a way that brought healing and joy. Showing compassion and tenderness during difficult moments can take a lot of effort for some, but God has taught us that compassion and humility are the keys to understanding each other's emotional needs. Many couples don't know how to feel intimate when tests and struggles come into their lives. When difficulty appears—such as a sick child, a death in the family, a chronic illness, or a lost job—spouses need to offer one another emotional and spiritual support. When I was struggling to conceive and carry a child full term, do you think I would have felt as spiritually intimate with my husband if he hadn't prayed with me? Probably not. The spiritual connection we shared filled me with hope. Connecting with him mentally or physically would have satisfied some of my needs, but I needed to know he cared about more than just my physical body; he also cared about my emotional and spiritual well-being. For us, our spiritual connection is the most important connection we have. God unites us through prayer, and as we humble ourselves by asking Him for what we need, He helps us deal with disagreements and conflict. We submit to Him and ask Him to continue leading us in our married life, and our spiritual connection with each other becomes stronger.

God Created Intimacy

Adam and Eve gave us a model of God's view of relationships and intimacy in marriage. In Genesis 2 we read about the creation of man and woman. The Lord God formed a man from the dust of the ground and breathed life into him, and he became a living being. He placed Adam in the Garden of Eden and, after a time, created Eve. What did God say? *"It is not good for the man to be alone. I will make a helper suitable for him"* (Genesis 2:18).

Not only did God see that man was in need of a partner, but He also determined how to create the perfect mate for him. This is one reason we need to allow God into the process of helping us choose our mates. The Lord knows who will be a suitable helper for you. He helped Adam achieve intimacy, and He can do the same for you.

As we follow the story, we discover Eve was special. God created every other creature from dust (Genesis 1:24), but she was more than that. She was what Adam was missing; she was the precise and perfect complement to his life. Scripture tells us God put Adam into a deep sleep, took one of his ribs, and with it created his bride. In other words, Eve was the completion of a creation already in progress.

She was his suitable helper and the longing of Adam's heart:

The man said,
"This is now bone of my bones
and flesh of my flesh;
she shall be called 'woman,'
for she was taken out of man."
— Genesis 2:23

When we marry and become one, a profound spiritual union takes place. They were two unique creations, but God bound Adam and Eve by a common identity that nothing else in creation had experienced. He declared them "one flesh" in Genesis 2:24. In biblical terms this is a covenant. The man and woman were both naked, and they felt no shame. That is God's definition of intimacy in marriage: a husband and wife knowing everything about each other and feeling no shame. In other words, it is total acceptance of one another. That is why a man leaves his father and mother and is united to his wife, and they become one flesh.

That is God's definition of intimacy in marriage: a husband and wife knowing everything about each other and feeling no shame. In other words, it is total acceptance of one another.

However, if we left the story there, we'd be omitting an important part. Adam and Eve sinned and it changed human history. Sin entered the world through Adam, and perfect intimacy between God and humankind was broken, as was the connection between husband and wife. Satan, the father of lies, was able to rule the earth through sin. His goal is to separate us from the Lord and each other, and to this day he still tries to separate, confuse, lie, kill, and destroy every human being and every marriage. The good news is that the fall of Adam and Eve didn't change God's role in the marriage relationship or His view of marriage. He still wants to have a say in whom we choose to marry. The Lord also desires that we become one flesh in a covenant relationship, so we can experience the same type of intimacy Adam and Eve did in the garden.

Discussion Questions:

1. Why do you want to get married? In your own words, what does it mean to live happily ever after?

2. Intimacy happens when we connect with our mates on three levels: spirit, soul, and body. Most couples need to have a soul connection to achieve intimacy. What's your definition of intimacy?

3. Do you think God has a perfect marriage match for you? Why or why not?

4. How can your relationship with God affect your choice of marriage partner?

5. After reading my parents' story at the beginning of the chapter, how important do you think it is to honor your parents and ultimately God in this decision to marry?

Prayer:

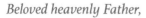

Beloved heavenly Father,

Please teach me what it means to have an intimate relationship with You. Heal my heart so I can learn to be intimate with my future spouse. I know Jesus came to give me an abundant life and the Holy Spirit will help me find the spouse of my dreams.

Chapter
3

THE SEX CHAPTER

Why You Should Avoid Living Together Before Marriage

How often do you think about sex?

A regular topic that comes up when I talk to young people about relationships is sexual activity. Having sex is, of course, on the minds of teens and young adults, and most people think about sex daily, including my husband and me.

In a recent study, researchers assessed how often college students think about sex. The study found that men think more about sex on a daily basis than women do. No surprise there, right? Women thought of sex from 1 to 140 times per day, while men thought of sex from 1 to 388 times per day.[1]

As much as we think about sex, it's strange how difficult it is for many people to discuss the topic. Was it easy for you to talk about sex with your parents? It wasn't for me. Most parents feel uneasy bringing up the topic of sexuality with their children. My parents let me learn about sex through television shows, movies, peers, and the school system.

In my interviews and conversations with young people, I've found that many teens grow up with a moral code that encourages promiscuity and sexual experimentation. Parents don't encourage abstinence or saving sex for the marriage bed; they let their children follow their own moral compasses and instruct them to use protection. They tell them it's okay to have sex but caution them to guard their hearts—and just don't get pregnant. More often than not, parents had sexual experiences before marriage and believe they don't have the moral authority to speak into their children's lives on this issue.

The pressure to have sex in a dating relationship is more common than most Christians think. The Kaiser Foundation states that "nearly half (47%) of all high

---

1 Kristen Jozkowski, "How Often Do We Think About Sex?...Results from a New Study," *Kinsey Confidential*: January 12, 2012, https://kinseyconfidential.org/sexresults-study.

school students report having had sexual intercourse."[2] A young woman I will call Ally felt this sexual pressure while growing up. Although she is happily married now, her sexual struggles started at age sixteen when she lost her virginity. She was unaware of the devastating effects of a sexual relationship. "The first time I had sex, I felt empty, lonely, and a desperate cloud of disappointment covered me," she told me. "I was ruined. I felt the most crushing pain in my heart after my first sexual encounter. No one ever told me that virginity was a treasure and that I was supposed to wait for the day of my wedding to give myself to a man."

Ally continued to participate in sexual relationships until she became a Christian and discovered the value of saving sex for her future husband. "Jesus came into my life and helped me to discover my identity in Him, His love, and forgiveness. That's when I also got out of my darkness and became pure again. Through the cross of Jesus, I became a new creature, a pure and valuable woman. Shortly after I made a commitment to the Lord, I met an amazing man and we got married."

According to the Center for Disease Control and Prevention, "many young people engage in sexual risk behaviors that can result in unintended health outcomes. For example, among U.S. high school students surveyed in 2015

- 41% had ever had sexual intercourse.
- 30% had had sexual intercourse during the previous 3 months, and, of these
  - 43% did not use a condom the last time they had sex.
  - 14% did not use any method to prevent pregnancy.
  - 21% had drunk alcohol or used drugs before last sexual intercourse.
- Only 10% of all students have ever been tested for human immunodeficiency virus (HIV)."[3]

As a mother and a Christian, my message to young people is simple on the topic of sex. The only way to avoid out-of-wedlock pregnancy, sexually transmitted diseases, and other associated health risks is to abstain from sexual activity before marriage. Even more important, the only way to avoid unhealthy soul ties and damaging emotional bonds with the opposite sex is by guarding your virginity. A soul tie is an emotional connection that unites you with someone else.

2 "Sexual Health of Adolescents and Young Adults in the United States," The Henry J. Kaiser Family Foundation: August 20, 2014, www.kff.org/womens-health-policy/fact-sheet/sexual-health-of-adolescents-and-young-adults-in-the-united-states.

3 "Sexual Risk Behaviors: HIV, STD, & Teen Pregnancy Prevention," Centers for Disease Control and Prevention, https://www.cdc.gov/healthyyouth/sexualbehaviors.

It is an automatic response during sex; your soul is "knit" with the soul of the other person. The soul is a composite of your will, thoughts, and emotions, and when you become "one flesh" with someone through sexual intercourse, you invite much of that person to live inside you. That is what we call a soul tie. This is obviously unhealthy when you are not married to that person. Bringing multiple soul ties from past relationships into your marriage is also unhealthy because these will affect your married life. Other people do not belong in your marriage.

On the other hand, there are healthy soul ties you can cultivate. For example, a friendship that is caring, generous, respectful, etc. can bring two people together in a healthy manner. Abstinence is an excellent family standard. A faithful monogamous relationship in the context of marriage is the best way to ensure a healthy, successful marriage.

Having said all of this, how do we become healthy and more educated in the area of sexuality? How do we talk to our parents and peers about it? The first step is going back and determining how our sexuality developed. How were we taught to think about it? Did we learn about it in a healthy way, understanding it is a good and beautiful thing? Or did we learn to shame it, thinking it is dirty and somehow unhealthy? Once we learn to recognize where we are in our understanding of sexuality, we can take the next step, which is realizing the beauty, purpose, and godliness of such a gift. When we are informed by the right sources, we can be more open minded about sexuality and begin to address others' questions.

How Did You Learn About Sex?

"If you kiss on the lips, you might get pregnant," a friend in first grade told me. A few years later in fifth grade, I remember a schoolmate trying to show me a pornographic magazine she'd found on her older brother's desk. I became so scared after looking at the first picture that we quickly hid the magazine. On another occasion, a middle school friend told me about the sexual abuse she'd endured only a few months earlier. As you can imagine, these experiences gave me a distorted view of sexuality. The word sex was something dirty to me.

I was a teenager when I first felt the urge to know more about the topic of sexuality. The place was my grandmother's house, and my teacher was a book with the words Educational Sexuality inscribed across the binding like a neon sign. I happened to be with my cousins that day, who were various ages, and we were giggling quite a bit. They wanted to take a look at the forbidden book as much as I did. As it turned out, they were the first to look through the pages, which made them giggle all the more. My heart pounded as I waited for my turn with the book. Looking at this book wouldn't mark my introduction to the topic, but no adult had ever explained to me what sex was all about. I may have sat through a class or two at school on human anatomy, but my information about sex came from what I'd heard from my young and uninformed friends and what I'd seen on television.

Finally it was my turn to thumb through the book's pages. I don't remember much except that there was more writing than illustrations, and I was disappointed—how boring! The figures in the pictures looked like cardboard cutouts, and everything was labeled. Reading about sex was a big letdown for me. For some reason, I'd expected the butterflies in my stomach to soar as I learned about the beauty of love.

There were, of course, other experiences as I matured into a teen and then an adult. I had many questions, but discussions about sexuality were taboo in my family, which only fueled the tension I felt about the topic. I began to wonder if a girl shouldn't ask these kinds of questions. Although my parents wouldn't talk about sex, they would let me watch all kinds of soap operas and movies that had kissing and content that was inappropriate for children.

Many young people have had similar experiences with friends and parents. Most of us discovered more about sex from movies than from our parents or mentors. Sadly, many families don't even teach their children about sexuality, and these days young people can log on to the computer and look up any topic they wish. The problem is that when we learn about sex from television shows, through movies, or by searching the internet, we probably aren't learning about sex and intimacy the way God intends. We are learning about the act of sex and not about why God created this wonderful expression of intimacy between a man and a woman. Intimacy is what we are really looking for as we grow older, but we are told the lie that sex will fill the need.

Why Abstain?

In a perfect world, we would enjoy our first sexual experience with our marriage partner after the wedding. My parents taught this standard to me, and it is the standard upheld by Scripture. However, this is obviously not the standard in most societies. Children and teenagers are not encouraged to treat their virginity as a treasure. In fact, virginity is scorned in many teenage peer groups. Although we don't live in a perfect world, God wants us to obey His leading and be righteous before Him. The Lord is the One we are to please, and He insists we save sex for the marriage bed.

Hebrews 13:4 is one verse that clearly states God's desire for our righteousness: *"Marriage should be honored by all, and the marriage bed kept pure, for God will judge the adulterer and all the sexually immoral."* God is a loving Father who gives us instructions for our own protection and benefit. Why should we abstain from sex before marriage? Why does God ask us not to have premarital sex? One important reason involves readiness. I was a senior in high school when I learned firsthand what it meant to be pursued by the opposite sex. I went out with my girlfriends and young men on several occasions, and when I turned seventeen, I thought I fell in love with a handsome young man I'd met through friends. In retrospect, this feeling wasn't love but more of an infatuation that felt so right at the time. Although I would have wanted to pursue a serious relationship with my suitor, there were two big problems. The first issue was that he was a charmer and popular with the girls. The second and more important issue to me was that he didn't have a relationship with Jesus.

The young man made every effort to get to know me, but looking back, I realize I wasn't ready to be in a relationship. Dating this man would have been a mistake and would have certainly left me heartbroken. At seventeen, most young people don't understand the commitment it takes to have a lasting relationship. I certainly didn't. Honestly, most teenagers are simply looking to have a good time. Young people don't realize their dating habits can have a big impact on their future relationships.

In 2014 the National Marriage Project at the University of Virginia published a study called "Before 'I Do'" and found that couples' actions before marriage actually matter. In other words, premarital experiences can end up haunting married couples. An important reason to abstain from sex involves the long-term consequences. Dr. Galena K. Rhoades and Dr. Scott M. Stanley put it this way: "What people do before marriage appears to matter. Specifically, how they conduct their romantic lives before they tie the knot is linked to their odds of having happy marriages."[4]

4 Galena K. Rhoades and Scott M. Stanley, "Before 'I Do,'" The National Marriage Project at the University of Virginia, accessed August 28, 2017, http://before-i-do.org.

If you knew that saving sex for marriage could heighten your sexual experience, create more stability, and result in greater relational satisfaction, wouldn't you wait to have sex? A study that illustrates the reasons to save sex for the marriage bed appeared in the Journal of Family Psychology and involved 2,035 married participants. According to the study, people who waited until marriage:

- "rated sexual quality 15 percent higher than people who had premarital sex
- rated relationship stability as 22 percent higher
- rated satisfaction with their relationships 20 percent higher

The benefits were about half as strong for couples who became sexually active later in their relationships but before marriage."[5]

Despite the harm it can wreak upon their relationships, many young people continue to have sex before marriage and move in together at alarming rates. God's heart is for people to know He can fill the void they feel. Having sex before marriage and living together are not going to help them have the good, abundant life He wants for them.

Living Together

Matt and Sarah met in college, began dating, and fell in love. Like many couples in this age group, they were eager to find intimacy and moved in together. As good as the idea of marriage sounded to them, living together first made more sense. Matt was looking for a companion, and Sarah was looking for a way to escape her parents' home. Cohabitation seemed like the natural next step in their relationship.

Sarah told me during our interview, "I was tired of being told what to do and didn't have a good relationship with my parents, especially with my dad. I wasn't loved the way I needed. My dad was more of a dictator at home. I didn't have a good sense of my worth."

Sarah went on to explain she had a relationship with Jesus but didn't attend church. "Living together seemed like a sensible choice," she said. "I found

---

5 Dean M. Busby, Jason S. Carroll, and Brian J. Willoughby, "**Compatibility or Restraint? The Effects of Sexual Timing on Marriage Relationships,**" *Journal of Family Psychology* 24, no. 6 (December 2010), 766–774, http://psycnet.apa.org/doiLanding?doi=10.1037%2Fa0021690.

Matt to be nurturing and, best of all, he knew how to rescue me. He didn't have a relationship with Jesus but knew how to rescue me!"

Unfortunately, Sarah and Matt traded one dysfunctional situation for another. Living together caused emotional confusion and despair in their relationship, and Sarah had to lie many times in order to keep her living arrangements from her parents.

When I asked how they could have avoided living together, they shared about their need for a mentor. "We needed someone willing to speak into our lives and help us. Some kind of mentoring on the topic of marriage would have helped us make better decisions. That would have changed a lot of things."

An increasing number of couples are moving in together, starting families, and even buying homes before marriage. Just as nobody buys a car without kicking the tires, researching the make and model, and taking the vehicle for a test drive, many couples don't get married until they've lived together. According to an article in the New York Times, cohabitation in the United States has increased by 1500 percent over the past fifty years. "The majority of young adults in their 20s will live with a romantic partner at least once, and more than half of all marriages will be preceded by cohabitation," writes Meg Jay.[6]

In a nationwide survey conducted in 2001 by the National Marriage Project, nearly half of the young people (in their twenties) who were surveyed agreed with this statement: "You would only marry someone if he or she agreed to live together with you first, so that you could find out whether you really get along." The majority believed that if they moved in together, they could avoid divorce.[7]

On the surface, living together before marriage could make sense to certain people. After all, marriage is a lifetime commitment that shouldn't be taken lightly—right? People choose to cohabit because they're searching for intimacy and are afraid of the commitment of marriage. Typically, young women are more eager to commit to a relationship and get married, but generalizations are not safe to make here. I've heard both young ladies and young men talk about how their partners are not ready for the responsibility of marriage. As a result, they don't pursue marriage and choose to live together instead. In many cases, bringing up the topic of marriage can cause conflict and even a breakup.

---

6 Jay, "Downside."

7 Meg Jay, "*The Downside of Cohabiting Before Marriage*," New York Times, April 14, 2012, http://www.nytimes.com/2012/04/15/opinion/sunday/the-downside-of-cohabiting-before-marriage.html.

I recently talked with a young woman I will call Lilly who shared about a breakup with her boyfriend. They were very much in love when they started dating and, like many couples, desired to move past a dating relationship. They moved in together, started their lives, and took a step toward a long-term commitment. Unfortunately, the relationship didn't last. According to Lilly, her boyfriend wasn't ready for a long-term commitment.

Naturally, this is concerning to many of us who are a little older and already married because we grew up with a different mindset. These trends have also drawn concern from social scientists, psychologists, and various agencies. What's behind this trend to "test the waters" of marriage before committing? The answer is fear. People are afraid that marriage won't work out and are reluctant to give up personal independence. Many couples look at the divorce rates and the challenges of relationships and figure the odds are against them. In other words, the prospect of divorce is driving more people to ask, "Will you move in with me?" instead of, "Will you marry me?"

It is true that marriage is a big commitment, and it's natural to be nervous before jumping into it, but research continues to show that marriage has measurable benefits over living together. As Linda Waite and Maggie Gallagher say, "Married people live longer, are healthier, have fewer heart attacks and other diseases, have fewer problems with alcohol, behave in less risky ways, have more sex—and more satisfying sex—and become much more wealthy than single people."[8]

Researchers have found several advantages to getting married over simply living together:

- Marriage creates not only a family unit but a safety net of relatives who can offer a couple the support they need.
- The commitment that comes with a marriage declaration gives your spouse a sense of security.
- The institution of marriage creates the social, economic, and emotional conditions for effective parenting.
- Married women are at lower risk for domestic violence than women in cohabiting or dating relationships.
- Married couples build more wealth on average than singles or cohabiting couples.

8 Linda J. Waite and Maggie Gallagher, *The Case for Marriage: Why Married People Are Happier, Healthier, and Better Off Financially* (New York: Broadway Books, 2002).

- On average, husbands and wives are healthier, happier, and enjoy longer lives than those who are not married.[9]

Children raised by their married parents have additional benefits:

- They are less likely to be poor or to experience persistent economic insecurity.
- They are more likely to stay in school, have fewer behavioral and attendance problems, and earn four-year college degrees.

Here are just a few of the practical benefits of saving sex for marriage:

- You have no risk of conceiving a child out of wedlock.
- You have no risk of STDs.
- Your relationship will be built on a love that is real, substantial, and stable.
- Waiting for sex teaches you how to control your sexual passions.
- Waiting for sex promotes good communication in dating.
- Your relationship with both sets of parents is improved.
- You have the freedom to question whether you should continue the relationship.
- You are more likely to succeed in marriage.[10]

The Cohabitation Effect

According to an article in the *Journal of Couple & Relationship Therapy*, premarital cohabitation has been shown to be associated with higher rates of divorce in several U.S. studies. The studies indicate links between premarital cohabitation and lower marital quality. Those who cohabit before marriage have lower marital satisfaction compared to those who do not cohabit before marriage. Researchers observed more negative communication, conflict, physical violence, and higher rates of infidelity in those who cohabit before marriage. This association between premarital cohabitation and marital distress and divorce has been termed the *cohabitation effect*.[11] Sociological evidence overwhelmingly demonstrates that living together can have detrimental effects. In fact, cohabitation not only fails to prepare couples for marriage, but it also contributes to decreased marital stability.[12]

9 Waite and Gallagher, *Marriage*.
10 Waite and Gallagher, *Marriage*.
11 Galena K. Rhoades, Scott M. Stanley, and Howard J. Markman, "Working with Cohabitation in Relationship Education and Therapy," *Journal of Couple & Relationship Therapy* 8, no. 2 (May 2009), 95–112, https://www.ncbi.nlm.nih.gov/pmc/articles/PMC2897720.
12 Rhoades, Stanley, and Markman, "Cohabitation."

The evidence for marriage, not cohabitation, is astounding. For the best possible sex life and marriage relationship, young people should avoid two things: living together before marriage and premarital sex. This decision is their choice, of course, but it will impact the rest of their lives.

Institution of Marriage

Another battlefront for marriage today is the belief that the institution of marriage is obsolete. Many couples don't believe in the importance of marriage and are content to live together. In November 2010 Time magazine and the Pew Research Center released a poll showing that nearly four in ten Americans believe marriage is old fashioned.[13] "Halting and reversing the sustained trends of nearly four decades will not happen by accident," researcher Chuck Donovan writes. "The nation needs to forge a fresh American consensus that rescuing marriage—a Marshall Plan to rebuild shattered American homes—is a matter of the highest national priority."[14]

Although marriage statistics have been called into question recently, the divorce rate is still alarming. But do we have all the facts? In her recent book, *The Good News About Marriage: Debunking Discouraging Myths About Marriage and Divorce*, Shaunti Feldhahn details groundbreaking findings from an extensive eight-year study on marriage and divorce:

- The actual divorce rate has never gotten close to 50 percent.
- Those who attend church regularly have a significantly lower divorce rate than those who don't.
- Most marriages are happy.
- Simple changes make a big difference in most marriage problems.
- Most remarriages succeed.[15]

We need to learn to embrace our sexuality in a healthy, positive way and realize it is an amazing gift from Heaven. God gave us a sex drive to teach us about His love and the love and passion we can have toward our spouses. Sex is a

13 "The Decline of Marriage and Rise of New Families," Pew Research Center: November 18, 2010, http://www.pewsocialtrends.org/2010/11/18/the-decline-of-marriage-and-rise-of-new-families/2/#ii-overview.
14 Chuck Donovan, "A Marshall Plan for Marriage: Rebuilding Our Shattered Homes," The Heritage Foundation, June 10, 2011, http://www.heritage.org/marriage-and-family/commentary/marshall-plan-ma-rriage-rebuilding-our-shattered-homes.
15 Shaunti Feldhahn, *The Good News About Marriage: Debunking Discouraging Myths About Marriage and Divorce* (Colorado Springs: Multnomah), 2014.

wonderful gift meant to be unwrapped on the wedding day, and viewing sex in this way helps us understand it is something beautiful and intimate to share with our lifelong partners. The reason our sex drive is aroused early in life isn't to torture us—it's there for us to learn to manage it. Using self-control in those moments will help us to be faithful during marriage.

Discussion Questions:

1. Why do people want to live together? Why is this trend on the rise in America?

2. What are the benefits of a marriage commitment in contrast to cohabitation?

3. If cohabitation is morally wrong, why do so many young people move in together?

4. How were you introduced to the topic of sexuality?

Prayer:

Dear heavenly Father,

I come to You in the name of Jesus to ask You to teach me what true intimacy means. I desire an intimate relationship with You first. Holy Spirit, heal me from any negative sexual habits. Please change the parts of my mind that don't go along with Yours, and give me Your mindset concerning sex.

Chapter

4

THE PURPOSE OF MARRIAGE

Why Your Marriage Will Bring Glory to God

When I was about four years old, I had the privilege of being one of the flower girls in my grandparents' fiftieth wedding anniversary ceremony. The magnitude of the anniversary party and the ceremony were lost on me at the time, but later in my childhood, I remember looking at the pictures and thinking about what a wonderful day it was. I wore a beautiful golden dress with a short veil, and I felt so pretty. Seeing my grandmother's elegance in those pictures filled me with hope for a wonderful marriage myself. That was how the concept of marriage first began to form in my young mind. I also remember my parents kissing and showing affection, and I never forgot the secure feeling this brought to my soul. Although their relationship had many difficulties, I wanted to capture those few precious moments like fireflies in a jar and never let them go.

My grandmother, Mama Lucita, married Papa Alonsito when she was fifteen years old and he was seventeen. From what I could tell, they had a beautiful marriage. I know they had some struggles, but the challenges they faced only increased their love for each other. My grandma was an awesome wife and mother, full of wisdom.

Although Grandma Lucita had ten children, she lost her first three children before she turned twenty-four and miscarried at least once. This alone was enough to devastate most marriages, but it served to make her commitment to her family stronger. My mother would often tell me they had a house full of laughter and, yes, mischief with six girls and one boy. Their marriage became even stronger once they met Jesus. I remember how my grandmother, then in her nineties, used to pray for every single member of the family. Referring to Leon, she would tell me, "I'm praying for your *gringuito*," and I knew she was. She was a great example of what a good wife and mother should be. She took great care of my grandfather to the last day of his life.

My grandfather was a great man of honor, very wise and loving. Perhaps one of the most enduring memories of Papa Alonsito was his last day on earth. My mother shared with me how he waited for each of his children to arrive, as some of them lived out of town and one was travelling out of the country. He hadn't been able to talk much and wasn't feeling well at all, but when all seven of them were there, he had them come into his bedroom so he could bless them. He died only after he'd blessed every single one of his children. After seventy-three years of marriage, at the age of ninety, my Papa Alonsito passed away. What a great legacy he and my grandmother left me.

Our perceptions and beliefs about marriage develop from the influence of our parents and family, peer groups, and the media. In rare moments we're instructed about married life by pastors, parents, and mentors, but many teens grow up learning about sex and marriage from unhealthy sources. As a result, a realistic view of the overall purpose of marriage is missing. In this chapter we will discuss why the institution of marriage exists and how it should function in society.

Bringing Glory to God

The mystery in a nutshell is just this: Christ is in you, so therefore you can look forward to sharing in God's glory. It's that simple.
— *Colossians 1:27 (MSG)*

At the most fundamental level, marriage exists to bring glory to God. That is its primary purpose. As we grow in our marriage relationships, treat our spouses in a godly manner, and develop Christlike character, God smiles. When we enjoy the intimacy and fulfillment He designed for marriage, He rejoices. No longer does He seem like a distant, faraway entity we cannot sense or see, but He is an active part of our lives. He is our center and the love that glues us together with our spouses. A marriage relationship can help us grow as disciples of Jesus so we can shine His light and make a huge difference in this world. There's no doubt in my mind that if we allow God's Spirit into our marriages, we will glorify His name.

The Lord established marriage as an institution for this very reason—to point to His love for all of us. God united Adam and Eve in holy matrimony, saying, *"Therefore a man leaves his father and his mother and cleaves to his wife, and they become one flesh"* (Genesis 2:24, RSV). This foundational statement about marriage is repeated several times in the Bible: first by Jesus in the context of His teachings on divorce (Matthew 19:5; Mark 10:7–8) and then by Paul to illustrate the relationship between Christ and His Church (Ephesians 5:31).

As you read this book on marriage, understand God is calling you to something that is beautiful but sometimes challenging. Though some of God's specific purposes for your life will be clear to you before you get married, some will be revealed only after you say, "I do," and keep walking with Him together with your spouse.

Marriage involves a call from God. Would you take a new job without researching your employer? Would you invest money without doing research or consulting an advisor? In the same way, it is wise to investigate marriage before stepping into it. In Starting Your Marriage Right, Dennis and Barbara Rainey explain it this way:

> God's first purpose for creating man and woman and joining them in marriage was to mirror His image on earth. Center your attention on those words, *mirror His image*. The Hebrew word for "mirror" means to reflect God, to magnify, exalt, and glorify Him. Your marriage should reflect God's image to a world that desperately needs to see who He is. Because we're created in the image of God, people who wouldn't otherwise know what God is like should be able to look at us and get a glimpse.[1]

Benefits and Purposes of Marriage

What has God put on your heart about marriage? Before you give a quick answer, consider a few of the many benefits of marriage.

Unity

> *Though one may be overpowered,*
> *two can defend themselves.*
> *A cord of three strands is not quickly broken.*
> *— Ecclesiastes 4:12*

---

1 Dennis and Barbara Rainey, *Starting Your Marriage Right: What You Need to Know in the Early Years to Make It Last a Lifetime* (Nashville: Thomas Nelson), 2006.

Marriage is a spiritual agreement unifying two people and two families. Being of the same mind in a relationship is crucial for its success. In marriage the focus should be on what a couple is together and the goals they have in common. It is about the team and not the individual. This doesn't mean we lose our individuality, but we are committed to helping each other succeed in every area of life, thereby increasing our intimacy together. A blessed marriage is one that experiences victory because there is a unity of purpose. Even if there are disagreements, knowing we share the same goals provides stability within the relationship. Whether the decisions are financial, family related, or concern another aspect of life, a couple who is unified will experience more happiness.

When a husband and wife regularly spend time in prayer and submit their decisions to the Lord, better decisions are made. Walking in unity takes humble hearts and surrendering to God's Spirit.

Love and Companionship

> *Do two walk together*
> *unless they have agreed to do so?*
> *— Amos 3:3*

Affection, love, and true companionship grow out of oneness of spirit as each partner models Christ's love. Drawing closer in a relationship involves growing intellectually, emotionally, sexually, and spiritually deeper with your partner. Being a true companion means, at times, sacrificing what you want to do and learning to appreciate what your spouse loves. Companions enjoy hanging out and sharing life's challenges, as well as making the time to create moments that keep renewing their love.

The New Testament describes three types of love:

- *Eros* (sexual love)
- *Phileo* (friendship and a companionable love)
- *Agape* (unconditional love)

These types of love produce incredible attributes in our lives. From *phileo* derives *philautia* or love of self. From *eros* derives *ludus* or playful love. Finally, *agape* is the most profound kind of love: that of dying to self in order for the other person to grow. It is selfless and sacrificial. The fruit of agape love is *pragma*, which is real, mature love that becomes an indestructible commitment.

Although *agape* love and *eros* love are key to establishing a marriage, the result is *phileo* love: an eternal and real commitment in which you can see your spouse not just as a lover and companion but also as your faithful friend. You are willing to give your life to protect and help your partner grow and increase in every area. This is the love that bonds a couple together. This love involves a deep understanding developed between both parties and only comes with time. We see this type of bond displayed between couples who have been married for decades.

The apostle Paul tells us what love looks like in 1 Corinthians 13. It is patient, kind, hopeful, and trusting; it never fails. For many this kind of love might seem impossible to demonstrate, but with the help of His Spirit, we can truly love the Lord's way.

Lineage

> *God blessed them and said to them, "Be fruitful and increase in number; fill the earth and subdue it. Rule over the fish in the sea and the birds in the sky and over every living creature that moves on the ground."*
> — *Genesis 1:28*

One characteristic of a successful marriage is a lasting legacy, which is often displayed in the caliber of a couple's children. The blessing of children allows a marriage to reproduce itself physically. There is nothing more fulfilling in a marriage than having children. It gives a couple a reason to get up every day and desire and dream for more. God finds great delight when a couple's children carry their legacy forward. Although children bring much joy, they also bring the responsibility to teach and train. Some couples opt not to have children for various reasons, and these couples often find joy and fulfillment in investing themselves in relationships and service.

Sexual Enjoyment

> *Marriage should be honored by all, and the marriage bed kept pure, for God will judge the adulterer and all the sexually immoral.*
> — *Hebrews 13:4*

The physical relationship is a reflection of the loyalty and affection shared between marriage partners who have become one flesh. God created marriage and, likewise, He created sexual relations. Once married, it is important to understand what will help your mate experience sexual pleasure. Although most of us think of sex in terms of enjoyment, keep in mind that sex is relational, too. When we become "one flesh" with our spouses, there is a blending of spirit, soul, and body. The more we work at trying to please our mates, the better sex will be. It is not just about your pleasure but about both partners feeling sexually satisfied. God designed lovemaking to be a manifestation of the unity a couple shares.

Protection

"A man's home is his fortress and refuge." That saying offers a glimpse into how a couple should manage their home. A husband and wife should both provide protection and instruction in their home, as God has given them the purpose of taking care of each other and the ones placed in their safekeeping. In most cases, it is the man's job to protect his family. When everyone is asleep upstairs and a couple hears a sound downstairs, the man doesn't turn to his wife and say how tired he is or how he got up last time. Typically, the man gets up to protect the family because it's part of his nature to protect. Similarly, a couple must be unified in protecting their family from emotional and spiritual dangers. In most cases, women are the ones who instinctively protect their children from unhealthy influences.

Men are called to be the head of the family. The word head in Scripture comes from the Greek word *kephalé*, a military term describing the first row of soldiers in a battalion. This row was formed by kings, generals, and valiant men who were experienced in the art of war. Behind them came the men with little experience in war, followed by the new soldiers just enlisted in the army. Therefore, when someone was called the "head," it was because this person was capable of giving his life for the ones behind him. That is the meaning of the word head in the New Testament.[2] As Jesus is the head of the man and the Church (1 Corinthians 11:3; Ephesians 5:23), God calls men to be submitted to Christ so they can be protectors and humble servants who pray fervently and bless their families. The husband protects the wife by laying down his life for her just as Jesus did for all of us on the cross, and together both parents are charged with protecting and raising godly children.

2 Cristian Canelos, "La Situación de la Mujer en la Iglesia del Siglo XXI," in *Biblia, Teología y Ministerios en Contextos*, edited by Ángel Manzo (Guayaquil, Ecuador: Publicaciones Seminario Bíblico Alianza del Ecuador, 2016), 30–34.

The wife protects the home by trusting and honoring God and her husband. She knows that *"charm is deceptive, and beauty is fleeting; but a woman who fears the Lord is to be praised"* (Proverbs 31:30). Both husband and wife are called to submit to each other according to Ephesians 5:21, which brings covering and protection to the couple. (We'll discuss submission in greater detail in a later chapter.)

Stewardship

> *A good person leaves an inheritance for their children's children,*
> *but a sinner's wealth is stored up for the righteous.*
> — *Proverbs 13:22*

God wants us to be good stewards. This means taking good care of the world around us, helping the poor and needy, and being wise with our own possessions. Together a couple can provide more financial stewardship and security for each other and their children. Whether a husband and wife both work or choose to have one spouse stay home, marriage is about teamwork. Ecclesiastes 4:9–10 states it this way:

> *Two are better than one,*
> *because they have a good return for their labor:*
> *If either of them falls down,*
> *one can help the other up.*
> *But pity anyone who falls*
> *and has no one to help them up.*

The purpose of earning money is to provide stability for the family, to bless those around us, and to give back to God. It is common knowledge that many marital arguments involve money. When we take our focus off the reasons we're earning income in the first place, it is easy to let money start to own us.

Resting in God's Presence

> *Yes, my soul, find rest in God;*
> *my hope comes from him.*
> — *Psalm 62:5*

We feel safe and free in a marriage when we rest in the assurance that we're under God's protection. It is easy for us to forget that God wants couples to relax, enjoy their lives, and rest in Him. Sometimes we think life is all about work, and we get so busy that we forget to enjoy the beautiful moments. We can become so entangled in our problems, bad thinking, and destructive behaviors that we forget God is in control of our marriages.

Your marriage should cultivate an atmosphere of rest where both husband and wife can take time off to enjoy God's presence, goodness, and beauty. Make sure to create this type of spiritual atmosphere for each other and your children.

Your marriage should cultivate an atmosphere of rest where both husband and wife can take time off to enjoy God's presence, goodness, and beauty. Make sure to create this type of spiritual atmosphere for each other and your children.

Expanding God's Kingdom

As followers of Christ, we need to be honest with God and ourselves. He called us to love the lost and has given us a commission to go out and shine His light. The Book of John says that just as the Father sent Jesus to the earth, Jesus has also sent us. This is a personal call we all need to heed. Being a disciple of Christ is the most amazing privilege we can have. He has given us absolutely everything we need for success, including the gift of His Holy Spirit, who helps us find victory through Jesus in any struggle or circumstance we go through.

What does this have to do with marriage? The world will know we are the children of God by the love we have for others; that is how we expand His Kingdom. One of the greatest testimonies to non-believers is a strong marriage.

The Purpose of Trials

One of the best moments in my life was when I married Leon. I clearly remember watching his eyes tear up as we stood together at the marriage altar, and this reminded me of God's love for me. God was the main party in our marriage covenant and had planned that day for Leon and me. I looked into Leon's eyes and acknowledged how God had brought us together, and for me that was a perfect moment. Three more perfect moments occurred when my kids were born. As they came out of my womb, I felt God's presence and a deep sense of love for them, because God was involved—He was a part of my experience.

Although we would like to have great moments all the time, the Lord uses challenges to help us grow. For Leon and me, one of our biggest challenges of late has been seeing our parents getting older; we are trying to find ways to help and bless them through this season of life. Knowing a parent is ill or dying is difficult, especially for me, as I am so far away from my family. This trial has brought Leon and me closer to each other in many ways. We've cried together and prayed without ceasing. Aging is part of life and something that has taught us to be aware of how short our lives are and how meaningful we want them to be.

Struggles will come to your married life, and during times of crisis, it is reassuring to know God has drawn you and your partner together to bring Him glory. Two of my friends, the "Smiths," understand a thing or two about developing Christlike character. Possibly their greatest challenge to this day involves raising their oldest son.

The Smiths' son began to show signs of autism and Asperger's syndrome at an early age. He was bullied in school, which added to the problem and caused him to withdraw academically and socially. Even after several years of special schools, homeschooling, and weekly visits to specialists, he didn't improve, and his list of disorders continued to grow. Countless times my friend and her husband considered putting him in an institutional setting. Mrs. Smith has been a strong believer for years, but in the midst of their crisis, God called Mr. Smith to faith in Christ as well, and he committed his life to the Lord.

Life for the Smiths smoothed out for a time until their son began to regress. He went through bouts of depression, talked about suicide, and refused to be a part of the family. He became more verbally and physically abusive. Again they began to consider sending him away for the good of the family. During one of his episodes, they made the decision to call an agency and send him to a ranch where he could get institutional help. As difficult as this decision was, they hoped and prayed the experience would result in real improvement. After their son had spent time at the ranch with medical assessments, daily evaluations, and psychological coaching, my friend shared some observations with me.

"He sounds more grateful over the phone," she told me. "He now understands that his problems aren't that bad. He finally has a little hope. He's eating their food and showering regularly. I really think he's starting to change."

Sometime later, the Smiths' son was ready to come home. His father drove to pick him up, and on the way home, they did some sightseeing. For a boy who had refused to get in a car and take a simple drive, this return trip was a step in the right direction and a signal of improvement. Needless to say, the decision to send him away paid off. In their final report, the organization recommended their son finish high school and ultimately college. For Mr. and Mrs. Smith, the biggest change was how their son started to talk about his future. Mr. Smith was even considering starting a tech company with him.

God is a good Father, and His intention is never for us to suffer, yet He uses struggles in our marriages to increase our faith and make our marriages stronger. In John 16:33 Jesus said, *"I have told you these things, so that in me you may have peace. In this world you will have trouble, but take heart! I have overcome the world."* Christ is saying God can use suffering as an opportunity for growth.

Teresa's Story

Years ago when I started a support group for women who had miscarried and wanted to get pregnant, I met a woman I will call Teresa. Some of the women who attended our prayer meetings got pregnant right away, and Teresa was one of them. Although she had miscarried a few times, one of her losses was particularly painful, as the child was born deformed and later died. As you can imagine, the situation left her feeling like God had abandoned her.

One of her children was born with Down syndrome and autism. She loved this baby so much and never considered him unwanted, but her husband greatly struggled with accepting and relating to this child. To him, the child was a mistake and caused him to question his faith. Although Teresa felt abandoned by her husband, she never doubted God's character as a good Father. Her struggle had more to do with the depression and anguish her husband endured because of the child. She had to be the strong one—and she was. As the process of healing continued, they were able to conceive three more beautiful children, all of them healthy.

When I asked her what kept them together, she said, "When we got married, we knew that this was God's will for us. My parents prayed for me since I was a little girl to marry the man that God had for me, and I did. When I dated other guys, my parents knew that they weren't God's will for me, and I listened to them and broke off the relationships. But with Randy, we all knew it was God's will."

She also explained that marriage is a covenant, and she told me one afternoon, "No matter what tests and struggles we encounter, we know that marriage is a covenant and a commitment for life. God is so good! Those prayers we prayed twenty years ago were answered. God has blessed me and my husband so much!"

Abba Father is crazy in love with all of His children. The presence of struggles and trials doesn't mean God loves us less. What it means is that we've been born into a fallen world where sin still exists. We have to learn to hang on to His loving arms no matter our circumstances. The truth of the matter is that with God's help, we can handle what life throws at us. We can actually grow in different areas of our lives with His guidance. As we walk through hardship, we can show a level of compassion and vulnerability toward each other that will help us understand our spouses' pain and the pain of others in a much deeper way. Some struggles can bring great blessing as we start to understand that God is always very close to us, even when we don't feel Him at all. The Word of God says that Jesus came to give us life in abundance. It is our job to trust Him, and it is His Spirit's job to teach us to live in that place of trust despite the trials we encounter in our marriages. In our weakness He is strong. When people see that our confidence and peace come from God, they will understand that His purpose was never to harm us but really to give us hope and a good future.

Marriage exists to bring glory to God, and as we trust Him in our marriages, we will see His blessings more and more.

Discussion Questions:

1. In this chapter I wrote about how the marriage relationship exists to bring glory to God. That is the primary purpose of marriage, and the Lord takes delight when we fulfill His will and get married. Do you agree or disagree with this thought? Why?

2. Which aspect of marriage are you looking forward to the most?

3. Does staying married forever sound scary to you? Why or why not?

4. What does unity mean to you, and why is it important?

5. Struggles and trials will come to all marriages. Why do you think this happens? How does God use these trials to help a marriage, or even a dating relationship, grow?

Prayer:

Dear heavenly Father,

Help me to have a teachable heart because I know that marriage requires learning and listening to You. Help me to grow closer to You and understand Your purpose in marriage for my life.

Chapter
5

THE MARRIAGE COVENANT

How Your Covenant with God and Your Spouse Will Change Everything

"Honey, do you really love me?"

I've asked Leon this question many times during our twenty-seven years of marriage, not just because I need to hear a sweet reply but also because I love being pursued and completely cherished by him. What all women want is the assurance that we're going to be loved and adored by our husbands for the rest of our lives.

He always replies, "Yes, sweetie, I love you a loooooot!" Or sometimes he'll say it in Spanish: "I love you muuuuuuucho!"

Men, meanwhile, need to ask other questions. "Will you honor and respect me for the rest of our lives? Will you encourage me and let me know I'm your hero?" They might not ask these questions aloud, but they need to know that they're honored and respected. Those are the words men need to hear. Unconditional love, commitment, and honor are the key components of the marriage covenant.

Most people have heard the word covenant but are unsure what it means. In the Bible a covenant was an agreement or sacred oath between God and His people, in which God made promises and required certain conduct from His people in return. Both in marriage and in Old Testament history, a covenant is the most sacred of all pledges and promises.

This is what a marriage covenant looks like:

- It is a commitment between a man and woman, as well as God Himself, made before family, friends, and the community to remain steadfast in unconditional love and sexual purity.
- It involves purposeful relational growth.
- It involves two people willing to love and honor each other and God for the rest of their lives.

- It involves sacrifice.

Covenant is how God has chosen to communicate to us, redeem us, and provide eternal life in Jesus. The Bible is a covenant document. The word *testament* is Latin for "covenant," and the Old and New Testaments are actually old and new covenants. Most people understand that marriage is a public declaration, but viewing the marriage ceremony as a covenant takes our vows a step further. One poetic example of covenant from Scripture is the Song of Songs.

Song of Songs

The Song of Songs is an Old Testament poem written by King Solomon about love and covenant marriage. Solomon and a Shulamite woman meet, fall in love, get married, and grow in their love for each other. More than just an interesting poem, the Song of Songs is also an allegory of God's love for Israel and addresses the relationship between Christ and His Church, which is His bride. I used the following two verses in my vows when I married Leon. As you read this passage, picture yourself on the receiving end of these sweet words. You will find they make you feel honored, cherished, and adored. This is at the heart of a covenant relationship:

> *Place me like a seal over your heart,*
> *like a seal on your arm;*
> *for love is as strong as death,*
> *its jealousy unyielding as the grave.*
> *It burns like blazing fire,*
> *like a mighty flame.*
> *Many waters cannot quench love;*
> *rivers cannot sweep it away*
> *If one were to give*
> *all the wealth of one's house for love,*
> *it would be utterly scorned.*
> *— Song of Songs 8:6–7*

Covenant History

Now that we've discussed how marriage is a covenant established by God, let's look at some of the most important covenants in Scripture. Notice how these examples reveal both God's character and the conduct He expects from us in return.

Creational Covenant

The first covenant in the Bible is the agreement between God and mankind. Humanity would represent God to His creation, express His authority, and take care of creation as His stewards. *"Be fruitful and increase in number; fill the earth and subdue it. Rule over the fish in the sea and the birds in the sky and over every living creature that moves on the ground"* (Genesis 1:28).

Adamic Covenant

God entered into a covenant with Adam and Eve when He told them that eating from the tree of the knowledge of good and evil was forbidden. He promised life for obedience and spiritual death for disobedience. *"And the Lord God commanded the man, 'You are free to eat from any tree in the garden; but you must not eat from the tree of the knowledge of good and evil, for when you eat of it you will surely die'"* (Genesis 2:16–17).

Noahic Covenant

God formed an agreement with Noah, telling him, *"Go into the ark, you and your whole family, because I have found you righteous in this generation"* (Genesis 7:1). Along with two of every animal, God spared Noah, his wife, and the rest of his family because they were righteous in the midst of great unrighteousness. After the rest of mankind was destroyed, God showed Noah the rainbow, which represented the covenant He made to Noah and his descendants.

Abrahamic Covenant

God promised land and descendants to Abraham in exchange for his obedience in leaving his home (Genesis 12:1–3). Three elements and three requirements ratified this covenant:

- The two parties had to be present at the time of the covenant.
- They had to bring an animal.
- They had to bring a knife for the sacrifice.

The two parties declared orally that a covenant was about to take place; then the animal was sacrificed and cut in half. Each covenant taker had to walk between the pieces of the sacrificed animal, and in this way, the covenant was ratified. If for any reason, one of the parties failed to follow through on the declared covenant, the faithful party could literally cut the covenant breaker in half and the covenant would remain honored.

The most interesting fact about this covenant is that Almighty God requested Abraham to bring the same elements mentioned here to seal and ratify the covenant God Himself declared and promised to him. God was the One who passed between the animals, not Abraham, and the covenant was sealed on God's side.

> *When the sun had set and darkness had fallen, a smoking firepot with a blazing torch appeared and passed between the pieces. On that day the Lord made a covenant with Abram [that is, Abraham] and said, "To your descendants I give this land, from the Wadi of Egypt to the great river."*
> — *Genesis 15:17–18*

In this covenant, we have to understand the great mercy God showed toward Abraham by not letting him walk in between the cut animals. God knew that Abraham was going to fail and, as a result, would have to die, but despite Abraham's failures, God kept His promise. Abraham's faith in God was an eminent part of his life. He knew the deep meaning of covenant and that God would never fail him, which was why he was obedient when God later asked him to sacrifice his son Isaac. No matter what happened, He knew God would be faithful to His promise.

Mosaic Covenant

After the Hebrew people were delivered from slavery in Egypt and went to look for the Promised Land, Moses received the Law on Sinai. This group of laws served as the universal moral code for all people and when followed ensured fellowship with God. However, this covenant was later transformed when Jeremiah 31:33 declared, *"This is the covenant I will make with the people of Israel after that time . . . I will put my law in their minds and write it on their hearts. I will be their God, and they will be my people."*

Each of these biblical covenants was ratified with blood, including the creational covenant, when God first created flesh and blood. The wages of sin is death, and man can approach God only through the sacrifice of innocent blood. That is why the Passover remains important to believers. The Israelites were slaves in Egypt when God called Moses to rescue them. Before the last plague in which every firstborn would die, God told Moses to have each Hebrew household sacrifice a lamb and cover their doorposts with its blood. That was the only way to keep the angel of death away from their homes and firstborns. Death "passed over" these homes. God's people were freed from slavery, walked through the parted waters of the Red Sea, and experienced other amazing miracles on their journey to the Promised Land.

In the Old Testament, the Passover marked the beginning of the deliverance of God's people and highlighted His unconditional love for them and the power of the blood. It might sound strange to our westernized ears, but blood played an important role in ancient times and it was considered to be full of power. There is life in the blood, according to Scripture. Following the Passover, all sacrifices in the Mosaic system are founded on this principle: Through the blood of sacrifice, there is deliverance, protection, and a God-provided future.

That principle was fulfilled in the Person of Jesus. Both the Son of God and God Himself, Jesus was conceived by the power of the Holy Spirit and born to the virgin Mary and Joseph the carpenter. He came to earth with flesh and bones. Jesus emptied Himself of His divine privileges and came as a humble human being, relying and depending completely on His relationship with His heavenly Father and the Holy Spirit. Christ had not even begun His ministry when John the Baptist announced, *"Look, the Lamb of God, who takes away the sin of the world"* (John 1:29). So from the very beginning, it was declared that Christ would die and shed His blood in order to take away sin.

Ultimately, God brought redemption to all people when He sent Jesus to earth to die on the cross. This new covenant fulfilled all other covenants. Because Christ shed His blood for all of us, animal sacrifices were no longer required for the forgiveness of sins. Further, His blood allows us to overcome the powers of darkness:

"Come now, let us settle the matter,"
says the Lord.

"Though your sins are like scarlet,
they shall be as white as snow;
though they are red as crimson,
they shall be like wool."
— *Isaiah 1:18*

The prophets knew that God's heart was for the people to repent and come back to Him, and Isaiah 1:18 represents the invitation Christ would make available to us. When Jesus died on the cross, He gave His life not just because He was obedient to His Father but also because He was expressing His unique and perfect love by willingly offering Himself for us. His sinless, spotless life was given as a ransom for our sins. His blood is His total and unfailing commitment to us. Jesus died an agonizing and cruel death. Not only this, but He was separated from the presence of His heavenly Father for a brief time. When we accept His sacrifice, repent, and invite Him to take our place as sinful people, we also accept that His atoning blood can rescue us from Satan's stranglehold. When we accept the power of His resurrection, we receive His victory.

Since we have been redeemed from the enemy, we are no longer our own; we belong to Jesus. His blood has returned to us everything that was lost when sin entered the heart of man. *"But if we walk in the light, as he is in the light, we have fellowship with one another, and the blood of Jesus, his Son, purifies us from all sin" (1 John 1:7). When we believe in Jesus, God's Spirit comes to live in us as a seal over our hearts. "Now it is God who makes both us and you stand firm in Christ. He anointed us, set his seal of ownership on us, and put his Spirit in our hearts as a deposit, guaranteeing what is to come"* (2 Corinthians 1:21–22).

Your Marriage and the Blood of Jesus

If we invite Jesus to be a part of our marriage covenants, He will give us everything we need to make them work. He is our foundation and the party who is fully committed to us. When we invite Him to be more than a guest in our marriages but to be our rock, our shield, our wisdom, the main part that glues a husband and wife together—we can know that He is 100 percent in. Jesus has given it all for us to have blessed marriages. We just have to learn to listen, trust, and obey. His precious blood and the power of His resurrection have brought us back to unlimited, intimate relationship with the heart of the Father. It is the same eternal spiritual state Adam and Eve experienced in the Garden of Eden. God's character through every covenant reminds us that He is the One who is faithful, and He will never back out. A marriage covenant is made with three parties: God, the husband, and the wife.

Some of us are a little squeamish, and blood is a topic we may not like to think or talk about. When Jesus described His coming blood sacrifice, many of His friends left Him. Blood at that time had a strong and sacred meaning, and not many understood or could even conceive of what the Savior was saying. In John 6:53–54 Jesus stated, *"Unless you eat the flesh of the Son of Man and drink his blood, you have no life in you."* Knowing what Jesus was talking about in this verse is crucial to understanding the idea of covenant.

When Jesus mentioned eating His body and drinking His blood, He was talking about a conviction or strong belief we all need in order to have eternal life: We believe that His death pays the penalty for our sins. His perfect righteousness is freely given to us in exchange for our unrighteousness. We "eat" Jesus' flesh and "drink" His blood by believing He did those things for us, and this forms the covenant we have with our Savior. He instituted the Lord's Supper because He didn't want us to forget the very core of what we believe: that Jesus saves us and we have a covenant with God.

The Power of Covenant

I recently met a man I will call John who shared with Leon and me about his sexual struggles. When he was twenty years old, he started dating someone, and as a Catholic, his desire was to stay pure, which meant abstaining from sex before marriage. However, despite his best efforts, he gave in to temptation.

"I mistook my girlfriend's need for affection as a sign that she wanted to have sex," he told us. "What she wanted was to please me and experience intimacy, but I interpreted that as, 'Let's do it.'"

They had sex several times and out of guilt, he decided to end the relationship. During the next few months, he became very close to God and studied the Bible. Feeling a new passion for living and relationships, he was discipled in the Christian faith and dedicated his life to the Lord, fully committed to following Him. Years later, John felt led by God to pursue someone, a different girl. They started a relationship in which they both committed to stay pure before God and each other. After months of purity, they passionately kissed on the day of their wedding, and John and his wife have been married now for many years. Because of their commitment to each other and the Lord, they've experienced God's faithfulness in their marriage. I love this story of forgiveness and restoration, and it highlights several aspects central to the idea of the marriage covenant:

- A personal covenant with God, accepting the sacrifice of Jesus and His forgiveness by repenting and committing to love and live for Him
- The covenant between the husband and wife, as well as between the couple and God
- A husband and wife who invite God to be part of their marriage covenant. They allow Him to speak to them and commit to receive His love, healing, and forgiveness so they can freely love Him and each other.

God always extends an open invitation for us to make Him part of our marriage covenants, and when we say, "Yes," we commit to trusting Him, understanding He will do anything to keep us together. Have you ever seen a candle ceremony at a wedding? Leon and I had three candles: one representing God and one for each of us. Leon and I took our candles and lit them, and then we lit God's candle with both of ours. We blew ours out, and the one candle remained lit as a symbol of the three of us becoming one. My marriage covenant is with Leon and God, and I would never want it any other way.

Even after a damaging relationship, when we know we've crossed the line, there is grace. If you are carrying guilt over a past relationship, repent for what happened and know you will be forgiven (Romans 10:9), washed clean by Jesus' blood. Ask Him to cleanse you from any soul ties or unhealthy emotional bonds in your life. Realize Christ passionately loves you and will always pursue you.

Even after a damaging relationship, when we know we've crossed the line, there is grace. If you are carrying guilt over a past relationship, repent for what happened and know you will be forgiven (Romans 10:9), washed clean by Jesus' blood. Ask Him to cleanse you from any soul ties or unhealthy emotional bonds in your life. Realize Christ passionately loves you and will always pursue you.

How a Covenant Works

When we get married, the words we speak serve as a commitment or covenant before God and man, similar to the covenants made by our spiritual fathers. According to Jewish custom, God's people signed a written agreement at the marriage to seal the covenant. In much the same way, in America and other countries the marriage ceremony is meant to be a public demonstration of a couple's commitment to a covenant relationship, and their vows activate the agreement. Although the marriage ceremony is a memorable way to mark the union of two souls, it is the couple's commitment before God and men that matters. We need to mean what we say in our vows at the altar. When a couple trades vows before God, the Bible tells us that God unites them. They are no longer two people but one. For many couples, this happens at the altar or when they enter into a legal marriage contract, but more and more frequently, couples are skipping the covenant and settling for cohabitation.

In most cultures marriage has two "steps" in order to be ratified: vows and sexual intercourse. Legally, the vows form a verbal contract to become one entity that shares property, debt, privileges, and other responsibilities. This is why a couple has to go through the court system and cannot abolish the marriage easily. It is also why a pastor, priest, or justice of the peace must officiate the wedding. Spiritually, the vows create the covenant. The couple is united, both in the eyes of the society in which they live and before God, who spiritually joins them together. Just as a legal agreement cannot be broken without consequences, so a covenant cannot be broken without consequences.

Biblically speaking, having sex before the wedding ceremony is morally wrong; however, sex is expected after the wedding. In most states a marriage that is not consummated can be annulled, which voids the marriage completely, making it as if it never happened. In ancient times the wedding celebration started once the guests were shown a bed sheet with blood on it—a sign the newly married couple had consummated their relationship. Remember a covenant in Scripture requires blood. The hymen is a thin membrane that covers all or part of the entrance to the vagina. Though this doesn't happen in all cases, the hymen usually breaks the first time a woman has intercourse; the blood is spilled and the hymen doesn't heal unless there is a miraculous intervention. I have heard testimonies of women who had intercourse before getting married, but they repented, asked Jesus to heal them, and then testified they bled the night of their wedding. That is an amazing testimony, but the biggest miracle is the forgiveness of God. When we ask Jesus to forgive us, we can know we are pure no matter what, because Jesus cleanses us from our sins. Many years ago the hymen was considered a symbol of covenant, which is one reason our virginity is a gift to save for our spouses.

When we remain pure for the day of the wedding, we are blessed. This kind of purity protects the couple from bringing unhealthy soul ties into the marriage that can cause significant problems. Staying pure also prevents children from being born outside of a covenant relationship, which makes them vulnerable to a cycle of unfaithfulness, one that repeats the same mistakes and behaviors and causes additional separation and destruction.

Chastity or moral purity in both men and women is a precious and valuable gift that should be developed. In their book Moral Revolution: *The Naked Truth About Sexual Purity*, Kris and Jason Vallotton say, "Anyone can give away something expensive, but only those who understand sacrifice can give away something valuable."[1] Knowing the deeper meanings behind the marriage covenant gives us a sense of purpose and helps us determine what God's will is for us in marriage, as well as how to prepare for it. It also helps us wait and learn patience as we trust that God has a special person picked out as our future partner.

If you have kept yourself pure, I applaud you because of the strength of your convictions. However, if you're like millions of people who have lost their virginity, not realizing it was a treasure worth saving for marriage—you get the chance to start over. Do you remember Ally's story from chapter 3? She represents many people who have found hope and restoration. What she told me rings true: "No one ever told me that virginity was a treasure and that I was supposed to wait for the day of my wedding to give myself to my spouse. Then Jesus came into my life and helped me to discover my identity in Him, His love, and forgiveness. That's when I also got out of my darkness and became pure again. Through the cross of Jesus, I became a new creature, a pure and valuable woman."

The great news is that with the help of God's Spirit, we can start over. If we acknowledge that His blood has the power to transform us, we can be made new. Choose to embrace forgiveness, live in a covenant relationship with Christ—and expect to have a covenant marriage with God at the center.

---

1 Kris Vallotton and Jason Vallotton, *Moral Revolution: The Naked Truth About Sexual Purity* (Grand Rapids, MI: Chosen Books, 2012).

Discussion Questions:

1. What is a covenant?

2. What does it mean to become one flesh?

3. What are the consequences of having sex outside of marriage? Do you feel guilty or ashamed because of a past relationship? Invite Jesus into the situation. Ask Him to wash you clean and remove all shame and guilt from you. Also ask Him to set you free from any unhealthy emotional bonds or soul ties.

4. Why is it important to wait to have sex until after marriage?

5. Do you have a covenant relationship with Jesus? Explain what this means to you.

Prayer:

Dear heavenly Father,

Teach me more about how to have a covenant relationship with You. Help me to treasure the idea of a marriage covenant. Teach me how the blood of Jesus can help me draw closer to You and make me pure.

II

LOOKING INWARD

Search me, God, and know my heart;
test me and know my anxious thoughts.
See if there is any offensive way in me,
and lead me in the way everlasting.
— Psalm 139:23–24

Do you understand you are the joy of God's heart?

To have a deep relationship with this God who loves us, our hearts need to be healed. All of us are in need of healing, and we are transformed as we learn how to see our Father, know Him, and love Him in a healthy way. The key to accessing God's heart is repentance, and the key to accessing His blessings is obedience. We don't obey Him out of obligation, because we think it's expected of us—we seek Him and do what He says because He is our joy, too.

As you trust Him from your heart, you will reap a huge reward. You will know who you truly are and what you were made for.

Chapter
6

BECOMING THE ONE

How You Can Be a Gift to Your Future Spouse

How do you know when you're ready for a relationship?

In matters of love and relationships, many people are reactive. They meet someone attractive and bam! They begin to date. One thing leads to another, and they're in an official relationship only a month or even a week later. Although my experience was more reactive, I'd been praying for a suitor for some time. When Leon asked me to be his girlfriend, I sensed the Lord was pleased with our relationship. I asked Him for confirmation and He clearly said, "Yes."

Sometime later I asked God if I was ready to take the next step: marriage. Like many young people, I had numerous questions and doubts, but I knew the most important thing was God's assurance that marriage was His will for my life. Involving the Lord in the decision gave me confidence in my choice and allowed me to prepare for my marriage. He led me through a process that helped me know I was following His will for me.

This is the process God took me on. It began when Leon was just a someday hope in my heart. Before I met my husband, I needed to shore up spiritual and emotional areas in my life, so my preparation for marriage started by looking inward. I identified the importance of my relationship with Jesus and realized how much God adores me. I needed to know how much I was loved and how much I loved God in return; that was the first step for me. Then the Lord put a desire in my heart to look outward and find a husband. I began to consider the qualities I desired in a man, and eventually I met Leon and made a commitment to him. Every time I look at the diamond I wear on my left hand, I thank God for the man He brought into my life.

To become the one for your future spouse, you begin by looking inward and addressing the following areas: your love for God, any spiritual and emotional healing that may be necessary, and your identity—who you actually are and not the person you may feel pressured into being. Only after that do you begin to look outward and consider issues of compatibility, expectation, and commitment. Let's take a look at the first step.

Loving God

And so we know and rely on the love God has for us. God is love. Whoever lives in love lives in God, and God in them.
— 1 John 4:16

You are God's delight. Do you understand how much you delight His heart? Giving and receiving love is one of the most fulfilling experiences a person can have. Both human and divine love have the power to transform, yet in its broadest sense, love is a choice. Love is something we choose to do, and it is tied to our faith. Before we can be ready to love another person, we must understand what love is and the source of all love. We need to start with God's perfect love.

Jesus had a deep, abiding relationship with His Father. He trusted Him the way a little child would trust their earthly father. To enter the Kingdom of Heaven, Jesus said we have to be like little children, which requires trust. Have you ever observed the adoration a young child has for their dad? Children know their fathers are there to love, help, and encourage them, and this is the way it should be. A child will jump into a father's arms from a high ledge or will laugh hysterically as they're thrown into the air and caught—all because of this trust. I remember watching my three children play the roughest games with Leon, knowing they wouldn't get hurt. Why? My children knew what I knew about Leon—that he is trustworthy and wouldn't put them in harm's way. This is the type of trust we should have for our heavenly Father.

I've observed through the years that people who don't trust God or don't feel loved by Him generally didn't have a good relationship with their earthly fathers while growing up. They might have been abandoned, ignored, neglected, physically and emotionally abused, or simply not loved the way a child needs to be loved.

A biblical story that emphasizes God's love for each of us is the parable of the prodigal son, which Jesus shares in the Gospel of Luke. A father has two sons, and the younger asks for his inheritance before the father dies, a dishonoring request that essentially removes the father from the son's life. The father, however, agrees and the son goes out and squanders his inheritance. Soon afterward, a severe famine hits the land, and the younger son becomes so destitute that he longs to eat the food he's feeding to pigs. He returns home with the intention of repenting and begging his father for forgiveness, expecting to be made a servant. But the father is waiting and watching for his son's return. When he sees him, he runs to meet his lost son on the road. In the culture of the day, rejecting the father as this son did was punishable by death; the neighbors could have stoned the son before he reached the house. But instead, in an overwhelming display of affection, the father gives his son his robe and ring and restores honor to him. The father welcomes him back as his son, not a servant, and holds a feast to celebrate his return.

Although this parable is about a man and his father, the central message is that God loves each of us unconditionally. His affection has no limits. God, like the father in the story, gives us everything when we come back to Him with a repentant heart. The Lord loves us perfectly, and all of us need to experience this type of affection without limits, letting go of any misconceptions we've adopted about the Lord's character. The parable tells us to accept His love and attention wholeheartedly, and it frees us up to love Him back. I know many people who are in search of this love, but they don't know how to find it because they haven't fully accepted the unconditional love of Christ. For some, it takes only moments to trust the Lord in this way, but for others, it's a lifelong journey.

Ask Father God to reveal His love to you. Wait before Him and seek Him in this matter. If you think you are not encountering God's love, or if you have any doubts about how much the Lord cherishes and delights in you, reach out to someone. Find a pastor, friend, parent, or teacher who knows God well and can help guide you into a better understanding of His love for you.

Ask Father God to reveal His love to you. Wait before Him and seek Him in this matter. If you think you are not encountering God's love, or if you have any doubts about how much the Lord cherishes and delights in you, reach out to someone. Find a pastor, friend, parent, or teacher who knows God well and can help guide you into a better understanding of His love for you.

Agape Love

God is love. He is full of unconditional, everlasting love that is meant to be experienced by every human heart, soul, and spirit. It is meant to go far beyond an "I know it in my head" kind of love. God's love is so much more than what any of us could explain. That is why the apostle Paul prays that we will be *"rooted and established in love"* and that we may have the power to grasp *"how wide and long and high and deep is the love of Christ"* (Ephesians 3:17–18). We need to know this love deeply in our hearts and feel it in the deepest part of our beings. God's love for us is what the Greeks called agape love. It is unconditional and the highest expression of love. Agape love is the foundation for Christian living and loving. What Paul wrote in 1 Corinthians 13:4–8 offers a glimpse of what this love looks like:

> *Love is patient, love is kind. It does not envy, it does not boast, it is not proud. It does not dishonor others, it is not self-seeking, it is not easily angered, it keeps no record of wrongs. Love does not delight in evil but rejoices with the truth. It always protects, always trusts, always hopes, always perseveres. Love never fails. But where there are prophecies, they will cease; where there are tongues, they will be stilled; where there is knowledge, it will pass away.*

Though a high mark for us all, 1 Corinthians 13 is the standard of love. Not many of us can say we show this kind of love every moment of every day, but if we have experienced God's love, we have the opportunity to express this kind of love to others. As the apostle John wrote, *"There is no fear in love. But perfect love drives out fear, because fear has to do with punishment. The one who fears is not made perfect in love"* (1 John 4:18). How do we drive out fear, experience God's love, gain a relationship with the Lord, and demonstrate the highest standard of love possible? It starts with repentance.

How I Met Jesus

Through my childhood and teenage years, there were many occasions when I felt close to God and was curious about spirituality. When I was about fourteen years old, a missionary came to speak at my school. He shared about his work with the lost, and my heart felt like it caught fire. I wanted to be a missionary to the world. Listening to this man created a desire within me to please God and do what was right, and for the most part I did, but I still felt the Lord was far away from me.

For years I thought I earned my salvation through good deeds, but at the end of my senior year in high school, I started watching a television show called *The 700 Club*. They regularly prayed for and talked about miracles, and this fascinated me. I remember thinking, *That is the Jesus I want to know! The Jesus who is alive and still heals people today, not just the One who suffered on the cross.*

I was seventeen years old when my mother invited me to an evening service at a small church about fifteen minutes away from our house. That was the evening my life changed forever. I was raised in the Christian faith and went to an all-girls Catholic school, but we never went to church on Sundays. My dad told us he wasn't accepted at church because he'd divorced his first wife. I realize now that the guilt and shame he carried haunted him, and that was why he didn't take us to church as a family. I always believed there was a mighty God, but I thought He was distant. With these reasons and assumptions piled on my shoulders, I didn't have a personal relationship with Jesus.

But at that evening service with my mother, I began to understand, really understand, what repentance meant and what Jesus did for me on the cross. The people in this little church appeared different to me. They were worshipping God in such a sincere way; some were crying, while others were quiet. Many were expressively worshipping God with their hands lifted high, as if they were trying to touch Him. I had never seen anything like it. They were in awe of God's presence in that place. By the time they finished their worship time, I was already feeling something different in my heart. I was ready. My heart completely surrendered to the unconditional love and acceptance of Christ. The pastor gave a short talk on what Jesus did on the cross, and when he asked if anyone wanted to accept Jesus into their heart, I said, "Yes!" Two pastors, Jim and Tom, led me through the prayer of salvation. As I prayed, I repented and gave Jesus all my shame, regrets, feelings of impurity, and all my sins. I quietly confessed the wrongs that were done to me and the wrongs I had committed, and everything was taken away. I asked Jesus to be my Savior, my King, and my Lord; the Holy Spirit came to live in me and gave me eternal life through His forgiveness, freedom, and eternal love. This was the most amazing spiritual experience I'd ever had. For the first time in my life, I felt completely loved. It was like a bright light had touched my heart. Almighty God became my Friend that day. The only thing I wanted to do after that experience was love Him back and thank Him for what He did for me on the cross.

Experiencing God's Love

God's love is available to everyone at every moment. You were in His heart even before you were born. He made this world thinking of you. Psalm 139 says that He wove you together in your mother's womb and you are fearfully and wonderfully made. It is all because He loves you.

Interestingly, the experience of God's love can be different for everyone. I know some people who didn't experience the love of God until later in their lives because of different reasons, a common one being past hurts. We've all had some kind of hurt or pain in our lives, and God wants to reveal His love by healing us and showing how vast His love is for us. Though God's love is always available to us, sometimes we can't "receive" that love because of pain in our lives or our disappointment with earthly fathers. A good friend of mine, whom I will call Don, falls into this category. He met Jesus as a young person, but he didn't experience God's love until much later in his life. He didn't have a good relationship with his father. In fact, his dad had such high expectations for him that Don believed his father wasn't proud of him. His dad made him feel like he could never accomplish anything, and he was constantly put down with words and actions. He never felt loved by his dad, and he built up a wall so he wouldn't be hurt anymore, refusing even to consider his need to feel loved. As I talked to him about this part of his life, he told me he had believed a lie. His faith made him miserable because he didn't feel loved by God, the people close to him, or his father. It took my friend decades to surrender, repent, and receive God's unconditional love and acceptance. He could preach about God's love—but he didn't feel loved by God until he understood what true repentance meant.

I clearly remember a sermon Don shared one Sunday about God's love. The way he explained it, repentance means agreeing with God and thinking the Lord's way. Any other thoughts are lies, and if we believe those lies, we can't honestly repent and feel loved by God. Unfortunately, Don learned what freedom looked like after a painful divorce. He told me he didn't really know anything about marriage when he married his first wife and was very immature, but once he repented, he found a joy and freedom he'd never experienced. He finally felt loved by his heavenly Father, and God recently blessed him with a second wife, who gets to reap the benefits of a husband who knows he is loved. Don is a living testimony of God's grace, second chances, freedom, and the restoration God has for all of us.

A Father's Love

Similarly, a woman's search for delight also begins with her earthly father. Although young girls learn about femininity, nurturing, and value from their mothers, a woman's sense of worth and identity is defined by her father. Often the question "Do you delight in me?" is answered with silence or unreasonable expectations from fathers. One woman I know understands this too well. I told you about my friend Sarah and her husband, Matt. The memories and traumas Sarah has from her childhood took years to heal, and at the center of her pain is her relationship with her father.

For much of Sarah's childhood, her father acted like an authoritarian. He was controlling, expected perfection, and caused Sarah to have an unhealthy fear of authority figures. Because of her father's emotional absence and lack of affection, Sarah never felt valued, and she carried much of this pain with her into her marriage. She had grown up watching her parents lash out at each other in order to resolve conflicts, so she did the same. That was just how disagreements were handled in her family. Her husband, however, came from a different family environment. In his family conflicts were pushed aside and not dealt with at all. As you can imagine, Matt didn't have any idea how to communicate with his new bride. So he retreated.

A few years ago, after a lot of relationship coaching, Matt realized Sarah had never received the right kind of love from her earthly father. As a result, she was unable to experience the true measure of God's love. Matt describes it this way: "When a conflict arose, like the wave of the ocean, it engulfed her. Naturally, she responded the only way she knew how. She fought! Sarah was out in a sea of emotion and needed me to get out there with her. Our relationship has become so much sweeter because I learned how to listen and empathize with Sarah."

For Matt, discovering how to help his wife has made a huge difference in their relationship. His understanding has also helped Sarah receive the love of her heavenly Father in greater ways.

Sarah and Matt represent many young people in search of true love, acceptance, and identity. They didn't get it from their earthly fathers, who in many cases didn't get it from their fathers either. They didn't know that to express agape love means to surround their children with encouragement, words of affirmation, hugs, and making them feel wanted as they grew up.

Your heavenly Abba Father is ready to show you how His love really looks and what it feels like. As you invite His love to surround you, you'll begin to understand His love like you never have before.

Total Surrender

When it comes to matters of the heart, never underestimate the power of prayer. A friend of mine, "Jenn," wanted to find her husband and she was talking to God

> *Your heavenly Abba Father is ready to show you how His love really looks and what it feels like. As you invite His love to surround you, you'll begin to understand His love like you never have before.*

about it. I remember a time when she prayed for a husband during one of our Bible study meetings. The prayer was simple, but it came from the deepest part of her heart: "I need a husband, Lord. Please send me one."

A few weeks later, God delivered Austin.

Austin and Jenn started dating, and as Jenn became more acquainted with him, she realized that his commitment to the Lord was a bit tepid. Although Austin was somewhat religious, he didn't fully accept the idea of a personal God and had no desire at all to submit his life to Him. Although Jenn knew she was in love with him, she heard God saying, "Don't marry him until he really commits his life to Me." So she obeyed and broke off the relationship. She couldn't have done such a selfless act if she didn't trust the Lord. She gave up what was most precious out of an obedient heart because of her convictions.

The Lord was at work. One afternoon while walking near a church, Austin's heart was stirred and he was drawn to go inside. He entered the church, encountered God's love, and surrendered his life to Jesus. Once Austin committed his life to the Lord, Jenn felt peace about reestablishing the relationship. She could have easily given in to her passions, stayed in the relationship with Austin, and settled. However, she knew that God had something better for her and Austin. She understood that her relationship with the Lord was the priority and Austin came second. She also understood that the Bible promises if we delight in the Lord, He will give us the desires of our hearts. Jenn surrendered Austin to the Lord—and this changed his life forever. Love and delight go hand in hand. Austin and Jenn have been married for many years now, and they know what the faithfulness of God looks like.

It is when we decide to delight in the Lord that we develop an intimate relationship with Him. He shows love toward us and asks that we love Him back. When someone asked Jesus what the greatest commandment was, He said we need to love God with all our hearts, souls, minds, and strength. The kind of love we receive from the Father must be reciprocal, and it involves a willingness from our hearts to show God gratitude.

So this becomes the important question: How much do we love Jesus? Are we willing to surrender to God's love and His purpose for our lives? This is the kind of love God wants His children to demonstrate—fully committed hearts for Him. Becoming the one means accepting God's love freely so you can love Him back, love yourself, and love others. It is only through this kind of selfless agape love that we can love our spouses the way we are called to love them.

Discussion Questions:

1. What is the highest form of love? How would you describe it in your own words?

2. After meeting Jesus, how do we maintain a healthy spiritual life?

3. Why is it important to experience God's love as you're preparing for marriage?

4. Read 1 Corinthians 13. Why is this passage a good example of what love looks like?

5. How do you show love toward God?

Prayer:

Father,

I ask You to touch my heart deeply, so I can really know how much You love me. Heal my heart if there are any areas that need healing. I forgive my earthly parents for any way in which they didn't love me the way I needed. Surround me with Your presence and lead me to love freely.

If you feel that your relationship with God is nonexistent or not where you want it to be, pray the following prayer:

Father,

I know my sins have separated me from You. I am truly sorry, and now I want to leave my sinful life behind and turn toward You instead. Please forgive me and help me avoid sinning again. I believe that Your Son, Jesus, died for my sins, was resurrected from the dead, is alive, and hears my prayers. I invite Jesus to become the Lord of my life and to dwell in my heart from this day forward. Please send Your Holy Spirit to help me obey Your commands and to fill me with Your love.

Chapter
7

HEALING FOR YOUR EMOTIONS
Your Journey to Wholeness and Hope

When I was six or seven years old, a traumatic experience altered my life. I was sexually molested at a sleepover party. Although the details of the abuse are hard to remember, I recall being isolated and sleepy when the man touched me. The emotional scars lingered well into my teens. I felt impure, dirty, damaged, insecure, and unprotected, and I started believing lies about myself. I began to think things like, *Who would want to be with an impure, damaged girl like me? I'm not pretty. Men will think I'm ugly because of this.*

After that experience I began to believe that most men were womanizers, abusive, overly interested in sex, controlling, and unfaithful. I saw them as chauvinistic, while I saw women as objects of lust. In addition to these negative views, I carried a great amount of shame that caused me to lose confidence in myself. On several levels I believed lies about my identity and the world around me.

Coupled with this shame and trauma, my family was filled with unrest. Although my parents adored me, they struggled in their own relationship. Our home was constantly filled with fighting, which made me feel powerless. A blended family, we dealt with rivalry and jealousy that fueled the tension we all felt. I probably *appeared* to be a happy and confident child, but the truth was that deep inside I was incredibly insecure.

My life began to change when I committed myself to Jesus and became a born-again Christian. God's healing came almost instantly after I asked Him to forgive my sins and gave my life to Him. His presence, love, and mercy took away all my heaviness, as well as the sins committed against me. The many lies I believed, the shame, guilt, and emotional trauma vanished when I felt God's love. I remember clearly thinking, *I feel so pure. There's nothing to compare to how I feel.*

When I gave Him my life, He deposited His truth and love in me. Even though I didn't know 2 Corinthians 5:17 at the time, this verse describes my experience: *"Therefore, if anyone is in Christ, the new creation has come: The old has gone, the new is here!"* That is exactly what happened to me. I felt clean, pure, and connected to the Lord. My perspective on men changed, and I began to understand they are honorable. That is when I started praying for a godly husband, and I knew God would answer my prayers.

Preparing ourselves for marriage involves opening up our hearts to the Lord, which means emotional healing. Perhaps one of the boldest scriptural statements uttered by Christ on the topic of healing is found in John 4:13–14. Jesus declared, *"Everyone who drinks this water will be thirsty again, but whoever drinks the water I give them will never thirst. Indeed, the water I give them will become in them a spring of water welling up to eternal life."*

Many of us are familiar with that verse, but what is sometimes overlooked is the woman with whom Jesus spoke. Like many of us, the woman at the well had a tragic story, and it was no accident that Jesus chose to meet with her. He knew she had emotional baggage and was in need of deep healing. His words carry more impact when we understand her situation.

When they reached Jacob's well, Jesus sent His disciples on ahead to buy food in the nearby town of Sychar, while He remained alone at the well. When a Samaritan woman showed up to draw water, she was surprised to see a Jewish man sitting next to the well in the harsh midday sun. Why was He alone, without any travel bag, food, or water jug for His journey? Didn't He know there was a town nearby?

As she approached the well and began to draw water with her rope and bucket, Jesus greeted her and started a conversation. According to the customs of the time, it was improper and even scandalous for a man to be seen in public with a woman who wasn't his wife. A proper woman would have run if a man who wasn't her husband tried to approach her in public, and rabbis especially were careful to avoid public contact with women. Jesus, however, deliberately sought to speak with this woman and treated her with special consideration, as if she were one of His close friends.

Another unusual twist to this story is that the woman chose to walk all the way to this remote well, at least a half-mile away from her village. She also picked the hottest time of day to travel—at midday when the sun is most intense. In other words, she was hiding. She was hoping to avoid contact with the other people in the village.

Jesus said to her, "Will you give Me a drink?"

Of all the people Jesus could have chosen to single out for a personal encounter that day, why did He choose to speak with a Samaritan woman? Wouldn't it have been more advantageous for Him to speak with one of the leading Samaritans— one of their elders, scribes, or teachers? What business could Jesus have had with a woman who'd never met Him or heard of Him?

The woman knew what people like Jesus typically thought of people like her. "Jews do not associate with Samaritans," she told Him.

But Jesus began to show her who He was, comparing Himself to the well right beside them. "Indeed, the water I give you will become in you a spring of water welling up to eternal life."

She wanted what He offered. "Sir, give me this water, so I won't keep getting thirsty and having to come here to draw water."

Jesus told her to go call her husband and return, and when she answered that she didn't have a husband, He gave her a word of knowledge—she'd had five husbands and wasn't married to the man she had now. They talked further and Jesus eventually revealed who He was.

"I know the Messiah is coming," the woman said. "When He comes, He will explain everything."

Jesus replied, "I am He."

Do you see what was happening here? Jesus looked past her circumstances to her heart. This story is a beautiful picture of the healing He offers each of us. Completely amazed, the woman left her water jar at the well and immediately returned to Sychar, and as soon as she arrived in town, she started telling everyone she met what had happened to her at Jacob's well, making her the first female evangelist. The villagers believed in Jesus and openly testified that this Man really was the Savior of the world.

103

How thirsty are we for healing? Are we seeking the living water that will quench our spiritual thirst? Are we ready to be healed from past hurts? Are we ready to let Jesus make us whole? In life and in love, wholeness always flows from the heart. So knowing the condition of our hearts is vital.

The Heart

Above all else, guard your heart,
for everything you do flows from it.
— *Proverbs 4:23*

I once heard my friend Jesica say that our hearts are the truest expression of who we really are. Physically, the heart is the central organ of the body, and morally, it is the seat of the affections and the center of our moral consciousness.

In Luke 10:27 Jesus said to *"love the Lord your God with all your heart and with all your soul and with all your strength and with all your mind."* He then said, *"Love your neighbor as yourself."* It follows that guarding our hearts means we must protect ourselves from the evil influences we face each day. What we allow inside of our heads forms our thoughts and attitudes and shapes the deepest parts of our beings. If we accept negative influences, they will become deeply rooted inside us and harder to deal with. The quicker we can detect an emotional condition and get it straightened out, the better off we are. Guarding our hearts, then, refers to how we live our lives in the present, yet it includes the past as well. In Proverbs 4:23 to guard also means identifying the areas of our lives that need healing and allowing God to heal them.

Most of us have been wounded in some way, whether by parents, those in authority over us, siblings, friends, other relatives, etc. But no matter what happened or how it happened, we can take heart because the Lord is our Healer. The woman at the well is a poignant example of how a hurting, injured life filled with shame can become something new. Divorced five times, living with a man who wasn't her husband, friendless, shunned by her neighbors—no doubt, she was plagued by a negative view of her circumstances. Yet Christ reached out to her. He actually sought her out, and in the same way, He reaches out to us to be healed because of His great love and the potential He sees in us.

Forgiveness

Do not be anxious about anything, but in every situation, by prayer and petition, with thanksgiving, present your requests to God. And the peace of God, which transcends all understanding, will guard your hearts and your minds in Christ Jesus.
— *Philippians 4:6–7*

Prayer is the pathway to guarding our hearts. Peace comes when we trust God, and trusting God is often expressed through prayer. But what do we do if our lives are in shambles? How do we get in communication with God when everything is falling apart and we realize we are in sin? In a word—*forgiveness*.

Like the woman at the well, we need to admit we are powerless to control our desire to sin. We also need to understand our lives are in desperate shape, and the Lord is the only force that can help us break free from sin. Once we commit our lives to Christ, it's time to confess our faults to ourselves, to the Lord, and to a mentor we trust, if necessary. As our hearts become open to change, we are ready to forgive those who have hurt us—this could include ourselves.

All human beings are broken people in need of the Lord's healing; we've all been wounded in some way. In a study entitled "When Hurt Will Not Heal: Exploring the Capacity to Relive Social and Physical Pain," researchers concluded that social or emotional pain "is as real and intense as physical pain" and that "individuals can relive and reexperience social pain more easily and more intensely than physical pain."[1]

Sadly, our wounds usually come from someone close to us, and as a result, forgiving those who have wronged us can be a challenge and take time. For most people, forgiving others is a struggle. Perhaps your mother made you feel that your best efforts weren't good enough. Maybe you were molested as a child or your father never told you he loved you. What harsh lessons did you learn? Were you cherished and delighted in, or were you disregarded? If there was absence or abuse in our childhoods, we are wounded, and those wounds entwine messages through the core of our beings, striking at our souls. The common result is unforgiveness,

---

1 Zhansheng Chen, Kipling D. Williams, Julie Fitness, and Nicola C. Newton, "When Hurt Will Not Heal: Exploring the Capacity to Relive Social and Physical Pain," *Psychological Science* 19, no. 8 (August 2008): 789–795, https://www.researchgate.net/publication/23282492_When_Hurt_Will_Not_Heal_Exploring_the_Capacity_to_Relive_Social_and_Physical_Pain.

which is the biggest blockage to hearing from the Lord. To be healed, we need to turn toward God's love and submit to the changes He wants to make in our lives. Then once our hearts are at peace, we can readily offer forgiveness to those who have hurt us, which opens the lines of communication with God. Forgiveness unlocks the door and allows us to transfer the shame, guilt, sorrow, and rejection to Jesus, and in exchange He offers us peace and freedom over pain. We are not prisoners of our hurts anymore.

The Power of Words

Some have deeper wounds than I did as a child, some not as deep; not all of us go through severe trauma, but everyone goes through some kind of trauma that causes them to think differently about themselves, others, and the world. Painful experiences can provoke young people to make negative vows—they say something negative about themselves or their lives, which they start believing and consequently living. There is power in the words we speak. Life and death are in the power of the tongue (Proverbs 18:21), so what is the outcome of declaring we will never get married? Or have children? What happens when we state that we are ugly or dumb? Negative self-talk may seem harmless, but it can keep individuals from breaking free into the victorious life God has for them.

Have you ever said or thought any of the following statements?

> *My parents don't love me. They've never told me they love me, and they've never tried to hug me or show me love. I'm unlovable.*
> *I'm so stupid. I'll never be as successful as this other person.*
> *No one listens to me because I'm not confident. I'm going to get fired.*
> *I'm not pretty enough. No one asks me on a date.*

Whatever the cause of our pain, the circumstances can become distorted, and we start seeing things in a way that is contrary to what God wants for us. The brain is like a plant that needs water, fertile soil, and sun. If we feed junk into our brains, we're going to produce negative thoughts and make unholy vows, such as the statements I just gave you. If we fill our minds with Scripture and see ourselves the way God sees us, our thoughts will be pure.

Dr. Paul Hegstrom of Life Skills International puts it this way:

The wounds of childhood will affect us for a lifetime. The brain freezes when we have been wounded by rejection, incest, molestation, emotional abuse, and physical abuse below the age of puberty. Traditional therapy calls this *fixation*. We call it *arrested development.*[2]

Identifying our core wounds is essential. Many experts say they come from the fear of being separated from unconditional love. Even in the womb, a child can be wounded if the parents don't want them or the mother considers getting an abortion. A person can need healing from this type of trauma and may not even know it. I'm always amazed at the healing God brings to people who feel rejected and abandoned because one of the parents, or both, didn't want the children or wanted them to be a different gender. I was one of those kids. My mom was eager to get pregnant, and even though she waited a few years for it, she was nervous about the pregnancy because my dad wasn't ready to have me yet. She waited quite a long time to tell him about me and harbored a lot of fear, which I believe I felt. Thank God that my dad was happy to hear she was pregnant and learned to love me in wonderful ways, but this didn't automatically undo the fear of rejection I struggled with. I carried this burden for years before God, through His Word and people who prayed for me, helped me understand the healing I needed. My parents later confirmed they both dealt with a lot of fear concerning what a pregnancy would bring to their already chaotic relationship. They asked me, and the Lord, for forgiveness.

Jesus is ready to heal us at any time. That is why Hebrews 4:12 says, *"For the word of God is alive and active. Sharper than any double-edged sword, it penetrates even to dividing soul and spirit, joints and marrow; it judges the thoughts and attitudes of the heart."* We just have to ask and be willing to be vulnerable with Him or others we trust.

Many ministries help people heal from past hurts. Don't be afraid to ask God where to go to find the inner healing He wants to bring to you. Ask Him to search your heart so there is nothing hidden. Dr. Gregory L. Jantz writes, "There comes a critical time in each person's life when the truth is

> *Many ministries help people heal from past hurts. Don't be afraid to ask God where to go to find the inner healing He wants to bring to you. Ask Him to search your heart so there is nothing hidden.*

2 Paul Hegstrom, "Wounds," Life Skills International. http://www.lifeskillsintl.org/Articles/Words_from_Paul/Wounds.html.

accessible. Faced with it, you can either run and hide, denying it, or you can face your truth, accept it, and grow stronger."[3] Healing can be a process, sometimes a long one, but I've learned that the sooner we let the Holy Spirit come heal us, the sooner we will be set free. As we discover and recognize there is an area that needs healing and we submit it to God, there is no doubt He will take care of it.

The mind, heart, emotions, and will are part of the soul. To be healthy, mature adults, we need to take care of these parts of who we are, allowing the Lord to work in every area of our lives. As Psalm 139:23–24 says, *"Search me, God, and know my heart; test me and know my anxious thoughts. See if there is any offensive way in me, and lead me in the way everlasting."*

Sally

"Sally," a friend of mine, remembers hearing "I love you" from her parents only a few times. Whenever she rode in the car with her father, he rarely spoke a word to her and always seemed preoccupied, but whenever they were at social events, his personality changed and he was the life of the party, talking to every adult he could find. When Sally had homework she didn't understand, her father did it for her instead of explaining it to her, which seemed strange to her since her father was a teacher. From an early age, Sally felt unloved because of her father's mental absence.

Although she grew up in a Christian home, Sally didn't know how much her heavenly Father loved her. Our families are meant to be representations of God. Our image of Father God deep in our hearts is formed by our childhood experiences with our earthly fathers. If our earthly fathers are absent, distant, or harsh, we believe the Lord is absent, distant, and harsh. Sally's experiences as a child resulted in an unmet need for love in her life. Though she professed faith in Christ, she didn't see the Lord as her Friend, Provider, and Healer. Church is a place to meet friends and form relationships, a place to find faith in God, yet Sally rarely found healing for the emotional pain she confronted daily. She just needed to hear the words "I love you." She graduated from high school and began looking for the love that was absent. She married and had children, but her marriage was unhealthy.

3 Gregory L. Jantz and Ann McMurray, *Healing the Scars of Emotional Abuse* (Grand Rapids, MI: Revel), 2009.

She told me, "I remember feeling as though my whole existence was to serve my husband and family. I felt lost, depressed, and invisible." She ended up going through a painful divorce and living for a season as a single mom.

She didn't feel cared for or loved for years after her divorce, even after she married the second time. However, as she really started to know the love her heavenly Father had for her, she changed and began believing how blessed and loved she was—even before, by her earthly dad who couldn't express his love verbally. Her breakthrough came when she stopped believing all those lies, the religious spirit, and legalism she learned at church. It was when she discovered her heavenly Father's love that she understood she was loved her entire life.

"It was during the darkest time of my life," she said, "that I began to rely on the Lord. He became my strength and provided what I needed at every turn. Life wasn't easy. I struggled to put food on the table and keep my home, but with the help of my parents, family, and friends, I began to thrive. It was during those years that I began to understand how much my parents did love me. Although they weren't outwardly affectionate, they loved me with financial gifts, they fixed my car, they helped pay for my children to go to a private school. My relationship with my father grew very sweet during those years."

Sally, like many people in tough circumstances, believed that somehow God was responsible for her heartache. She felt ashamed and embarrassed after the divorce and blamed God. When we're visited by devastation and financial insecurity, many of us wonder why God allows it, but this is what Sally realized: The Lord blessed her in the years following her divorce and used the tragedy in her life to teach her about His love. Now she's happily married, involved in Christian work, and enjoying life.

"Most of my healing came from knowing how God really sees me," she said. "Nothing is ever wasted with the Lord. He uses failures and every struggle to build character. As Christians, the way to maintain your emotional health is to remind yourself how God sees you. And the Lord is crazy about you."

Maintaining Your Healing

As difficult as finding healing may seem, it is actually simple, because God is always willing and ready to pour out His healing within us. When struggles come, we can take heart—what God has started, He will finish.

A breakthrough from a past hurt or overcoming a bad habit produces a sense of victory, but what some do not understand is that with victories come more battles. Therefore, be prepared to maintain your healing. This simply means walking in what God has done for you. The problem I've seen is the enemy wants you to think God didn't totally heal you or that you don't deserve your healing. The enemy will try to steal it from you, but if God heals you, He won't take the healing away. Once it's done, it is yours to keep. Isaiah 53:5 goes to the heart of it: *"But he was pierced for our rebellion, crushed for our sins. He was beaten so we could be whole. He was whipped so we could be healed"* (NLT). Remember Jesus won your victory for you.

Every day we need to remember what God did for us. Really, it is when we stop coming to Jesus consistently that we forget what He has done for us and start believing lies. When we remain in Him, we walk in His emotional healing. Hanging out with Jesus twenty-four seven is the best thing we can do to be healed and maintain our healing. John 15:4 says it very clearly: *"Remain in me, as I also remain in you. No branch can bear fruit by itself; it must remain in the vine. Neither can you bear fruit unless you remain in me."*

In addition to healing our pain, God never wastes a hurt or sorrow. He will turn that pain into joy if we let Him. We get to live in a continual lifestyle of exchange as we move from our brokenness to His wholeness, crying out, "Create in me a clean heart, O God!"

Many of us have suffered and are still suffering from a high level of emotional pain. Some of us feel abandoned, rejected, controlled, lonely, abused, bullied, unattractive, unloved. The list goes on. But Jesus is in the business of healing the root of every negative thing that has happened to us. In the rest of the chapter, we'll look at a few amazing stories of how people have encountered breakthrough in their lives.

The Pornography Struggle

Ben struggled with a pornography addiction from the age of ten when a friend introduced him to pornographic magazines. As he grew into adolescence, he became more entranced with girls and often kept dirty magazines under his bed. Then Ben discovered the internet, where he found a feast for his sexual appetites. Although he tried to break the cycle of addiction, he never truly found success.

His problem with porn followed him into his marriage—until he discovered how to battle the emotional issues resting behind his addiction.

For Ben, the breakthrough came when he admitted he was powerless to control his desire to sin. He understood after years of anguish that his life was out of control and the only force that could help him break free from sin was a relationship with the Lord. Ben recommitted his life to Christ, confessed his faults, and reached out to an accountability partner. Through regular group meetings, he began to identify areas of his life that were lacking. Relationships were hard for Ben because he saw himself as unlovable. He made a commitment to resist porn on a daily basis and to affirm the Lord had a wonderful plan for his life. Although Ben still faces daily temptations, he remembers that temptations are not sin. He understands how to avoid porn by relying on the Holy Spirit for guidance and by reaching out to his accountability partner.

"When it comes to my addiction with pornography, I live one day at a time," he told me. "When I reach out and find quality relationships, I tend to feel more positive about myself and I'm less likely to use pornography to medicate. I pray that God will take away the desire to view porn. I pray to the Lord to help me resist the devil, but I know that I'm the only one that can flee from evil. Besides having regular conversations with the Lord, I find that having a mentor to talk to about my struggles has made a big difference with this addiction."

Ben is still on the journey of finding complete healing, but this he knows—his identity comes from feeling loved by Jesus and knowing he belongs to Him. The desire to be totally loved, cherished, and accepted can be fulfilled by God alone.

Am I Beautiful?

From an early age, Madeline wanted to look like her older sister, Mary. Madeline never felt beautiful next to her sister, who was athletic, popular, and thin. Every time Madeline looked in the mirror, she saw a fat, ugly, untalented girl—the opposite of her sister.

"Someday you'll blossom, Maddy!" her sister would say.

Madeline didn't believe her. She grew jealous not only of her sister's looks but of Mary's entire life. Madeline decided in her teenage years that she was going to take matters into her own hands, and she began to develop an eating disorder. Although her parents and sister told her she looked fine, she continued to see herself as fat and a loser. Due to her distorted view of herself and extreme weight swings, her parents eventually forced her to see a psychologist.

After several sessions, Madeline's breakthrough came when her psychologist told her she was beautiful. Her counselor also told her the meaning of her name and the story of Mary Magdalene from the Bible.

"Your name means 'tower' and 'full of strength,'" her counselor told her. "Mary Magdalene was a devout follower of Jesus Christ, who cast seven demons from her. Mary Magdalene was present at the cross during the hours of agony of Christ and waited until the body was taken down and placed in a cave. She bought sweet spices to anoint the body. The next morning Mary Magdalene was the first to arrive at the tomb to find it empty. She saw the vision of angels and was the first person to see Jesus after His resurrection."

Madeline finally understood that it didn't matter so much how people saw her, but it was the opinion of her heavenly Father that mattered. She began to read the Bible and really internalized how much God loved her—He loved her so much that He sent Jesus to die for her. At last she could forgive those who had wronged her and let go of the jealousy she felt toward her sister.

Today Madeline maintains her healing by affirming each day that God made her wonderfully. When she looks in the mirror and sees imperfections, she reminds herself that her name means tower and strength. She tells herself that the inner qualities a person develops matter most. Beauty fades and weight fluctuates, but the fruit of the Spirit is more important; those are the qualities God wants each person to develop:

> *But the fruit of the Spirit is love, joy, peace, forbearance, kindness, goodness, faithfulness, gentleness, and self-control. Against such things there is no law.*
> — *Galatians 5:22–23*

Abandoned

When Grace was five years old, her drug-addicted, single mother abandoned her in their apartment, never to return. Grace was accustomed to being left alone, but after several hours she became concerned and went down the hall to tell the neighbors, who called the police. She ended up in a foster home full of other children in similar circumstances. Retreating into books, she became shy, withdrawn, and full of fear. Her peer relationships never lasted because she carried the weight of abandonment into every friendship she had. As she developed distrust of adults and people in general, she began to fill her need for care and companionship with male relationships. Fearing abandonment, she became extremely jealous of her boyfriends and would accuse them of cheating on her, which would drive them away. This pattern of starting a relationship, fearing abandonment, becoming jealous, and going through a breakup pursued Grace into adulthood.

Grace's breakthrough came when a coworker invited her to church. There she met people who had suffered in similar ways but found peace with Jesus. The pastor shared that Jesus had suffered in the same ways we do and He'd felt the sting of abandonment. His own Father, it seemed, had forsaken Him.

"My God, my God, why have you forsaken me?" (See Matthew 27:46.)

The pastor went on to explain that Jesus was crying out in anguish because of the separation He experienced from His heavenly Father. It was the only time Jesus did not address God as Father. He had taken our transgressions and iniquities upon Himself so we could be free from sin, and as Jesus carried our sin, the Father turned His back on Him.

But that wasn't the end of the story—Jesus rose from the dead, and this was all part of God's plan. *"God raised him from the dead, freeing him from the agony of death, because it was impossible for death to keep its hold on him"* (Acts 2:24).

Grace understood. Christ had experienced abandonment, just like she had, and she didn't need to fear any longer. God would never forsake her if she committed her life to Him. He will never forsake any of us because His Son was forsaken in our place.

Grace maintains her healing by remembering that Christ suffered for her. When she experiences fear, she goes straight to Scripture and renews her mind:

- *"Never will I leave you; never will I forsake you"* (Hebrews 13:5).
- *For the Spirit God gave us does not make us timid, but gives us power, love and*

self-discipline (2 Timothy 1:7).
- *It is better to take refuge in the Lord than to trust in humans* (Psalm 118:8).

God can bring emotional healing to people in so many ways. Just as the Lord can use doctors, healing prayers, or other means to bring the physical healing we need, emotional healing can come instantly or happen over time in phases, based on what God reveals to us and how open and ready we are to receive His healing. What I know for sure is that God is a good Father who wants to see His children healthy in every area of their lives. He wants us to be transformed by the renewing of our minds, with thoughts that are pure and right. Do you want to taste His goodness and healing?

The Power of Testimony

> *They triumphed over*
> *[the enemy]*
> *by the blood of the Lamb*
> *and by the word of their testimony;*
> *they did not love their lives so much*
> *as to shrink from death.*
> *— Revelation 12:11*

A testimony is based on an experience. It's a personal story of how God restored us and brought victory into our lives. It's what we have seen and heard the Lord do in those moments when we knew there was no way out. Testimony is the result of God using what was meant for evil in our lives for our good instead. The more Christians who come forward and talk about how God has intervened in their lives, the more people begin to realize that God is real, miracles do happen, and prayer works. This inspires others to seek Him and find the hope so needed in a world full of sin, hurt, and sadness. Our message is that if God did it for us, He could also do it for you—just give Him a chance.

Your testimony can never be stolen from you. The enemy can't take it. When God does something in your life, it's yours and no one can cut it away from you. The brokenness you've gone through in the past is what will give you a good future.

"Which of you, if your son asks for bread, will give him a stone? Or if he asks for a fish, will give him a snake? If you, then, though you are evil, know how to give good gifts to your children, how much more will your Father in heaven give good gifts to those who ask him!"
— *Matthew 7:9–10*

Jesus is the only One who can turn bad into good. God can use even the tragedies in your life for His purposes. Your testimony of victory in Jesus is His gift to you.

Miriam's Testimony

A friend of mine, a woman I will call Miriam, understands the power of testimony. She grew up in a Christian home. In fact, her parents were the pastors of a church. They were loving people toward others, but they were rarely affectionate toward her. Their approach to living emphasized the Christian faith as a set of rules; it focused on God's judgment and offered little grace for mistakes. Miriam needed to know she was loved, but her parents were strict and withheld physical affection from her, which made her feel abandoned. As a result, she began to look for the love she didn't get from her parents in relationships with men, which eventually led to drugs and drinking.

"I was curious about the non-Christian world," she told me. "I saw non-Christians having more fun than my family, and they seemed to care about each other more. As a child and teenager, my life was about following rules. That is when I began to believe the lie that the world had more to offer me than God did."

She hoped to fill the void in her life with drugs, alcohol, and physical relationships and lived this lifestyle for almost a decade. When she discovered her boyfriend was cheating on her, she left him. After years of decadence and failed relationships, she realized she'd hit rock bottom and that the void in her heart would only be filled with a relationship with Jesus.

"I realized God was the only One that could offer a perfect and unconditional love," she said. "Because I'd grown up in the church, I knew how to find a way back to the Lord and so I started to pray. The Lord showed me an invisible wall that was protecting me from evil and I started praying more. I prayed a simple prayer: 'Jesus, You get me out of this and I will be forever Yours.' That was it. My

115

eyes were open and I literally packed my bags and left, not looking back. I was completely healed! All my life I tried to run from God, but He never let me go. His love won my heart and now I am forever His."

Not only did Miriam find the love of Jesus, but she also reconciled with her parents and turned from her destructive lifestyle. She completely surrendered to God and started going to church again. She stopped drinking, doing drugs, and having extramarital sex. God removed her addictions and restored her. He gave her a healing experience that can never be taken from her. She now knows that her relationship with Jesus is the most amazing and fun part of her life and that her testimony brings hope and restoration to others who have gone through similar experiences.

God is the Healer, and He is the first One interested in making us whole. Healing brings restoration, and restoration brings freedom to become more like Jesus. And as we become more like Jesus, we become better people, better companions, and better spouses.

Discussion Questions:

1. Our hearts are the truest expression of who we really are. Physically, the heart is the central organ of the body. Morally, the heart is the seat of our affections and the center of our moral consciousness. Why does the Bible tell us to guard our hearts?

2. Why do you think the woman at the well was so vulnerable with Jesus? What does this story teach us?

3. Have you experienced trauma in your life? What lies have you believed? What would the future be like if you believed God's truth in these areas instead?

4. Which of the stories in this chapter do you relate to the most and why?

5. Do you need to forgive anyone? If it is difficult, ask Jesus to help you.

6. Many of us conceal our victories in Christ because we are embarrassed or uncomfortable with the past. A long time passed before I shared the testimonies of God's power in my life because those stories involved my family, and I didn't want to offend them. Are you willing to share the testimony of your emotional healing? Are you aware of how God could use it to bring healing and restoration to others?

Prayer:

Dear heavenly Father,

I come to You in the name of Your Son, Jesus. I am part of Your family. Jesus is not just my Brother but also my Savior and best Friend. Could You please come and surround me with Your presence, love, and mercy so I can be healed? Holy Spirit, empower me so I can be transformed and stand firm in the knowledge of what You have done for me.

Chapter
8

THE TRUTH ABOUT WHO YOU ARE

Believing What God Says About You

When it came time for our son to go to college, I drove him to his chosen school in Southern California and dropped him off. On the way we talked about everything. I really wanted to make sure we covered every topic necessary so he could make the best choices in this new season of his life. We both laughed and I, of course, cried a few times. He surprised me with some of my favorite songs in Spanish that he had downloaded for the trip.

As we got closer to his new school, I just said, "Son, remember who you are and how much God loves you. We will always love you, no matter what."

Being a parent is the most amazing blessing anyone can have, and raising children is one of the most challenging and rewarding experiences in life. It is incredibly difficult when we have to let our children go. This has happened to me twice, and in another year I will have to do it again. While they are safe and protected under our roofs, we need to teach them about their identity. There are times we do well with this and other times when we don't, but the important thing is to communicate this truth to our children: The best way to see yourself is with the eyes of Jesus.

The Truth About Identity

God gives us our status. He has made us His beloved children, His heirs, and He is the One who has given us our identity. In the previous chapter, we discussed the human soul and the need to allow God to heal our hearts through three things: repentance, renewing our minds, and the help of mentors. This chapter is focused on the human spirit and learning to connect our spirits to the Spirit of mighty God. Knowing God's nature and understanding the way the Lord sees us are pivotal in capturing the new identity we've been given.

In psychology your identity is defined as the conceptions, qualities, beliefs, and expressions that make you who you are. John Locke, an English philosopher and physician, held that personal identity is a matter of mental continuity and believed it was founded on consciousness or the memory, not on the substance of the soul or body. He argued that the "associations of ideas" we make when we are young are more important than those made later because they are the foundation of the self. Those associations are what first mark the *tabula rasa* or blank slate.[1] Although there is much truth in Locke's definition, I believe our identity encompasses more than our memories. Our identity touches all parts of our spiritual and mental consciousness.

Perhaps your identity is that you are a female who is honest, warm, caring, intelligent, and sometimes moody. You enjoy relationships, going to the gym, and volunteering at a soup kitchen on Sundays. You visit your family frequently and pray every night before you go to bed. When it comes to your passions, you are completely focused on the fifth grade class you are teaching. Those kids are the reason you get up every morning. Each of these things helps form your identity, and you carry that identity with you wherever you go. The way we perceive ourselves, the way we act, the way we think, and the way we interact with others are all influenced by our identity, which is further defined by our relationships.

As I was growing up, one of the things that gave me the greatest satisfaction in life was having straight As on my report card. I loved the feeling of being known as a smart kid, and I enjoyed being admired by others. I can remember the first time a classmate was honored because of her grades, and I wanted to have what she had—the honor and admiration of my peers and teachers. My school life was about studying and being the smartest kid in school. My identity was based on performance for many years, and inside I was an insecure teen.

If I asked you to describe your identity, what would you say? Perhaps you would tell me your occupation or a hobby you love. Perhaps you would describe your hopes, dreams, and the future. Drilling down even further to the core of who you are, one of the most important qualities you possess is your spiritual drive. Spiritual development is an aspect of life that many people overlook, but it's a part of our identity that needs to be grown or we will never find happiness.

---

1 John Locke, *An Essay Concerning Human Understanding* (1689).

Led By the Spirit

When we accept Christ into our hearts, our spirits become alive to the things of God, to His love and purpose. Our spirits connect with God's Spirit, and the Lord shapes our destinies in new ways.

Training our souls can be difficult, but it isn't impossible if we allow God's Spirit to lead us. *"For those who are led by the Spirit of God are the children of God"* (Romans 8:14). One way I let the Spirit of God lead me every day is through honestly believing what God says about me and reading aloud my true identity statement, especially when I sense I need a reminder. My identity statement is my written reminder of God's destiny for my life, my calling as a Christian, and how God sees me. This is a portion of it:

> I am a beloved daughter of the Living God. I am a living fragrance of His love because He has chosen me and anointed me to live for Him. I am completely His. Christ paid the price for my sin with His blood. His blood gives me forgiveness and allows me to live in His shelter, under the covering of His wings. God gives me free access to seek Him and see His face. Jesus' blood gives me victory and security, and I know that nothing can ever separate me from God's love. I live every day knowing that I am a branch of the true vine and a channel of life to others. I am more than a conqueror, and His strength is made perfect in my weakness.[2]

Many people base their identity in their performance or productivity, or they find their identity in external beauty, in their work and careers, their families, friends, hobbies, etc. God wants us to find our identity in Him and use the many gifts and talents He has deposited in us to help others and accomplish His will for us on earth. God wants us to find fulfillment in our callings and really love who we are and what we do. When we find our identity in Christ, we act upon who we truly are and not upon what other people want us to be. Our identity shouldn't be based on striving for what we do not have but in knowing who we are and what we have in God, so we can live with purpose.

One morning while I was praying, God revealed this truth of who I am. He clearly said to me, "Tell Me who I am to you."

2 I wrote this identity statement following the Bible-based format taught by Chris Hogan, Noble Call Institute Inc., and Relate 20/20. For more information, visit their websites at www.noblecall.org and www. relate2020.com. Also see the appendix at the back of this book.

I started by declaring all the amazing things God represents to me. With much joy, I declared, "You are the Alpha and the Omega, the beginning and the end, my heavenly Father, my Savior, my Prince of Peace, God Almighty, merciful and loving. You are here with me, in me, and You never change."

Then God reminded me of the qualities He'd developed in me. The realization struck me and I declared, "I am Your beloved daughter. I belong to You, Lord. I am Your princess; I am good, merciful, and loving."

Joy filled my heart as I sensed the truth. The words I'd received from the Lord became a powerful declaration that transformed me and my day. My morning was totally changed, but more than anything, my heart was transformed as I believed and accepted who I was once again. I am on a journey of learning to see myself and others the way God does, and reminders always help. This is what identity is truly about. It is bestowed from God, and what God wants is our hearts. Really, God is after a relationship with us. He's not so concerned with everything we do but with a relationship where we share our hopes, dreams, fears, and ultimately our hearts.

Another way I remember who I am in Christ is by emphasizing core principles based in Scripture. Reviewing the following steps always helps me find my peace during struggles.

Believe What God Says About You

> *For we are God's handiwork.*
> — *Ephesians 2:10*

God is pleased with how He created us. We are valuable to Him and to others, and His opinion of us is the most important one. He sees us as a product of the many qualities, gifts, and talents He's given us, and—most important—He sees Jesus in us all, which makes us look amazingly beautiful in every area of life. Wherever you are in your walk with Him, you get to lay aside the worst habits and the mistakes

You get to lay aside the worst habits and the mistakes made in the past, and embrace your best qualities instead. When you're struggling, repeat Psalm 139:14 to yourself: "I praise you because I am fearfully and wonderfully made; your works are wonderful, I know that full well."

made in the past, and embrace your best qualities instead. When you're struggling, repeat Psalm 139:14 to yourself: *"I praise you because I am fearfully and wonderfully made; your works are wonderful, I know that full well."*

God takes the concept of identity even further with the names our parents give us. They have meaning and can also be considered part of our identity in Christ. When my husband and I named each of our kids, we researched the meanings of the names we'd chosen or were thinking of choosing. *Christian* means "follower of Christ." *Amy* means "beloved," and *Jessica* means "blessed one." My first name, *María*, means "living fragrance," while *Salomé* means "peace" and "princess." Leon's name means "courageous." Every name has a meaning that plays a part of who we are. In fact, the names that don't have the best meaning for whatever reason, He changes and gives them a better meaning. That is why the name *Jacob* doesn't mean "supplanter" anymore. God changed his name. In a heavenly encounter, Jacob refused to let go of the angel of God until he received a blessing, and God gave Jacob the name *Israel*, which means "the one who has prevailed with God."

One thing that keeps us from committing in relationships is the stories we tell ourselves, not realizing what God says about us instead. For example, a young man may not believe he's good enough for a successful young woman, and feelings of inadequacy that stem from a childhood experience could make him break up with God's destiny, rather than sharing his true feelings and committing. Living in our identity as God's children means believing what God says about us.

Let Go of False Accusations

> *"Don't hurt your friend,*
> *don't blame your neighbor."*
> — Psalm 15:3 (MSG)

It is unfortunately common for us to allow others to define the way we think of ourselves, and quite often their opinions are not based on Scripture. If authority figures tell us we're incompatible, ugly, or damaged, this can become part of our self-concept. A young woman can believe she has no value because she doesn't think she's pretty or successful. "Who would want to marry me?" she asks. A young man who had trouble in grade school says, "I am unintelligent. That is what I am. How could I possibly get a good job and be able to support a family?"

Don't let what people say about you define how you see yourself. Abandon any image that is not from God, and stop accepting the false characterizations others make. Let God's opinion be the one that defines you. Pray to the Father and ask Him about His plans for you.

Cultivate a Relationship with the Holy Spirit

Now it is God who makes both us and you stand firm in Christ. He anointed us, set his seal of ownership on us, and put his Spirit in our hearts as a deposit, guaranteeing what is to come.
— *2 Corinthians 1:21–22*

Don't let what people say about you define how you see yourself. Abandon any image that is not from God, and stop accepting the false characterizations others make. Let God's opinion be the one that defines you. Pray to the Father and ask Him about His plans for you.

We are God's precious children, and He created us in a way that pleases Him. We are now identified with Christ and have the power of the Holy Spirit within us. We determine our identity with the help of the Holy Spirit in two ways. First, His Word helps us learn who we are. We can meditate on His Word and ask the Holy Spirit to give us the revelation needed so we can believe and treasure what God says about us. Second, He shows us who we are as we allow Him to speak to us personally. This can happen when we are alone with Him and also when other believers speak words of true encouragement into our lives. If we don't know what the Holy Spirit thinks of us, we can ask Him, and He will make Himself known. We just need to give Him some time to speak to us.

Know Your Core Values

Do you know someone who's made a major life decision based on the need to please a parent? Perhaps this person works hard and excels because of the expectations of a hard-to-please mother or father. It is true that many great things are accomplished because of high expectations. It is also true that the pressure of parents can sometimes produce positive outcomes. However, you need to embrace who you are. In many cases, your identity is not what others say it is. Are you listening to the voice of the Holy Spirit as He leads you toward your passions in life?

To give you an example, think about a young man who wants to get married. His mother keeps pushing him to find a wife because she wants grandchildren and thinks he will be happier when he is married. Because of his mother's expectations and pressure, he may be willing to settle for someone who shares only a few of the same core values he does, instead of seeking God for the person who would be a better match for him.

Core values help determine your behaviors and actions. They are the highest morals and principles you carry inside you, and through this inner part of yourself, you can say "yes" or "no" to the many temptations and tests of life. Being true to yourself is one of the strongest pieces of advice a parent, leader, or mentor can offer someone when that person encounters a major life decision.

To figure out your true identity, you need to know who made you—the One who loves you more than anyone else could ever love you. You belong to Him. When you discover that you truly are God's child and that He loves you with everlasting love, that He accepts you the way you are and considers you the most wonderful treasure He has, you begin to understand who you are. This is the beginning of staying true to yourself as a believer in Christ. Don't let others define you or make decisions for you that you should make yourself. You are God's masterpiece, and He will help you to live according to *His* highest values and beliefs. Life is a journey to becoming the person you were created to be; it is the process of discovering who you truly are and where you come from. Once you understand these things, being true to yourself becomes simple.

Expect Great Things from God

> . . . *being confident of this, that he who began a good work in you will carry it on to completion until the day of Christ Jesus.*
> — *Philippians 1:6*

Remember, God's plans are always good; they are not harmful for you. His plans are designed to bring you hope and a future.

Why are you on this earth? God is the only One who can give you the right answer to that question. He's equipped you with unique skills and talents, and He will use these things for His Kingdom and eternity. You may be a teacher, CPA, gardener, social worker, or entrepreneur—whatever your calling in life, begin to realize God can use your special talents for His purposes. Once you know who you are and what God has called you to do, you are enabled to understand how you can impact the world around you.

Expect great things from God because the specific purpose you have in life goes along with the gifts He has given you. However He's gifted you—if you have great discernment and wisdom to counsel others, if you are able to inspire people and change their lives—you can catch a glimpse of His purpose for you within your gifts. Depending on the situation, it can take some time to know what your gifts are and how to use them, which is why you need the Holy Spirit's help and the input of encouraging believers who know you and can encourage you in the gifts they see in you.

When people or spiritual forces look to damage you, they attack those aspects of your character you hold most dear; they attack your identity, which is the core of who you are. When this happens, respond the same way Jesus did: with God's Word and the truth you know about yourself (Matthew 4:4). Reminding yourself of how God sees you can be a balm for any traumas in your life. In a marriage, having your mate lovingly remind you of what they know to be true about you helps fight negative thoughts. Whenever I am counseling someone, I encourage them to become an expert on identity and listen to what God says about them.[3]

I encourage you to find someone who understands how God sees you. Marrying someone who sees you the way God does is one of the greatest blessings marriage provides.

---

3 According to Chris Hogan at Noble Call Institute Inc., four words help us understand our identity: *safety, security, sufficiency, and significance*. When God meets us in these four core needs, we are on the path to having a truly noble identity. See the appendix at the back of this book for more information about finding your identity.

Discussion Questions:

1. How would you describe your identity?

2. Describe how you connect with God.

3. Describe how God sees you.

4. Below are the key ways to develop your spiritual identity. Meditate on each area and write what it means to you:

      a. What Scripture says
      b. What others say
      c. The Holy Spirit's role
      d. God-given talents
      e. God's plans for you
      f. Strong core values
      g. Remaining in His love

Prayer:

Dear heavenly Father,

I admit that without You I'm nothing, but with You I am everything. Please show me who I am in You and how You see me. Help me come up with an identity statement that is based on how You see me, and help me believe and live every part of it.

III

LOOKING OUTWARD

"My Father is glorified by this, that you bear much fruit, and so prove to be My disciples."
— John 15:8 (NASB)

Your choices manifest the healthy state of your heart. This is the time when the great foundation you have laid will be revealed in your everyday life. Your decision concerning the person you want to marry comes out of your true identity and the core values you carry within you.

Chapter
9

COMPATIBILITY

What Is It and How Does It Work?

Wouldn't relationships be boring if we were all the same? Fortunately, God has made each of us unique. In relationships most people are drawn to their opposite or to a person who is somewhat different. Because we're often blind to our own negative traits, we seek out mates who have strengths to augment our weaknesses.

Becoming the one involves preparing for your future mate by finding your passion in life and understanding personal strengths and weaknesses. Perhaps God has called you to be an engineer, architect, teacher, or missionary; moving into God's plan for your life will allow you to cross paths with the one you are set apart for. When you and that person meet, you can be emotionally and spiritually ready.

Finding a mate isn't so much about going out and hunting a person down with a lasso. Instead, focus on becoming who God wants you to be, and from there put yourself in the right social circles as you trust that God has a plan for you. If you put yourself on the right path, the right person is bound to walk along and join you. Many find their spouses through mutual friends who know them well and tell them, "You have to meet this person!" You'd be surprised how often this happens. Many have met in college, at work, church activities, conferences, on mission trips or the internet. A couple who made a big impression on me met over the phone. The gentleman called for a work-related question, and he was so interested in the way the woman communicated that after some phone conversations, he asked her out.

Compatibility

Compatibility is a common topic when discussing relationships. Simply put, it means how capable you and your partner are at existing together in unity. The online dating site eHarmony describes compatibility in terms of twenty-nine dimensions with two overarching principles: core traits and vital attributes. The company explains, "Your core traits are defining aspects of who you are that remain largely unchanged throughout your adult life. Vital attributes are based on learning experience, and are more likely to change based on life events and decisions you make as an adult."[1] Compatibility is a complicated topic. Finding a person who meets even most of your personal needs may seem unattainable, but once again this is a matter of trust. Press in and trust that the Lord will guide you to the love of your life.

Whether you are looking for areas of difference or similarity, try to be open to uncovering aspects of your own personality that will allow you to know the other person better. Being transparent and your true self will take you to amazing places in your relationship. Be true to the awesome self God gave you. This is an excellent trait.

No couple will ever be completely compatible, and it actually is healthy to seek out a marriage partner who is different than you are. Differences in personality, gender, personal habits, culture, and family backgrounds are often the components that bring us together and attract us to each other. But sometimes they can also pull us apart. Knowing your personality type can help you navigate relationships. You might be more of an introvert or extrovert, a thinker or feeler. Do you focus on the basic information you take in or do you prefer to interpret and add meaning?[2] Do you make snap judgments or stay open to new ideas?

What makes someone a good match for you? Think about a quiet and introspective teacher from a small family who is dating an adventurous young woman from a big family. The young man may be looking for someone to liven up his life. What about a young woman who lives at home with parents who are overprotective and have failing health? She feels a sense of obligation to take care of them, but when she's twenty-four a man with children comes along, and she finds love, a family unit, and a way of escape. What about two college students who meet in youth group? They come from good Christian families and are about to embark on their careers. What a match . . . right? My husband is eight-and-a-half years older than I am. When we met, I was in my second year of college, and he had already been out of college for five years and held a steady job. He was from a different country and had a different family background, but God still brought us together. Despite our many differences, God still had a plan to make it work.

1 "Relationship Compatibility: A Guide to Finding 'The One' (Part I)," Dating Advice, eHarmony, accessed August 28, 2017, http://www.eharmony.ca/dating-advice/about-you/dating-advice/relationship-compatibility-a-guide-to-finding-the-one-part-i%C2%AD.
2 For more information about these personality types, visit www.myersbriggs.org/my-mbti-personality-type/mbti-basics.

Obviously, couples should have some things in common. A friend of mine puts it this way: If two logs are floating down a stream—one log down the middle of the stream and the other along the shore—the middle-of-the-stream log will make the journey much more quickly and leave the shore-hugging log behind in the brush. In the same way, when couples aren't compatible in certain areas, the results can bring challenges and conflict. As David Augsburger writes:

> The very same differences that initially drew us together later pull us apart and still later may draw us near again. Differences first attract, then irritate, then frustrate, then illuminate, and finally may unite us. Those traits that intrigue in courtship, amuse in early marriage, begin to chafe in time and infuriate in conflicts of middle marriages; but maturation begins to change their meaning and the uniqueness of the other person becomes prized, even in the very differences that were primary irritants.[3]

Because Leon and I had a long-distance relationship, we spent a lot of time considering the decision we were making. We knew deep in our hearts that God wanted to bless our lives with a healthy marriage. We both had the desire to listen to our mentors and to follow what God was saying about our future together, and we enrolled in a pre-marriage class with an experienced couple, which gave Leon and me the start we needed. Part of the class involved reading a marriage book and discussing specific topics during weekly meetings so by the time we said, "I do," we knew what the words really meant. Much of the class also focused on uncovering our similarities and differences. Discovering areas of compatibility, or the lack thereof, is an important part of any pre-marriage class.

I needed time to develop into the woman God wanted me to be for Leon. Through correspondence, several trips back and forth, and many phone calls, Leon and I became more familiar with each other and very good friends. Eventually I was ready to become a wife, but I will be honest and tell you the process of learning to become the one continues to this day. God is always willing to teach us how to have a better and more intimate connection with one another. Leon and I are compatible in many ways but different in others. Knowing our differences has helped us be more creative in learning how to understand and accept each other unconditionally.

---

3 David Augsburger, *Sustaining Love: Healing & Growing in the Passages of Marriage* (Ventura, CA: Regal Books, 1988), 40.

Without a doubt, our strongest point of compatibility is values and beliefs. We place our relationship with God, church involvement, and Christian values as a high priority. Although our lives have changed through the years, one thing remains the same: the emphasis Leon and I put on living out the Christian faith. Another area of compatibility we share is temperament. Leon is seldom in a hurry. When he sits down for a meal, he takes his time. He is patient with people, very social, and enjoys spending time with family and friends. When the world around me is moving at a breakneck pace, I am able to slow down and enjoy time with my friends and family.

One way to discover how compatible you are with someone is by spending time with each other's family and friends. This is, actually, one of the best ways to get to know someone because it can tell you a lot about the person. The more couples talk and communicate about their family backgrounds, the more prepared they are to handle family differences. My husband had the opportunity to learn so much about my family background when he came to live in Ecuador during our courtship. He saw my family at their best and worst, and coming into our marriage, he knew my family was dysfunctional in many ways. Because I shared my family life with Leon early in our relationship, he was better prepared to understand God's heart for me as his wife and his role as a godly husband. He used to tell me, "My family background is so different than yours. The way your parents relate to each other compared to my parents is so different." He was right. My parents solved problems with yelling, while Leon's parents avoided conflict and didn't talk much about pressing issues.

He also told me his parents' ways were much simpler than those of my parents. The "salt of the earth," his grandparents were farmers, and most of his family worked the land. His parents maintained their fairly simple lifestyle even though Leon's dad was an engineer and his mom was an architect, and they both left small towns to move to Northern California. My parents, on the other hand, had maids and servants and lived with some luxuries.

So as you can see, Leon and I knew each other well before marriage, and in a way we knew what to expect. He spent time with my family, learned Spanish, and lived in Ecuador in order to make sure I was the one God had chosen for him. I also made a trip to America with my mother to feel out what life would be like in the United States.

In their marriage book *Fit to Be Tied*, Bill and Lynne Hybels explain the role of communication in building a marriage relationship. The first decade of their marriage was difficult because of assumptions and lack of communication. The Hybels realized early on that they were radically different. They went into marriage not knowing their family backgrounds and how those backgrounds would affect them, so for about ten years, their marriage was a disaster. They write, "The courtship era is the time to get serious about communication. Don't assume that quantity automatically produces quality. Don't settle for relating on the surface."[4] They suggest couples spend time with the families to get to know why their future spouses act in certain ways. This is important to do *before* you get married, and the only way to do it is by hanging out with both families.

The Hybels go on to explain the need to express honest feelings, confront, dig deep, and ask probing questions. They say the goal of marriage is to find intimacy. "You will never find genuine intimacy with an uncommunicative partner."[5] This is the reason I insist that couples spend some time with each other's families so they can get to know this part of one another that is often missed and can cause problems in a marriage.

When you discover why your partner acts a certain way, it's easier to pray about it, asking the Lord for healing. Find communication tools that can help you bring clarity, and fix any unhealthy patterns you might have learned from your parents.

> *When you discover why your partner acts a certain way, it's easier to pray about it, asking the Lord for healing. Find communication tools that can help you bring clarity, and fix any unhealthy patterns you might have learned from your parents.*

Areas of Compatibility

After much research, I've identified seven key areas of compatibility that are listed below. Generally, it's a good idea to take a compatibility test in order to determine the type of person you're most aligned with. Such tests can also help you get to know someone better. No matter how compatible or incompatible you think you are with the person you want to marry, you need to "get your feet wet" and look

---

4 Bill and Lynne Hybels, *Fit to Be Tied: Making Marriage Last a Lifetime* (Grand Rapids, MI: Zondervan, 1993).
5 Hybels, Fit.

at the details. Really get to know each other. Some people think about having a big house with land and animals, while others want to live in the suburbs. Most couples have lofty financial goals, but they haven't always given much thought as to how they will achieve those goals. Like points of compatibility, differences are important in a relationship, but they can also be an unwelcome surprise. The more you uncover about your partner's personality and habits, the better prepared you are to handle incompatibility.

Think through the following categories of compatibility, ask questions, and consider your current or future relationship:

- Values and beliefs: What are your core values? Do you want to have children, for instance? How should they be raised? Are your spiritual development and relationship with God important parts of your life?
- Relational skills: How skilled are you at verbalizing your thoughts and feelings? How do you handle your temper and your overall mood? Is conflict resolution easy or difficult for you?
- Physical nature: Are you physically active? Do you enjoy hikes and sports, or do you prefer to stay around the home? Are you always on the go? Do you thrive on being in shape? When you get married, how often do you want to have sex?
- Temperament: Do you have a positive or negative view of yourself and the world around you? Do you find fault easily? Are you happy, fulfilled, and hopeful, or are you moody?
- Intellectual nature: How interested are you in learning? How would you like living with an artist? How much would you enjoy living with someone who is pursuing a political position? Do you like comedies, dramas, or action-adventure movies? Do you prefer to read at night, go to a musical, or watch television?
- Social capacity: Do you prefer to be around people, or do you prefer solitude? Relationships work best when both people can be dominant at different times and submissive at other times. (We'll talk more about submission in a later chapter.)
- Goals: What are your goals for the future? If you have a similar life plan as your future mate, you'll experience less conflict. For some couples, life goals are the conduit that brings them together. Though no one can predict the future, seeking out a marriage partner who has similar professional goals can be a benefit. Discussing financial goals gives a couple further insights

into their compatibility. Some people want to live in a big house on several acres; others are content with a condo in the city. Which one are you?

Faith and Compatibility

When they are considering a mate for life, many people of faith put a high rank on the area of values and beliefs. Although it would be a mistake for values and beliefs to be the only criterion in the search for a life partner, it should be near the top of the list, if not the most important criterion.

According to a Pew Research Center survey conducted in 2014, Americans agree that the role of faith in marriage is important: "Marrying within the faith is still common in the United States, with nearly seven-in-ten married people (69%) saying that their spouse shares their religion."[6] Whether the marriage is between Christians, Catholics, Muslims, Hindus, or another religious group, only 30 percent of married people get married outside of the faith. However, the survey notes that interfaith marriages seem to be on the rise.[7]

Why is faith such an important area of compatibility? All people are on a spiritual journey. For those of us who know Jesus, this journey requires daily focus as we work out our relationship with Him. This translates into a lifestyle; it determines our social interactions, affects our ways of thinking, and dramatically impacts our everyday beliefs. Faith is about how we live our lives.

As you become the one, you will realize how important God is in your life. There are many benefits to this realization, but one of them in particular has a direct impact on your marriage. Knowing how important God is to you will keep you from settling for less than what God has

> *As you become the one, you will realize how important God is in your life. There are many benefits to this realization, but one of them in particular has a direct impact on your marriage. Knowing how important God is to you will keep you from settling for less than what God has for you—and what He has for you is a godly, loving spouse.*

---

6 Caryle Murphy, *"Interfaith Marriage Is Common in U.S., Particularly Among the Recently Wed,"* Pew Research Center, June 2, 2015, http://www.pewresearch.org/fact-tank/2015/06/02/interfaith-marriage.

7 For more information on this topic, go to http://www.pewforum.org/2015/05/12/americas-changing-religious-landscape.

for you—and what He has for you is a godly, loving spouse.

Be willing to ask the person you are interested in what their faith means to them. Many people call themselves Christians because of the way their parents raised them, but they may not have any idea what it really means to accept Jesus as their Lord. Obviously, all of us are sinners saved by grace and are on a pilgrimage of learning to become more like Jesus, but if you don't see this desire for spiritual growth and intimacy with God in your date, a long-term path with that person may be harder. It is important for both of you to believe that a loving God is bringing the two of you together. Then for the rest of your lives, you will know you are compatible in the one thing that will keep you together even if everything else fails: your faith.

> *Be willing to ask the person you are interested in what their faith means to them. Many people call themselves Christians because of the way their parents raised them, but they may not have any idea what it really means to accept Jesus as their Lord.*

Gender Differences

Another area that cannot be overemphasized in compatibility is gender differences. Men and women have the obvious differences, of course, but it is important to be aware of how the internal differences can affect a marriage. Many empirical studies have documented gender differences in personality, and two classes of theories—biological and social psychological—have sought to explain these differences. Although couples can share many of the same qualities, men and women look at the world from unique perspectives. From a very early age, men and women are trained to view life in contrasting ways. The biggest proof of gender differences is found in brain science, which shows the interesting ways we are wired. The female brain is wired to process externally for the most part, so women tend to solve issues by talking. The male brain, generally speaking, is structured to think things through internally, so most men process mentally or quietly.[8]

---

8 Paul T. Costa Jr., Antonio Terracciano, and Robert R. McCrae, "Gender Differences in Personality Traits Across Cultures: Robust and Surprising Findings," *Journal of Personality and Social Psychology* 81, no. 2 (2001): 322–331, http://www.cin.ufpe.br/~ssj/Genderdifferences%20in%20personality%20traits%20across%20cultures%20Robust%20andsurprising%20findings.pdf.

Dr. Terri Orbuch reached similar conclusions about how men and women view life in her twenty-seven-year study on married couples. She wrote, "Men and women have real differences when it comes to what they want and need in order to stay happy and together in the relationship."[9]

In general, men are more "logical" and women are more "emotional," meaning that men tend to compartmentalize life issues and women tend to blend life together, viewing everything as connected. In his lecture "Laugh Your Way to a Better Marriage," Mark Gungor explores the differences between men and women with humor and many generalizations but also a lot of truth:

> Men's brains are made up of little boxes. And we have a box for everything. We've got a box for the car, we've got a box for the money. We've got a box for the job, we've got a box for you, we've got a box for the kids. . . We got boxes everywhere. And the rule is: the boxes don't touch . . . Women's brains are made up of a big ball of wire. And everything is connected to everything. The money's connected to the car and the car's connected to your job. . . It's like the internet superhighway, okay? And it's all driven by energy that we call emotion.[10]

Men tend to be more independent and need their own space, while women often fill up the closet, the bathroom, and the kitchen with knick-knacks. Women need the reassurance of their man's love every day; men are happy with a little sex and then bed. Women are deeply pleased by simple actions, such as when their husband reaches out to take their hand or when he texts simple notes like, "I'm just thinking about you." Why is this? Because it says, "Yes, you're lovable and I choose you!" Men, meanwhile, need to hear, "Great job!" and "You amaze me!"

Concerning sex, a husband needs to know that his wife desires him. Sexual affirmation gives a man a sense of confidence that carries over into every other area of his life. Sex is powerful. If a wife says, "I'm too tired," men can feel depressed or undesirable. Those three words can ruin a man's day or even his week. On the other hand, women get more satisfaction from touch, cuddling, words, and the effort a man puts into the sexual experience.

When it comes to gender differences, couples are unique. No two couples are alike in the way they work out their relationship, but perhaps the one aspect that all

9 Terri Orbuch, "What Keeps Marriages Together? It Depends on Your Gender!" *Hitched*, http://www.hitchedmag.com/article.php?id=1703.
10 Mark Gungor, "Laugh Your Way to a Better Marriage" (lecture), https://vimeo.com/77545336.

couples have in common is insecurities. Though we learn to live with insecurities, men and women deal with them in contrasting ways; however, we can bring these issues to the Lord, remembering they can be difficult to recognize at times.

Women tend to ask, "Am I lovable? Will he choose me again? Am I cherished?"

Men tend to ask, "Am I capable? I want to be a great husband, but am I?" Most men constantly question how others view them, so their hearts are filled when they know their wives believe in them and notice what they do.

Another difference between men and women is the ability women possess to take care of others or to nurture. Women are the primary caregivers, while men have to learn how to be caregivers. I have met some amazing men who have learned to be aware of their nurturing potential, but in most cases, it is something they still need to learn.

Be open to what is needed in order to complement and bless your spouse. This is why being a student of your future spouse is crucial. It's by learning about your spouse's perspectives, dreams, abilities, strengths, and even weaknesses that you grow closer to them. Learning about your spouse helps build patience and character, and it also helps establish unity.

Be open to what is needed in order to complement and bless your spouse. This is why being a student of your future spouse is crucial. It's by learning about your spouse's perspectives, dreams, abilities, strengths, and even weaknesses that you grow closer to them. Learning about your spouse helps build patience and character, and it also helps establish unity.

Positive Incompatibility

For many women, myself included, the home is one area where easy compatibility goes out the window. Leon and I have struggled throughout our married life in the area of making decisions about home improvements. Of all the potential conflicts in a marriage, one would think that "home improvements" would be low on the list, but somehow it still causes tension between us. Some might say this is a communication issue, as we often disagree about the topic, but I see it more as a matter of our upbringing and compatibility.

Let's say I want to fix up the backyard, buy new furniture, or redecorate the living room. Maybe I want to remodel the kitchen because it's looking outdated. This is typically a decision the couple makes together. What if one spouse is adamant the money should be saved or that the kitchen and backyard look fine the way they are? Leon is the one who sometimes opposes home or yard renovations, and I am the one pushing the project. What's a couple to do?

Taking a step back from the situation for a moment, let's look at family background. Leon comes from a farming family. His parents lived through the Great Depression and learned to live within their means and sacrifice financially, and they viewed saving and investing as a priority for a better future. They didn't see the value of buying better furniture or improving the yard because of financial pressures. Be content with what you have no matter its condition; that was how farming families survived.

I was raised by parents who achieved financial success as a result of hard work and sound investments. In Ecuador my dad worked more than one job as a young man and started his own financial consulting business a few years after I was born. He was a saver, but both of my parents liked buying new things, especially during my teenage years. They vacationed frequently and even had some fine furniture delivered from Europe. Though my dad considered saving and investments a priority, my parents still enjoyed a lavish lifestyle.

As a young newlywed, I had a level of expectation when it came to living arrangements, and I was used to a certain type of lifestyle. I knew Leon had financial goals that were akin to mine, and I also understood life in America would be much different than what I was used to in Ecuador. At the beginning of our marriage, I knew we couldn't always afford new things, but I was content to wait. What I didn't plan on was how this would affect me emotionally. If my home didn't look a certain way or if I couldn't landscape the backyard, I became a bit moody. On many occasions, I expressed to Leon that I wanted to buy new furniture and redecorate the living room so our house would look better, but he didn't see this as a priority and was indifferent. For many women, the home is an extension of who we are. We desire to look around and see pretty things. We want to make the home look beautiful for ourselves, our families, and our husbands.

Both Leon and I wanted to achieve financial independence and pass that on to our children, but to Leon, achieving these goals required sacrifice in the present.

For a few years, I had to let go of my desire to buy nicer things for our home. Leon placed the priority on saving first and having a plan before buying anything. I couldn't really see this at the time, but now I realize the wisdom in managing money that way. In those early years of my marriage, I became accustomed to having a budget and spending a set amount of money, and I learned to be content with what God provided.

Spending habits and personality styles regarding money could be a great source of distress if you don't learn to communicate well and to live within your means, planning for the future. Millennials like to have things instantly, and many fall into the trap of borrowing too much money and paying high interest rates. Credit cards are an irresponsible answer. Take an honest look at yourself and ask if you are the kind of person who spends money on unnecessary things and easily gets into debt. On the other extreme, are you someone who doesn't want to spend money on anything? Where can you find balance?

> *Spending habits and personality styles regarding money could be a great source of distress if you don't learn to communicate well and to live within your means, planning for the future.*

Although Leon and I may never be totally compatible when it comes to money management and home improvements, we've learned to accept each other's differences and balance each other. Compatibility differences don't have to mean that the relationship will never work. In fact, some compatibility differences can help you grow closer to God and each other, as long as both of you maintain a heart of love, humility, and unity. Though these differences can frustrate us, they will help us grow in many other areas if we learn to communicate well. I encourage you to look for some meaningful areas of compatibility with your loved one, especially those areas that go to the core of who you are. Some areas of incompatibility, such as differences in faith, should never be considered; they are sincerely "incompatible." However, other compatibility differences allow room for growth and will help mold you into a better person and spouse.

Discussion Questions:

1. Why is it important to ask God for His will as you choose a marriage partner?

2. If you're in a relationship, describe your partner in the following areas of compatibility:

      a. Values and beliefs
      b. Relational skills
      c. Physical nature
      d. Temperament
      e. Intellectual nature
      f. Social capacity
      g. Future goals

3. How can differences in a relationship be a good thing?

4. What are the most important aspects of compatibly for you?

Prayer:

Dear heavenly Father,

Teach me to live in Your Spirit and show me how to hear Your voice. I pray I will learn to hear You and be able to make decisions led by Your Spirit, not my flesh. Help my future spouse do the same. Holy Spirit, transform us to be more like Jesus. I love You, and I choose to trust You so I can act in a loving manner toward my future spouse.

Chapter
10

DATING WITH PURPOSE

Knowing What You Want in Your Future Spouse

A few weeks ago, my young friend "Ryan" was excited. He had recently met "Hope," and it seemed they were perfect for one another. When I saw them together, they were beaming and appeared incredibly happy, but a short time later, Ryan came to see me, trying to pick up the pieces after the relationship had fallen apart. It started and ended quickly.

What happened?

Unfortunately, I see this pattern all the time. Many people who find themselves here get caught up in the infatuation and physical stage of a new relationship and don't stop to consider the deeper issues of why they feel they need to rush. Was it wise for Ryan and Hope to jump headfirst into a relationship? She had just broken up with someone a month before she and Ryan met. Did they have peace about the timing of their relationship, knowing God was giving them the go-ahead? Or was it unwise for them to start dating so soon?

That said, I have also seen emotionally and spiritually healthy, mature people who have been praying for a long time about this process. When God brought someone into their lives, He confirmed to both of them through their personal relationship with Him and wise counselors that it was the right time for them to start dating.

You're on a path to find the perfect mate—the one God has designed for you. Be patient. Harness your passions before making a lifelong commitment. Your path has crossed with this other person's for a reason, but God is giving you and that person a choice. You can throw yourself into a situation you may not be ready for. Or you can take a step back

> *You're on a path to find the perfect mate—the one God has designed for you. Be patient. Harness your passions before making a lifelong commitment.*

145

from the situation and the person just for a moment to pray and evaluate whether they could be Mr. or Miss Right.

Leon and I met when he was on a mission trip in my country. We exchanged contact information, and then he returned to his home several thousand miles away. He and I didn't see each other again for a year and a half, and though I liked him and hoped and prayed for something more than friendship with him, I was not ready for a relationship with him. I knew I was young, and I was only in my second year of law school. When he asked if he could come visit me, he told me three different months

Your path has crossed with this other person's for a reason, but God is giving you and that person a choice. You can throw yourself into a situation you may not be ready for. Or you can take a step back from the situation and the person just for a moment to pray and evaluate whether they could be Mr. or Miss Right.

that would work for him, and I chose the one that was the furthest away. It is astounding how important timing can be in a relationship. If we had rushed it, I think we would have discovered what countless other potential couples have discovered—that it wasn't the right time.

Though Leon and I wrote each other several times a week after meeting, I had reservations about a relationship with an American man who would take me to his country and away from my family. I knew that if I married Leon, God wanted us to live in the United States. It was just one of those things you know deep in your heart. I planned to fall in love one day, but I never expected it would be with an American guy. Although the thought of being with a man from America felt exotic and exciting, when I considered the long-term consequences, my mind raced. How would I handle life in America, and how would Leon manage living in Ecuador for a season?

There was also the issue of escaping the dysfunction of my home life. I knew my parents didn't have a happy marriage. If I continued to live with them or near them, would it take a toll on me? This may not be true for every person, but for me, I knew the answer was "yes." I didn't want to continue to be the person who always brought them back together. I really wanted them to depend on God, make that decision by themselves, and find restoration in their marriage. For this reason, I prayed even more for God's confirmation and peace to let me know if Leon was His will for me.

Leon was nervous, too. Without saying much of our expectations, we were both praying and hoping the Lord would lead us to something deeper. In the meantime, we built an excellent friendship. I had someone I could write to about the many things in my heart. He heard about my family, my friends, and my relationship with the Lord. It was wonderful to receive his letters and hear about his life, too. Our friendship was pure and sweet during that first year of writing and talking a few times over the phone. Getting to know each other at this first level was important and beautiful. We were friends, as well as brother and sister in Christ, and had the hope that God would do something in His right timing. As I look back on that season, I'm even more in awe of how God is so faithful with everyone who waits for Him. Jesus knows what we need.

One of the most important things we have to deal with in a new or potential relationship is our expectations. Leon is a wonderful man, and he met many of my expectations. As we built our friendship, I saw he loved God, treated people with respect, and wasn't the type to bounce from relationship to relationship. In fact, he had been praying for a wife for quite a while and hadn't been in a romantic relationship for many years. His best friend used to tease him and say, "All the girls here, and you have to go all the way to Ecuador to pursue a relationship." I like to think he was waiting and becoming the one for me. Not only did he love his parents and have a solid relationship with his whole family, but he also had a passion for missionary work.

However, one area of compatibility we struggled with was communication. Leon didn't speak Spanish fluently until he lived in Ecuador before we married. I was concerned about communication barriers, and even though many of my expectations were met, the idea of a cross-cultural marriage brought some unwanted thoughts.

The first week in August when Leon came to visit me, I was praying about our relationship because the pressure was mounting. I knew Leon had feelings for me, but I was terrified of the future and what it would be like with someone from a different country, culture, and background. My fears kept me from feeling anything for Leon at all, and I completely forgot about the spiritual connection I felt the first time I saw him. When he arrived, I was kind and polite, but I did not have any romantic feelings for him. Instead, I was more concerned that he would go back home feeling hurt because I had turned him down. I even asked my cousin to date him because he was a great guy and I thought she really liked him. So she tried to get his attention, which made me jealous. Later I found out she was praying for me and hoping that God would do something so I could fall in love with this handsome American. God used all of this to help me understand what "true love" from Him is like.

In this strange place of feeling and not feeling for Leon, I prayed hard. There was one day in particular when I remember getting on my knees and literally crying out to God to give me His special kind of love for Leon—but only if he was the one God had chosen for me to marry. That is exactly what happened. After almost a week of activities and family outings with Leon, I sensed God's voice. All at once, after a few days of being sure Leon was not the person I wanted to date for life, I received the most amazing gift of knowing he was the one for me. That Saturday morning when we went on a boat ride with my family all around, I knew deep in my heart that God had answered my prayers and I truly had found the one I wanted.

During this time, I learned that prayer and listening to God make finding a mate much easier. The Lord will even give us a deeper love for that special person because His love is perfect. His love is unconditional. Being able to care about another person unconditionally will help us through the different stages of married life. That is what happened with me. I learned to love Leon with an unconditional love. In my heart I knew he was the one I would be with for the rest of my life.

With quiet confidence, allow the Lord into your process of choosing a mate. If you're dating someone, make sure you have God's peace about the relationship, which means that your mind and spirit are synced with assurance.

With quiet confidence, allow the Lord into your process of choosing a mate. If you're dating someone, make sure you have God's peace about the relationship, which means that your mind and spirit are synced with assurance.

Personal Expectations

Read the list of expectations below and gauge both your relationship readiness and the caliber of the person you want to date. Be honest with yourself and God, and write down the things you desire the most and what you know you wouldn't settle for.

A woman should seek a man who . . .

- Loves God and treats people with respect. Treating others with respect shows reverence for God.
- Shows commitment. A man who is ready to marry is not bouncing from relationship to relationship and tepid about commitments.
- Shows how to forgive. Marriage is full of opportunities to offer and receive forgiveness. If a man can't forgive, the marriage will be stunted.
- Can control his passions. If a potential mate wants to stay late at your place and continually puts you in compromising situations, he's not in control. If he looks at other women, even though he's in a committed relationship with you, or watches pornographic movies, he could be in need of deeper healing.
- Honors his parents. God tells us to honor our parents so our lives may be long and things will go well with us.
- Is comfortable being a leader with a humble heart. Being a husband and father means having spiritual authority through his relationship with Jesus. Being a leader also means having a servant heart.
- Communicates well. He should know how to ask questions and engage as a listener. Is he eager to listen to your heart?
- Can hold down a job and is responsible.
- Values your opinions and can manage disagreements.
- Knows his identity comes from Christ.

A man should seek a woman who . . .

- Loves and fears God and hopes in the Lord.
- Honors her parents. Determine the kind of relationship she has with her father, because this will foreshadow her relationship with you, her husband. If she has a hard time honoring her parents, she likely will have a hard time honoring you.
- Knows how to give and ask for forgiveness. Marriage is full of opportunities to offer and receive forgiveness. A woman should know how to ask for forgiveness, admit she's wrong, grant forgiveness, and give grace when you fail her.
- Shares your desires for family. Some women choose careers over children, and you may have a different concept of what family looks like.
- Displays modesty. A woman's character is displayed in how she handles the power of her femininity and sexuality.

- Has a humble heart and is willing to trust her husband's spiritual guidance. If you are a godly man and willing to give your life up for your wife, it should be easy for her to trust you.
- Communicates well and is genuinely interested in your life.
- Is unafraid to voice her opinion. She should know what she thinks and needs and can communicate these things to you.
- Knows her identity comes from Christ.

Finding Mr. or Miss Right

When we talk about matters of the heart, falling in love, or giving someone the keys to our souls, we also need to talk about blind spots. We all have them. As we talked about at the beginning of this chapter, couples often want to rush into physical and emotional commitments without giving much thought to the long-term impact. We need to consider a few things as we step onto the dating field. First, God is the One who created us, and He wants only goodness for us and our relationships. That is the reason we commit to pray ahead of time and ask God for His counsel in what to do when we think there is someone on the horizon. We don't jump off the cliff of love and act on pure instinct when we meet someone we feel attracted to. That is what most people do, and it doesn't always end well because we need more than instinct. Instead, we understand that if we wait for God's right timing, the start of a meaningful friendship could lead to a wonderful marriage that lasts forever.

Second, starting a relationship leads to an emotional attachment. Song of Songs 2:7 states it this way: *"Do not arouse or awaken love until it so desires."* Sadly, many young people have experienced heartbreak because they decided to start an exclusive, emotional, and sometimes physical relationship too early in the process of getting to know a person.

For many young people, the road to finding Mr. or Miss Right is strewn with multiple relationships and heartbreaks. Most people would prefer to meet their prince or princess on the first date, but the road to marital bliss is usually more complicated. One struggle young people go through is the waiting game. Many times they find themselves in serious relationships and are unsure if they are dating the right person. I can relate to this concern, as my husband and I were in a long-distance relationship for several years. Waiting to get married and even spending time away from my future spouse were important parts of determining if Leon was the right man for me, even though at the time it was hard and felt like an emotional strain. Many of us end up settling because we think the perfect match isn't out there. I've known many people who met, fell in love, and got married despite the warning signs, and they found themselves in poor or even devastating marriages. This is sad because it can be avoided. Many pre-marrieds don't seek the guidance of the Holy Spirit in their marriage decisions at all. Young people sometimes see marriage as their salvation because of the many traumas in their lives, and they tend to believe that marriage is the answer to their emotional healing, which leads them to reject the voice of the Lord and the warnings of family and friends.

How can these difficult situations be avoided?

1. Pray about the person you're considering marrying. What is God saying about your spending the rest of your life with this person?
2. Spend some time apart from each other and get God's perspective on the relationship.
3. Get the advice and counsel of mentors, parents, and people who know you well. Those closest to you can usually see potential problems more clearly.

The good news is that God is always willing to help us find our way, even after we've taken a wrong turn. Singleness may feel unending, but it won't last forever. Use this time to prepare for marriage and enjoy this stage of your life. Be comfortable being single—because your identity is in Jesus and not in a marriage status. Don't settle for less than God's best. You're worth it.

Hope in the Waiting

Wait for the Lord;
be strong and take heart
and wait for the Lord.
— Psalm 27:14

Personally, I believe if someone has the desire to marry, it is because God gave them that desire. The people I know who haven't married are usually older and fall in different categories. I remember going out with a girlfriend who wanted to get married, but as she sat across from me at the table, I was surprised and then alarmed by her eating habits. I couldn't imagine a guy going on a dinner date with her and being attracted by her poor manners. It's possible for us to adopt some bad habits we don't notice, but someone interested in us would definitely notice. First impressions can make a big difference. They are like external beauty. Should a person's "cute factor" be the main or only reason we're interested in them? No, but it is a very important reason at the same time.

Second, a person who wants to marry but is still single might have expectations that are too high. This can be a sensitive topic, because God wants to give us the desires of our hearts and it's important to know what those desires are and be clear about what we're looking for. At the same time, we also have to remember that people are people. We're just normal. Anyone we're interested in will just be normal, too. We are looking for a person to spend life with, not a movie character who doesn't make mistakes and always knows what to say. Minor relationship issues can be magnified into major flaws when we hold them up to an impossible standard.

A person could also be single because they aren't exposing themselves to places where they can meet more people: conferences, mission trips, fun activities, etc. They also might need to ask their family, mentors, and friends to pray for them in this area and even help them find someone. Why not? God has a way of using people to help us find the right path for our lives. He did it in the past, and He does it now as well.

Finally it could also be a matter of God's timing. Perhaps that right person just hasn't come along yet. What if you are in love with Jesus and doing everything you can to meet someone, and it just hasn't happened? I know some ladies who are gorgeous in every aspect and love Jesus so much, yet they are still waiting, all the while feeling their biological clocks ticking away. What do we do with this? We keep on trusting God. I know of people who found their perfect match in their fifties and sixties—and to them, the wait was worth it. One of the ladies in my women's group recently got married after a long wait. She is thirty-eight years old and God has been faithful to her. She went on a mission trip and trusted Him; she wasn't even looking for someone, yet that is when He brought her husband.

With the Lord, it is a mystery and a beautiful journey of knowing His heart personally.

If you are about to lose hope in this area of marriage, the best advice I can give you is to be active in your first love. Pursue Jesus and, second, pray about which doors God is opening for you and which circles He wants you to enter to meet someone. Pray for godly encounters. Let Him lead you, knowing He wants to.

Dating with Purpose

Personal boundaries are the physical, emotional, and mental limits we establish to protect ourselves from being intentionally or accidentally manipulated by others. Boundaries allow us to separate who we are and what we think and feel from the thoughts and feelings of others. Learning to set healthy personal boundaries is necessary for maintaining a positive self-image. It is our way of communicating to others that we have self-respect, self-worth, and will not allow others to define us.

> *If you are about to lose hope in this area of marriage, the best advice I can give you is to be active in your first love. Pursue Jesus and, second, pray about which doors God is opening for you and which circles He wants you to enter to meet someone. Pray for godly encounters. Let Him lead you, knowing He wants to.*

Boundaries are an important part of protecting and caring for ourselves. If we're not getting the respect we deserve in a relationship, we need to look at our personal boundaries. Boundaries help us define our core beliefs as well as our limits. Boundaries also help minimize stress and conflict in a relationship. With clear boundaries, there's nothing to argue about.

With that in mind, it's important to establish a philosophy of dating that may be different than what many of us have experienced or watched occurring in other people's lives. I call it dating with purpose. Dating can be a confusing topic for many young people. Often in matters of dating, parents either encourage sexual freedom and don't offer any clear guidelines, or they are too strict and don't allow any interaction with the opposite sex. In an effort to fit in with their peers, many young people follow their friends' lead or mimic what they see on television. Like a boat lost at sea, young people set sail in turbulent waters and learn about dating and sexuality on their own. Much of the time, this results in brokenness.

Keep in mind that we will never get married if we don't date or our expectations are too high. At the same time, we'll probably experience heartbreak if we date too frequently because we think this is "normal" and dating fills an emotional need in our lives. Instead, a third option—think of it as friendship dating—is best. If you're going out on a date, go out to deepen or start a friendship. Hormones may push you to desire more from the relationship right away, but avoid this slope. The key is to compose your boundaries before you go out with someone, not as the relationship is developing. Here are some personal boundary suggestions, as well as signs of unhealthy boundaries:

1. Maintain Your Identity

Be aware of who you are, know what you believe, and don't be defined by others. How do you feel about important matters? What are your values, morals, and goals? Don't change who you are and what you want to make a relationship work. Continue to have a life that is independent of your dating relationship. Pursue interests and activities you enjoy and time with your good friends. Remember this simple truth: Happiness comes from the Lord, not only from a relationship.

Signs of Unhealthy Boundaries Concerning Your Identity

- Feeling pressured to go against your values so you can please others
- Feeling pressured to adopt another person's beliefs or ideas in order to be accepted

2. Have a Healthy Respect for Yourself

All of us have thoughts, feelings, plans, dreams, and hopes. We want to be heard and accepted as we are. With these things in mind, you can set boundaries that establish a level of respect for your emotional and physical needs, as well as your personal time. Be clear about availability when dating. If you've made plans, a date shouldn't expect you to change them just because they asked you to. You should be able to state your thoughts and feelings without being judged.

Signs of Unhealthy Boundaries Concerning Respect

- Not responding when someone mistreats you

- Not speaking up when you have something to say
- Struggling to say "no"[1]

3. Set Your Standard for Physical Space and Intimacy

Never do anything you're uncomfortable with on a date. Set a standard of physical intimacy before dating and stick with that standard. You should never feel uncomfortable because someone is sitting or standing too close to you. If your date is in your personal space, let them know.

Keep in mind that your physical boundaries may be different than other people's. For instance, you may decide that holding hands and kissing are acceptable as the relationship progresses, but another couple may decide that kissing leads to too much physical contact.

Signs of Unhealthy Boundaries Concerning Physical Space and Intimacy

- Becoming overly involved in someone's problems
- Struggling to communicate your emotional needs or define sexual boundaries
- Acting on your first sexual impulse

4. Know What You Want

What do you want in a significant other? Decide what is negotiable and non-negotiable. Are you willing to date someone who is divorced or has children? Are you willing to move to another country to be with that person? Know the values and personality characteristics you are interested in.

God knows your heart, and understanding how much He loves you and how interested He is in your desires gives you the opportunity to make choices about what you do or do not want in your future spouse. For instance, I never wanted a "macho man," and in Ecuador there are plenty of them. God knew my heart in this matter, and so He sent someone different to Ecuador for me. I also thought I wouldn't want to marry a divorced man because I had witnessed my mother's anguish over my dad's first marriage, and I can still see the painful effects of that divorce. God heard the desires of my heart, and Leon was never married before he married me.

---

1 "Signs of Healthy/Unhealthy Boundaries – Blueprint for a New Life Style," Sexual Assault Support Centre of Waterloo Region,
http://www.sascwr.org/files/www/resources_pdfs/incest/Signs_of_healthyunhealthy_boundaries.pdf.

I fully believe that if you say, "No," to certain things concerning your future spouse, God will honor your heart. He knows what's best for you. Do not feel obligated to date someone you weren't hoping for, and don't change your mind unless you sense God giving you the go-ahead to do so.

One key in this process is knowing the person, their character, and their walk with Jesus well. God restores and brings healing. A divorced person who encounters God's love, walks with Him, lives in integrity and purity, and has received emotional healing would be a better mate than a single person who's never been married but doesn't walk with Jesus or live in purity. Therefore, knowing the person well is vital, as is hearing God's voice to know if the relationship is in His will.

> *I fully believe that if you say, "No," to certain things concerning your future spouse, God will honor your heart. He knows what's best for you. Do not feel obligated to date someone you weren't hoping for, and don't change your mind unless you sense God giving you the go-ahead to do so.*

As you become the one, you can trust that God will lead you to someone special because He wants the best for you. That is what God did for me, and if He did it for me, why wouldn't He do it for you? He is ready to provide in every single need, even if we have to wait to see His provision.

Signs of Unhealthy Boundaries Concerning What You Want

* Willing to go out with anyone who asks
* Having a hard time breaking off negative relationships
* Changing your boundaries because you're attracted to someone

What Does Friendship Dating Look Like?

Friendship dating is a safe and meaningful way to get to know the opposite sex. As the friendship grows and both people mature and become healthier, friendship dating naturally moves into more serious dating, where two people get to know each other one on one. Friendship dating is vital because it allows you to relax. It is a joyful, fun experience in which you are becoming better friends with someone. The Christian community is filled with pressure to find "the one," jump into a relationship, get married, and have babies. But God knows your heart, so you don't have to rush the process.

This is what I think healthy friendship dating looks like. The first few dates should be casual. Go out with a group of friends to dinner and a movie or out for coffee. Avoid conversation about past relationships or controversial topics. Even excessive work talk can make the date feel more like an interview than a love connection. Talk about hobbies, interests, travel, and music. Smile, laugh, and have fun. Share enough about yourself that the other person can get to know you. You are on the date to get to know someone and establish a friendship.

Sharing should be mutual and reciprocal, not a one-way conversation. This isn't an audition. Be yourself and get to know your date. You wouldn't believe how often people tell me they went on a date and the person didn't ask them a single question but just rambled on about themselves. If someone is speaking too much, be sure you say something. Especially if you are more reserved or on the quiet side, make an effort to communicate your thoughts.

Pace the relationship. It's not a good idea, even after several dates, to spend the whole weekend with someone in a love bubble, staying up until late hours. While this can be romantic and thrilling, you're setting yourself up to feel overwhelmed and vulnerable, and you're also setting the stage for a sexual situation. End the date at a reasonable time and give it a few days before the next outing. This will allow your heart and mind to process your feelings and give you some clarity about how to proceed at a healthy rate. Share important information at a time that is appropriate. You may feel the need to share about medical, financial, emotional, or health conditions, but wait until the time is right.

Once you've had a chance to establish a friendship and the relationship is progressing, only then consider a stronger commitment.

Take It Slow

Many young people rush into a romantic relationship and later wish they hadn't. We are surrounded by painful breakups and heartbroken people, all of which prove that starting an exclusive dating relationship too soon isn't a good idea. It is better to wait and move forward when you are sure of what God is telling you. A young man I will call Jessie broke off a relationship for a variety of reasons. He was actually very much in love with his girlfriend, but as often happens, physical boundaries were not set at the beginning of the relationship. Within a short period of time, there was so much physical closeness that Jessie knew sex could easily be the next step, and he wanted to preserve his purity.

"The best advice I can give to young people is to take relationships slow," he told me. "Next time I will commit to be her friend first and not make the relationship exclusive right away. My first mistake was to tell her that I liked her during our first few dates. My recommendation is to wait to say things like 'I really like you' or 'let's start dating.' Go out as friends until you know that the relationship will work and is blessed by God."

I agree with him. The best way to have a lasting romantic relationship is not to rush it. And if you have an urge to rush it, examine your heart. Ask yourself why you are doing this. It is true that when you enter the infatuation stage, waiting to define your relationship can feel agonizing, but trust that God has a plan for you. Tune your ears to God as this will really help you determine if the relationship is His will for you.

> *The best way to have a lasting romantic relationship is not to rush it. And if you have an urge to rush it, examine your heart. Ask yourself why you are doing this. It is true that when you enter the infatuation stage, waiting to define your relationship can feel agonizing, but trust that God has a plan for you. Tune your ears to God as this will really help you determine if the relationship is His will for you.*

Dating and Faith

As a Christian, should you date only Christians? Is interfaith dating and marriage okay? The short answer is found in 2 Corinthians 6:14: *"Do not be yoked together with unbelievers. For what do righteousness and wickedness have in common? Or what fellowship can light have with darkness?"* In The Message these verses read, *"Don't become partners with those who reject God. How can you make a partnership out of right and wrong? That's not partnership; that's war. Is light best friends with dark? Does Christ go strolling with the Devil?"*

The apostle Paul gave a clear warning to avoid intermarriage with those who reject God. This command is offered for our own protection; God knows that we can't have the best possible marriage if we are with someone who has different beliefs, values, and priorities.

What is it about being "unequally yoked" that produces challenging consequences? It's not that couples spend their marriage arguing about doctrine. Rather, religion affects how we spend our time, how we spend our money, and how we raise our children, and disagreements over such issues can lead to unhappiness and divorce. However, we also need to remember we don't marry a faith—we marry a man or a woman. In many ways, we marry imperfections, beauty, and changes we don't see coming.

Paul's thoughts on this subject also speak to the idea of spiritual commitment. The question daters should be asking is this: "Where is my partner on their spiritual journey?" We shouldn't look at the person with a checklist in our hands, thinking, *Okay, they say they're a Christian, so I can check that off.* When we meet someone special, we want to understand their level of commitment to spiritual growth and to the Christian faith. They may say they are a Christian because their parents are, but are they committed to Christian living? It is best to date a man or woman who can express why they became a Christian and how they live out their faith on a daily basis.

The Power of Attraction

Typically, physical attraction is what brings people together. Let's be honest—we're not going to marry someone we find physically unattractive, boring, or socially flat. However, it is important to look past the outward appearance and to the heart. That is how we get to know a person's true character. If looks are the only criterion for dating someone, we will eventually have trouble because beauty fades. When couples connect solely through physical attraction, the relationship is based on some level of lust, and when the attraction wears off, the relationship will fail.

Do you remember the first time you had a crush or felt like you were in love? The thrill of a relationship with someone who can meet your needs is exhilarating. Once this idea of love enters the heart, it doesn't easily leave. For me, the occasion of my first crush was my seventeenth birthday party. The object of my affection was a handsome Latino boy who'd been invited by some friends of mine. He was dreamy and very available. His dark hair, brown eyes, and pleasing features made me feel warm all over. We met, and I instantly wanted to get to know him better. After my party we did go out on a few group dates. He came to my graduation party and I saw him at college. On several occasions he came over to my home to hang out with friends. I knew he had feelings for me, but our relationship never went past friendship because of my shyness. At the time I thought it was true love, but really, I was more infatuated with the person I thought he was. He would open doors for me, show concern, listen to me, and bring me gifts. The idea of going out with him felt appealing, but I wasn't ready for a relationship.

During this time in my life, I met and fell in love with Jesus. Growing in the Lord helped me understand love in a deeper way, which in turn helped me define what I wanted in a husband. After much prayer, and because this young man didn't have a personal relationship with Jesus, I made the decision not to pursue a relationship with him. This young man and I were attracted to each other and I thought about him a lot, but was it love? We often call it "love," but going through experiences like this serves to deepen our awareness of what true love looks like. Longing for love, romance, and someone to date is normal. These "almost love" experiences show us that many of our expectations may be incorrect, and we learn that love comes from the Lord and He should be involved in helping us find the perfect mate.

I believe the Lord honored my obedience and rewarded me for my convictions by bringing Leon into my life. Leon was my first boyfriend, my first kiss, my first everything. After Jesus, he has been my most precious gift from God. While dating we prayed a lot together and wanted to follow God's will for our lives. We had so much fun and learned to spend a good amount of time with family and friends. Today as we keep God at the center of our relationship, we watch as our love continues to grow and mature steadily.

I understand that marrying your first boyfriend or girlfriend may not be the case for everyone, but as we trust in God, we can relax and find a perfect match without enduring heartache.

The Three Stages of Romance

As many of us have a tendency to fall in love, it's important to be aware of the three stages of marriage and relationships. Knowing how romance "works" can help young people interpret their emotions more effectively and avoid unnecessary heartache. According to Jeffry H. Larson, most marriages go through the following stages:

1. Romantic love
2. Disillusionment and distraction
3. Dissolution or adjustment with resignation or contentment[2]

I label these stages *enchantment*, *adjustment*, and *mature love*. We tend to follow the order Larson lays out here, moving from one stage to the next. If we don't understand where we are in this progression, it is possible for us to misinterpret our feelings and not comprehend why we are behaving a certain way. When we understand this progression and where we are within it, we are better prepared to keep moving forward, while deepening our commitments to the people we love.

The Enchantment Stage

This stage is perhaps the most exciting and most dangerous. When a couple first meets, everything is wonderful in the relationship. Excitement and a sense of newness sustain the couple with immensely positive feelings. Logic gets pushed aside, and a couple can talk with each other for hours about things they've never shared with another person. They feel heard, valued, and understood. Infatuation makes your dopamine levels soar, producing a full-body euphoria that causes humans to desire sexual intimacy. Romantic love is deeply embedded in the pathways and chemistry of the brain. Do you remember the story of Romeo and Juliet? Their entire romance occurred in the enchantment stage. We're driven in this stage to idealize a potential partner. The novelty of a new love leads us to think about this person day and night, imagining all the ways they could fulfill our deepest desires. We want to spend every moment of every day with them.

However, we need to be careful because in this stage of romance, the brain struggles to incorporate red flags or flaws in a potential partner. We see only their favorable qualities, which feel great, but they aren't always a true representation of that person. Our brains are literally addicted to the feeling of love. In this stage the thinking, logical part of the brain gets put away in the attic.

---

2 Jeffry H. Larson, *The Great Marriage Tune-Up Book: A Proven Program for Evaluating and Renewing Your Relationship* (San Francisco: Jossey-Bass, 2002), p. 2.

How to Deal with Infatuation

1. Understand that infatuation is based on physical appearance and flawed perceptions.
2. Be aware that dopamine, a natural stimulant, is responsible for the infatuation high, and it can actually change the wiring in the brain the same way cocaine affects the personality.[3]
3. If you're feeling sexually aroused, one sure way to lower the emotional intensity is to think about how much you honor the other person and care about their well-being. Consider what a worthy endeavor it is to save each other's purity for marriage. Ask God to help you, and ask trusted friends to pray for you. Expose the thoughts you are dealing with and seek God's truth. Keep in mind that what you are feeling is normal and shouldn't be shamed; God gave every person a sexual drive as a gift to enjoy in the fullness of a marriage covenant.
4. Try shifting your focus by starting a new project or joining a workout class, a book group, a cooking class, etc. Ask God to replace any anxiety within you with His love.
5. Make sure to share these feelings with someone who can pray and encourage you to make good decisions about the relationship. Be vulnerable, ask for prayer, and share when you're feeling confused about the many facets of relationships.
6. Most important of all, ask God to heal any brokenness within you and keep seeking to know His love.

Although this stage of romance makes for great novels and movies, it will eventually end and give way to the next stage: realistic love or the adjustment stage.

The Adjustment Stage

In this stage we tend to get emotionally stuck or "fall out" of love. We begin to see who our partners really are and they begin to see us. All flaws are exposed. The relationship is not easy anymore and we start to experience challenges.

---

3 Scott Edwards, "Love and the Brain," *On the Brain: The Harvard Mahoney Neuroscience Institute Letter,* http://neuro.hms.harvard.edu/harvard-mahoney-neuroscience-institute/brain-newsletter/and-brain-series/love-and-brain.

The length of this stage varies wildly. Some relationships end immediately; some endure bickering and unmet needs for years, while others adjust and thrive. If you believe only in romantic love, your bubble will undoubtedly burst in this stage. You'll begin to feel cheated or that you settled for a partner who is not the person you fell in love with. You could begin to feel resentful and resort to blaming your partner for your unmet needs.

Some couples can get all the way to marriage and start their lives together totally enchanted with each other. Then, as the relationship grows, disenchantment sets in. Talks become strained, fascination is replaced by put-downs, and ecstasy is pushed aside. However, many couples make it through this stage and enter the next: mature love.

Mature Love

This stage is marked by safety and security in the relationship. Both of you feel fulfilled and cared for by your partner. In this stage you know each other at a deep, intrinsic level. You know your own desires, and you choose to accept your partner's desires, too. You have each other's backs—for better or worse. There is a sense of hope, thankfulness, and encouragement. When a couple becomes mature in their relationship, they understand how to love each other and how to be loved.

Unfortunately, many couples give up before reaching the maturity stage because it requires a lot of personal growth and two mature people who are willing to love and accept each other unconditionally. Each person needs an unselfish heart that genuinely wants to see their partner grow and is willing to make sacrifices for them. Though the maturity stage can be a distant dream for many, when you are in a committed relationship and both of you are willing to grow and learn, this stage can be reached—and it isn't even difficult. In a covenant marriage, you know that with God's help, you won't have to give up and your relationship won't become stagnant.

When your path crosses with that of a potential partner, be aware of the three stages of romance. Guard yourself from slipping into enchantment until you have evaluated your readiness and God's blessing over the relationship.

When your path crosses with that of a potential partner, be aware of the three stages

163

of romance. Guard yourself from slipping into enchantment until you have evaluated your readiness and God's blessing over the relationship. Becoming infatuated with a person is a side effect of emotions and not necessarily an indication that you've found your perfect match. Allow God to speak to you before you rush into an exclusive relationship.

> *Becoming infatuated with a person is a side effect of emotions and not necessarily an indication that you've found your perfect match. Allow God to speak to you before you rush into an exclusive relationship.*

Clear, godly expectations and boundaries are key to a successful dating relationship and a blessed marriage. Remember, love is not just a feeling. It truly is an action word that will manifest in many different ways as you get to know each other better. Seek out and develop the kind of mature, healthy, passionate, fun, and unconditional love only God can give you for your future spouse. This is the love that lasts forever.

Discussion Questions:

1. Have you ever been in love? If so, how did it impact your life?

2. Why is it important to know about the stages of love?

3. Have you ever been in a relationship where you felt enchanted with your partner? Did this feeling last?

4. Do you think it's okay to have high expectations when seeking a marriage partner?

5. Write down a list of attributes you would like in a spouse.

6. Write down the positive attributes you see in yourself.

Prayer:

Dear heavenly Father,

Lead me into knowing Your will for me in the area of love. May my heart be pleasing to You. Search my heart and help me to know how to wait on You. Teach me how to develop healthy expectations for my current or future relationship. Thank You, Lord, for Your love and great faithfulness toward me.

Chapter

II

COMMITTING TO YOUR SPOUSE

What Commitment Really Means

Do you think a relationship should happen naturally without any effort on your part? Or do you think a good, solid, amazing, for-the-books relationship takes effort?

Commitment is one of the most important aspects in building a strong relationship. If a couple wants to have a strong connection and experience intimacy, it will require the same kind of dedication, planning, and deliberate attention that one gives to physical health, a career, and a financial portfolio. Relationships require a type of commitment that says, "I'm with you no matter what, come what may, through thick and through thin." The commitment to marry takes most couples to a completely new level of personal interaction and faithfulness. A marriage commitment is a promise a couple makes to be together until death separates them. It requires a fierce devotion to one person. Many people think romantic relationships should just happen with minimal effort, and yes, we want our connections with people to flow, but relationships take work and a marriage commitment will test the resolve of both parties.

What does being committed to your marriage and spouse really mean? Commitment is a mindset or the strong belief that you will be faithful to the end. My commitment to my husband is a promise that goes to the core of who I am as a person. Before Leon and I started dating, we knew two important things deep in our hearts and committed to act upon them: First, we would not play with each other's feelings but care for each other in a healthy, godly way. Second, we knew a healthy relationship would lead us to marriage. That understanding is essential because it helps you evaluate how ready you are for a romantic relationship.

Let's unpack what commitment means in the context of the journey from dating to marriage. Commitment has four stages: friendship, courtship, exclusivity, and betrothal.

Friendship

The friendship stage involves getting to know another person in a group setting as well as in some one-on-one encounters. In this phase you get to relax and enjoy each other as friends without feeling any pressure. Remember, you are just trying to get to know each other in a fun and safe environment. This friendship will eventually help you establish whether or not the next step—a relationship—is God's will for the two of you. You learn some of the other person's likes and dislikes, get a better understanding of values and beliefs you wouldn't settle for, and experience some moments that allow you to realize if the two of you are compatible. You start to wonder in this phase if this is the person you have been praying and waiting for, yet there should be no pressure to take that next step.

The friendship stage is important because strong marriages are built between two people who are best friends, which means the friendship lasts throughout the marriage. The friendship stage shouldn't include any type of sexual activity. You aren't "friends with benefits." Instead, you are focused on getting to know each other and protecting the other person's purity.

Courtship

The courtship stage is where you acknowledge you are interested in someone and find out if the other person is equally interested in you. Again, avoid becoming anxious and rushing into love. Men sometimes don't wait for a woman to show that she's interested and they take off, running in pursuit. Ladies can become impatient and try to hurry things along. Some people take their time, choosing not to do anything until they are convinced they should pursue a serious, committed relationship. Ladies and gentlemen both need to be patient and allow God to take the lead because this will set the tone for the duration of the relationship.

After praying about the relationship to discern if it is God's will for you, talk to people who know you well and determine if this is the time to define the relationship. When you know the answer deep in your heart and there is peace about it, and you know the other person has the same feelings and desires to have this conversation with you, take the next step.

Exclusivity

The exclusive stage is where a boy becomes a man. Personally, I feel like a young woman needs to wait in this stage and be patient as a young man takes the initiative and begins to lead the relationship. I know that can be difficult for some women, but letting the man initiate helps the relationship and causes it to grow. Here's how this works: If a woman is willing to wait for her partner to pursue her and commit to a deeper relationship, she is allowing him to hear God's voice for himself and act upon it. There is such a thing as "women's intuition"; in many cases, women seem to be able to hear God and discern certain things quickly, so the young lady may already know how the relationship will turn out. She may have the answer, but if she can give the young man time to hear from God for himself, and to act upon what he has heard, it will bless the relationship and help the man trust that he can hear God's voice, too. In addition, waiting on God like this helps the young lady to trust Him in His perfect timing and not take matters into her own hands.

This stage requires the most communication, which can be hard for some men. Depending on what has or has not been discussed, it is wise for women to keep up their boundaries in order to guard their hearts. Remember, the most attractive thing to a Christian man is a woman who stands her ground with boundaries.

Betrothal

At the betrothal stage, you establish a committed relationship with the end goal of marriage. During this stage you have a sense of peace in knowing that God has confirmed the relationship and it is His will. Prayer is essential during this stage because you will encounter next-step questions: When is the wedding date? How long should you wait to marry? Make sure even this time of preparation is steered by God.

Establishing boundaries is important because now you are committed to one another, and the thoughts of being more physical with each other will become stronger. However, this stage is all about learning one another and not about physical contact. Typically, you get to spend more time with your partner's family during this stage, too.

Building the commitment required to succeed in a relationship is a process that can take months or even years, but once a couple is at this stage of devotion, they know they have what it takes. Like drawing back the curtains of a window, committing your life to another allows the sunlight to stream in. Couples on the verge of marriage know deep in their hearts that their lives will never be the same.

Waiting for God's Best

One of the first tests in my commitment to Leon happened when we were apart. We were in an exclusive relationship at the time but living in different countries— he was in America and I was in Ecuador. I clearly remember what a young man said to me at my best friend's birthday party.

"Do you really believe your relationship with your American boyfriend will work? What do you see in him that you can't find in an Ecuadorian guy like me?" He was interested in me and his words were meant to hurt. The young man didn't give me a chance to reply but followed with something even more cutting. "I bet he has already been unfaithful to you as you are so far away from each other."

Sometimes it's better not even to reply when people are trying to provoke you, but I couldn't let that go. I told him, "I know in my heart that Leon wouldn't consider seeing anyone else, just as I wouldn't. My boyfriend is the kind I can trust completely, and we trust each other."

As a couple, Leon and I had made a 100 percent commitment to each other to be exclusive. I never had a single fear throughout our relationship that he or I would fall for someone else. We'd begun to make plans and were looking forward to a life together. The guy who was hitting on me got the message. He could see from my confidence that my commitment to Leon was strong.

As our relationship grew, Leon began to pursue me more openly. The problem was that an ocean separated us. This didn't stop Leon, who shelled out a lot of money flying to Ecuador every chance he got. Initially I thought he had a flexible job that allowed him to visit me every few months, but it finally occurred to me that he was spending a lot of money to win my heart and get to know my family. The magnitude of his devotion still astounds me. For a period of about two years, Leon made several trips from the United States to Ecuador to visit me. Four months before the wedding, he resigned from a great job in order to spend more time with me in Ecuador. He wrote hundreds of long letters and called me countless times to talk. What I didn't understand at the time was that Leon was a big saver—he didn't spend his money at the drop of a hat. Even though long-distance phone calls weren't cheap, he would have me listen to full songs that spoke of his love for me. He would send me little gifts here and there by airmail. Mr. Savings had opened the vault in order to pursue me.

My good friend "Mary" had a much different courtship and marriage experience than I did. She couldn't wait to get married because at the time, she believed marriage was the key to her happiness. I'm sure you know someone like this. They are in love with the idea of falling in love but have little experience in what it takes to be in a relationship. Mary found a marriage partner not once, not twice, but three times, and every time she asked the Lord if the marriage was His will. The first time she felt Him answer, "Don't do it!" But she questioned whether or not that was His direction and married the man anyway. This was devastating to the people around her and the church where she was a member. After their divorce she met another man, and when she went to God about marrying him, she again felt like God was saying, "No." Again she doubted. She didn't know the man very well, and after marrying him she discovered he was unmotivated and didn't feel like working. She ended up being the one who maintained their home in every possible sense. She continued with him for as long as she could until her father finally told her to do something before her marriage killed her.

I am always amazed when I talk to young adults who think the people they are dating are their only possibilities. They aren't willing to wait for God's best because their vision is narrow. It was during a time of singleness that my friend Mary met a very special man. She asked the Lord if this was His perfect will for her, and this time she heard Him say, "Yes." An overwhelming peace surrounded her, and she knew that this time was different and that trusting in God completely changed everything. She is happily married to this day.

God in His great love has given us the ability to choose. That is His gift to us. Yes, there may be many choices for a spouse, but God knows who the best person is for you. He will tell you when to take action, and He will lead you just as He led my husband and me. You want God's perfect match. Both men and women want to find the one who will adore them for the rest of their lives, and God wants the same thing. He has a great plan for you in this area of your life.

I have seen so many people who committed to wait and trust God, and their reward was marrying the right person. One of the greatest privileges I have in life is mentoring young women, and I've been able to cross paths with so many different and wonderful people who are on the road to marriage. Several have married already, but those who haven't often struggle with how and where to find that special person. One young woman in particular had to call off her wedding and break up with her fiancé. As heartbreaking as it sounds, she discovered she wasn't ready for marriage. She told me, "I cannot live with him for the rest of my life. He is so different than what I thought he was."

For a time she mistakenly thought that if she didn't marry this gentleman, she would never have the chance for marriage again; however, through much discussion and prayer, she understood this wasn't God's best for her. She needed to figure out why she felt this desperation to marry, and she discovered her heart needed a lot of healing before she committed to marry again. Though she and this young man both had similar goals, they were incompatible in many other areas. More than anything, she admitted she needed to do some personal work on herself.

I've found there are many lies women in particular entertain when they think about relationships and marriage. We often struggle with issues of identity and accepting love, and we tell ourselves we aren't loveable or worthwhile. Often this leads to negative relationships with men and settling for the wrong man. God's solution is simple: accepting the unconditional love He offers us, falling in love with Him, and discovering our value as His children.

When you know to whom you belong, and you know God treasures you, the Lord can heal your heart from lies and past hurts. Only then will you be able to commit and choose a person who will love and treasure you the way God intended.

When you know to whom you belong, and you know God treasures you, the Lord can heal your heart from lies and past hurts. Only then will you be able to commit and choose a person who will love and treasure you the way God intended.

How to Strengthen Your Commitment

Here are some ways to strengthen and nourish your future marital commitment. Turn these into habits and then a lifestyle because they will help you through the different phases of commitment and into your married life:

- Pray. Develop a personal prayer life and spend time in honest reflection, asking God to show you how to be the person He wants you to be. Also, pray with your future spouse. If you can learn to pray before your marriage (alone in your quiet time as well as with your significant other), this healthy, loving habit will continue through your married life.
- Say it with actions. Let your behavior reflect your commitment. Make yourself available when the other person wants to talk, and be a good listener. Spend time alone with your partner talking about issues that are important to both of you. Try to find solutions to pressing issues.
- Say it with words. Constantly tell your future spouse you are committed to the relationship and marriage for the rest of your lives.
- Get others involved. Surround yourself with supportive individuals who share your values and want to see your marriage succeed. Have accountability partners.
- Get both sets of parents involved. Ask them for prayer and counsel. When the time is right, the man should ask the woman's parents for their blessing to start a relationship and later for their blessing to marry. It isn't so much about getting permission as it is receiving blessing. Asking for the parents' blessing is a way of honoring them and making them part of one of the most important decisions of your life. Many people don't want their parents to be involved, but I fully believe that if you choose to seek their blessing, you will be blessed even more.
- Learn to actively listen (listen in such a way that the speaker feels heard), communicate effectively, and have a plan to resolve conflicts.
- Discuss important money-related topics such as spending, saving, investing, debt, budgeting, tithing, entertainment, vacations, and financial goals.
- Discuss living expectations such as where to live, household chores and who will do them, etc.
- Discuss past sexual experiences and expectations regarding children.
- Discuss spending time with family and friends on the holidays.

God's Perfect Timing

Once you have found God's first choice for you, the next step is to pursue marriage. Here are the issues to consider before and while you plan the wedding:

1. Maturity

Marriage is a huge commitment in all areas of life and obviously requires a level of maturity in both partners. Parental involvement and quality premarital counseling are important parts of the maturing process. If a couple is young or immature, it's wise to suggest a waiting period in order to allow each person to develop social experiences, occupational skills, and potentially finish schooling.

2. Independence

Marriage establishes a couple's independence. Before the wedding day, both partners should be developed as individuals and as part of their family unit. How experienced is each partner when it comes to living on their own? Have they been on their own for a while, or is this their first time? The key concern is if they are responsible and are able to demonstrate they can be independent from their parents. Leaving father and mother to be united to each other is a psychological transition as much as a geographical one.

3. Parental/Guardian Support

Again, it is wise for young people who are considering marriage to seek their parents' counsel and blessing. This includes asking for their input with the wedding. If parents see benefits in waiting, they should express their opinions and explain them clearly, while the children should appreciate and respect their parents' honest input. At the same time, parents should remember that they don't own their children—God does.

4. Sexual Desire

In our culture some would say the gap between puberty and marriage is longer than it should be, which creates sexual temptation. The Bible clearly indicates that a couple planning to be married and struggling with strong sexual temptation should not delay their wedding date (1 Corinthians 7:9).

5. Emotional Longing

When two people know they will be married, their thoughts and feelings naturally focus upon each other and their approaching marriage, which can create an emotional longing. If the betrothal is brief, this longing is a healthy part of waiting, but a lengthy betrothal can lead to frustration.

6. School

Finishing college is an important rite of passage in the lives of many young people. Obtaining higher education is often part of the process of maturing and learning skills for the future. Therefore, it may be unwise for a couple to enter marriage when beginning college. The pressures and adjustments of classes and study require long hours and wholehearted determination. Once a couple has completed school or established themselves in an occupation, marriage will be an easier adjustment. However, this is not always the case. I also know of very mature people who married young and have a blessed and committed relationship.

7. Finances

Many couples prolong their engagements because of a lack of money. There are two key issues where finances are concerned: How much money do you have now, and how well do you handle the money you have? It's important to understand that living simply, shopping for bargains, and saving are important goals when starting a marriage.

In contrast, some couples get married with high incomes and face financial crisis within a few months. Discipline is the problem, not dollars. If a couple cannot live on their income, it's usually not because it's too low but because their standard of living is too high.

Parents should realize that nothing is wrong if the new couple struggles a bit with finances. Parents should be generous but should help only with needs, not subsidizing a young couple's ability to live beyond their means.[1]

God Wants to Give You a Beautiful Love Story

Many people hope for a fairytale romance. When my friend "Sian" first told me her love story, it was easy to see she was blessed with a special relationship, as many couples are, yet it seemed to me that her success in choosing her husband had less to do with being "rescued" by Prince Charming and more to do with her relationship

1 For additional information on this topic, check out Christian Courtship at http://www.christian-courtship. com.

with the Prince of Peace: Jesus. Sian's story is a remarkable tale that spans two continents and much soul searching, and it sounds like an arranged marriage. Her story also underscores my belief that God desires for each of us to find a marriage partner.

Sian and her parents are from India. After living for several years in America, they moved back to India to plant a church. When Sian finished her schooling, she returned to California and as God would have it, in India her parents were at a wedding and met a man named Justin. After much prayer, they felt strongly that Sian and Justin should meet. Sian had recently ended a relationship with an American she was in love with, and she was still healing from the breakup when God suddenly revealed His plans to her. He showed her an image of her husband. She saw a picture of him in her mind, and deep in her heart, she knew the man she was in love with wasn't the person God had for her.

Following the leading of God and her parents, she called Justin, who was living in Boston, and when she saw his picture, God's plan became clear—it was the man she had seen in her vision.

Their relationship grew over the phone until they decided to meet in India. After that initial meeting and a family get-together, they exchanged promise rings, as they both knew that God was the One who had brought them together to pursue marriage. They continued growing in their friendship over the course of a year through phone calls, Skype, and in-person visits. Now Sian and Justin are happily married and living in Dubai.

"I prayed to find the perfect partner ever since I was young," Sian told me. "And I truly believed that God would provide the best for me. Even after God had revealed 'the one' to me, it took immense faith to believe. My understanding was not enough. I had to lean on His understanding, though it seemed many times like the opposite of my personal hopes and dreams. God had a plan, a larger plan that I could not see with my tunnel vision. God always sees the bigger picture and knows what is best for us. Making a life decision of this magnitude was not easy. If it weren't for my faith in God and the spiritual guidance of my parents, I would have failed. Today I can say that because of my obedience and faith, I am blessed with a man that not only keeps me beyond happy, but I am privileged to share a home with a man whose heart is for God. He is a leader, my best friend, and most importantly, I am blessed with God's will in my life."

Your story will probably be different than Sian's, as God knows what each of us desires and needs, but He wants to help you pick a mate and give you a story that is truly unique and beautiful. I believe He already has someone chosen for you who will be just what you need in a spouse.

Discussion Questions:

1. What does commitment mean to you?

2. Are you ready to make a marriage commitment? Why or why not?

3. Are you willing to wait for God's perfect match? What are the benefits of waiting?

Prayer:

Holy Spirit,

Please guide me to the person You know I will be a blessing to for the rest of our lives. Help me to know the qualities to look for in a spouse, and help me to commit to trusting You and waiting for Your timing.

Chapter

12

TWO PEOPLE, ONE HEART

How to Become Truly One with Your Spouse

"Where you go I will go, and where you stay I will stay. Your people will be my people and your God my God."
— *Ruth 1:16*

I spoke Ruth 1:16 to Leon on our wedding day, and I meant every word. Choosing the God of my husband was easy, as we'd both had a fervent faith and deep love for our Savior Jesus even before we met. However, for me marriage also meant leaving Ecuador and moving to California. Leon's people, the Americans, became my people, and I chose to follow Leon as he pursued a career in financial advising. This involved making many changes in my life, but God has given us success and blessed our decision. It may be your turn to make a similar vow. My hope is that God will use this book to help you prepare for your wedding day.

The Art of Cleaving

There I stood, a newly married woman. The ceremony had gone by quickly, and the reception left me feeling a bit tired and elated at the same time. Leon and I were about to embark on a life together, and one of the best parts of marriage was about to happen. After years of waiting, I would get to consummate my marriage with the man of my dreams. My heart still flutters when I remember that special time following the reception. I gave my mom and dad a big hug and thanked them for the amazing love they'd poured out on me through the years. Then Leon and I waved goodbye to all our guests and made our exit.

This experience of becoming one or uniting with your spouse can be called cleaving. In Spanish the word is *unificación*, but the English word cleave comes from the Greek word *kolló*, which means to bond, unite, or join with. Cleaving is what you do on your wedding day when you leave your mother and father and unite with your mate for life. *"For this cause a man shall leave his father and mother, and shall cleave to his wife; and they shall become one flesh"* (Genesis 2:24, NASB). I learned about this concept the day I married Leon. When two people get married, they're pledging to become one. This creates unity in several ways. It's not my house or my bank account or my church anymore. It's our house, our bank accounts, our church. Each party is putting their spouse's needs before their own. Lives naturally blend when a marriage covenant is formed, but being united creates a spiritual union as well.

Cleaving includes talking things out, praying through challenges, and showing humility; it means being willing to admit when you are wrong, asking forgiveness, and seeking God's input and counsel regularly through Scripture and personal encounters with Him. It involves asking others for help and having a learning, teachable heart.

When we cleave to each other, we become dependent on one another. I have talked to many young people about this aspect of marriage, and dependence is a factor that discourages many from making a commitment. We have switched from a society in which women depend primarily on men to a society of self-reliance. As we become parents, one of our goals should be to teach our children to become independent and self-sufficient, but we must also teach them about the importance of relying on others. "*Nevertheless, in the Lord woman is not independent of man, nor is man independent of woman. For as woman came from man, so also man is born of woman. But everything comes from God*" (1 Corinthians 11:11–12). There is no room for any kind of superiority here, since men and women cannot exist without each other.

Oneness in Marriage

In a marriage unity and oneness are like rain boots and snow boots. Though they are similar to each other, you need both to be adequately prepared for the elements. Many of us have a pretty good understanding of what it means to be united with another person—we agree with them on several key points, love the same things, pursue the same things, are going the same basic direction—but the full concept of "becoming one" is often a little harder to understand.

Jesus talked about being one with God and others in John 17. This passage is a favorite of mine because of the picture it paints of marriage:

"May they also be in us so that the world may believe that you have sent me. I have given them the glory that you gave me, that they may be one as we are one—I in them and you in me—so that they may be brought to complete unity. Then the world will know that you sent me and have loved them even as you have loved me."
—John 17:21–23

One reason this passage impacts me is that Jesus was not just praying about His disciples, men who lived two thousand years ago, but He was also praying for you and me, His future disciples. If oneness is God's heart for His people, how important it is for oneness to occur in a marriage. We are called to be one with God and one with our spouses. *"But whoever is united with the Lord is one with him in spirit"* (1 Corinthians 6:17). When you and your spouse are one, you're doing what Jesus did and listening to the Father's heart. You are a team with God at the center, and you're living in the unity of His Spirit. That is the fulfillment of Jesus' prayer, which He took the time to pray just hours before He was arrested and condemned to die on the cross.

Besides the obvious, how do you move beyond unity ("I like what you like") to become truly one with your spouse? Sexual intercourse consummates a marriage and makes one flesh out of two people, but it is not the ultimate goal for becoming one with that person. In marriage you will encounter plenty of opportunities to come humbly to Jesus and ask His Spirit to help you maintain unity with your spouse.

Two issues couples regularly encounter in their relationship are abandonment and control, which bring disunity and do not enable them to become one with the other person. The sense of abandonment is a secondary emotion that comes from feeling ignored or rejected because you didn't get the attention you were hoping for. Adam was supposed to stop Eve from eating the forbidden fruit and he didn't do it. In other words, he ignored the important call he had of protecting her; he abandoned her when she needed him.

The second issue is the sense of control that comes from the curse following Adam and Eve's sin and the fact that husbands were called to rule over their wives from that point forward. Men and women have been competing and trying to control each other for thousands of years. This is the kind of separation the enemy wants to see in every married couple. The good news is that Jesus came to bring us back to God's initial plan of unity and oneness with Him, and even though we may struggle at times with certain issues, we can trust God has the answer for us. We have the freedom to choose to trust Him and to believe it doesn't have to be the old way anymore—it gets to be the way God desires for us. I love what Danny Silk says in his book *Keep Your Love On*: "Powerful people do not try to control other people. They know it doesn't work, and that it's not their job. Their job is to control themselves."[1]

If you are aware of the enemy's schemes, and you and your spouse are united in one spirit while calling out to God for help, you won't find yourself falling into the trap of control and abandonment. You will be able to catch these things early on and correct them, allowing God to heal your heart from past hurts, and He will draw you even closer to the intimate connection He means you to have with your spouse.

My friend Tammy loves the Lord with all her heart, and her desire to be one with God spills over into her relationship with her husband. She told me, "The best way I can be in total unity with my husband is when I do what the Father says to do. As I have been meditating in Ephesians 5, I realize that Craig has many more responsibilities than me as a husband, and I just have to honor him and, yes, submit to him. But we both do. The truth is I also have to die to myself and give my life for my husband, so I can see him grow and be the man God wants him to be."

A great marriage takes two people who are willing to die to themselves and their selfishness, so they can be united together in the Spirit of the Lord. Our Father wants every couple who loves Him to know each other better and in an intimate manner. What has helped my husband and I be successful as a couple? Knowing each other's strengths and weaknesses, so we are able to help each other, and understanding each other's differences, attributes, and strengths. This is the secret: The closer we grow to Jesus, the more united and intimate we will be with each other. The glue that holds us together is the Spirit of the Living God within us. In Him we become truly one.

Learning to Be One Through Prayer

Husbands, in the same way be considerate as you live with your wives, and treat them with respect as the weaker partner and as heirs with you of the gracious gift

---

1 Danny Silk, *Keep Your Love On* (Redding, CA: Red Arrow Publishing, 2013).

of life, so that nothing will hinder your prayers.
— 1 Peter 3:7

The apostle Peter was clear that if you want your prayers to be answered, you have to start by honoring your spouse. Both husbands and wives have a huge opportunity to honor each other through prayer. Prayer is the key to having a good relationship with your spouse because you learn to listen to God's heart for you, your spouse, and your marriage. Hearing God's voice is the most important aspect of a healthy and thriving marriage. There will be times when you and your spouse have opposing desires, and depending on the circumstances, you may be tempted to start hiding things from one another; however, when you hear the voice of God's Spirit, you will be prompted to think about your spouse first and begin a powerful journey in which you will see amazing blessings and favor from God.

Many of the women I talk to express a desire for that special time of prayer with their husbands. When couples start praying together, the wives feel honored, loved, and cared for. Prayer trains our hearts and minds to understand how God sees our spouses and how we can improve our relationships. Praying regularly also brings both parties a sense of humility and knowledge of God's will. Jesus says that if two of us agree about anything, we should ask for it—and it will be done. He also says that whatever we bind on earth will be bound in Heaven and whatever we loose on earth will be loosed in Heaven. This is a picture of what unity with God's Spirit looks like, and it is incredibly powerful when we pray this way with our best friends: our spouses. Praying with my husband has been one of the greatest joys in my life.

Prayer also has a lot to do with submitting to God and each other. When I pray with Leon, I am surrendering to God and my husband's desire to be in communion with Him. As a result, it becomes a blessed way of communicating with each other and the One who can hear us best.

Prayer also has a lot to do with submitting to God and each other. When I pray with Leon, I am surrendering to God and my husband's desire to be in communion with Him. As a result, it becomes a blessed way of communication with each other and the One who can hear us best.

The Art of Submission

As a woman, I know the word submission can be a point of controversy in a marriage or even in a dating relationship. Many people today don't understand the concept of submission and how the apostle Paul used it in that infamous passage in Ephesians: *"Wives, submit yourselves to your own husbands."* What? Why? That lovely little word submission has been misconstrued and misused for thousands of years.

I spent years pondering the meaning of Paul's teaching on submission and asking the Lord what it really means, and eventually He gave me this approach. We know that demanding someone's submission is not the heart of Scripture. Submission is a humble attitude of surrendering our selfish nature for the benefit of the person we love. It has more to do with humility and the desire to serve each other than it does imposing our will over another person.

The best example of humility and true servanthood comes from Jesus, who washed His disciples' feet during the Passover meal. Our King and Savior demonstrated the full extent of His love and humility by not acting like a king but like a servant. Peter was concerned when he saw Jesus washing their feet, and he tried to tell Him not to do it. However, when Jesus was finished, He explained:

> *"You call me 'Teacher' and 'Lord,' and rightly so, for that is what I am. Now that I, your Lord and Teacher, have washed your feet, you also should wash one another's feet. I have set you an example that you should do as I have done for you."*
> — *John 13:13–15*

That is what true submission looks like. Both the husband and wife submit to one another out of reverence for Christ. Those of us who know Jesus and have a part with Him, like Peter did, are called to demonstrate this kind of humility and submission to each other, just as Christ demonstrated it to us.

Ephesians 5:25–27 develops this theme even further and addresses the way a man should treat his wife. It is a new command that involves responsibility:

> *Husbands, love your wives, just as Christ loved the church and gave himself up for her to make her holy, cleansing her by the washing with water through the word, and to present her to himself as a radiant church, without stain or wrinkle or any other blemish, but holy and blameless.*

This type of love was a radical idea in Jewish and Greek society. By using the word love, Paul was essentially telling husbands to submit to the needs of their wives. In other words, Paul wanted husbands and wives to be unified. Marriage is always about coming together in mutual submission and understanding. This doesn't mean we have to think exactly alike and agree on everything, because God made us different in many ways. However, being one as husband and wife means being together in thought and heart and committed to one another. It means being humble and having the heart of a servant the way Jesus does; it means being willing to die for your spouse if necessary. This kind of love understands what both spouses are built to desire and helps bring those desires to fruition.

The Delight of God in Marriage

Not long ago, I had to choose between two important celebrations happening on the same day, at the same time. Guess which one I chose? The wedding, of course! I'm a hopeless romantic. I have faith that marriages will work out, especially if the couple follows the words of the greatest romantic of all time: God. The Lord does not want us to be alone. He desires that we find partners suitable for our every need (Genesis 1:26–28, 2:18–24).

God created marriage and delights in seeing couples come together. The Bible begins with the Lord blessing the union of Adam and Eve, and Jesus' first miracle in the New Testament was at a wedding in Cana of Galilee, where He learned from His mother there was no more wine for the guests. Even though providing more wine wasn't His first impulse, He honored His mom and graciously turned the contents of six stone water jars, each holding twenty or thirty gallons, into wine. It was a generous gift for the couple's wedding. God's blessings are always overflowing and more than we could ever imagine. At the end of the Bible, God completes all history with a wedding—the wedding of the Lamb. His Son is the Bridegroom and is committed to a pure and spotless bride, which is His Church— all those who believe in Him. I eagerly await that glorious day! God is all about marriage, and as He says in Proverbs 18:22, *"He who finds a wife finds what is good and receives favor from the Lord."*

I think Mary, the mother of Jesus, knew this aspect of God's heart better than most people, but her trip to the marriage altar took an unexpected turn. Think of her unexpected story and what it would have been like. Let's say you grew up in an extremely conservative culture and you've known the man you were going to marry ever since your childhood. Growing up together, it was the most natural thing to fall in love—everyone always knew the two of you would end up together. You bring out the best in each other and have a similar commitment to your faith. But then one night about four months before your wedding, an angel of the Lord appears to you and messes up everything.

"Greetings, you who are highly favored! The Lord is with you."

He then explains you are about to be something your culture does not accept: a pregnant, unmarried woman. How in the world are you going to tell Joseph? The man you love will naturally think you've been unfaithful. Everything you've wanted and longed for is suddenly at risk.

Hoping to come up with a brilliant plan, you go stay with your cousin Elizabeth for three months. It is now a month before your wedding, and by the time you return, you are starting to show clear signs of the angel's words. When the man you love comes to see you, he knows. You can see it in his eyes. You try to explain, but he doesn't believe you. Instead, he plans to divorce you quietly, so as not to shame you more than you already are.

You're devastated. Joseph is your closest friend and he has walked away. All your plans are about to burn. You're about to have nothing left.

That night you can't sleep or eat, and you wonder what you're going to do.

But then the next morning, everything changes again.

Joseph shows up at your parents' house early—he's had a dream from God. A month later, you marry the one your heart loves, and the two of you raise the Son of God together.

In every love story and at every wedding, there's always a little bit of drama. Although Mary's story is unique, it emphasizes that the Lord had a specific plan for her life with Joseph. Sure, there was tension and doubt between Mary and Joseph prior to the wedding, but the Lord assured both of them that their relationship was blessed. He chose Mary and Joseph to be Jesus' parents. It was God's perfect will, and in the same way, He also has a perfect plan for your marriage story.

Forecast: Rain!

I've known McKenna her entire life. The daughter of one of Leon's best friends since childhood, she met her sweetheart, Steven, when she was in high school. She instantly liked him but wasn't sure if the feeling was mutual. About a decade later, she signed up for a mission trip to India and the two of them connected and became good friends. The Christian mission field was the perfect place for them to learn more about each other. The trip must have gone well, because Steven asked McKenna out a few months later and they hit it off. Although this wasn't McKenna's first date, Steven was her first boyfriend.

Sometime later I invited McKenna to be a part of my first Becoming the One group. One thing led to another, and she began to help me co-lead the group. All the while, her love for Steven grew, but McKenna was patient. She wanted to have a relationship with him that pleased God, and she was willing to wait. And wait she did! Four years later, McKenna and Steven got engaged. The turning point, as she describes it, was when her parents blessed her and Steven, telling them they were very pleased with their relationship and would love to see them get married.

After the engagement they hurried to make wedding plans. They chose a day in October because McKenna wanted a fall wedding with an outdoor ceremony at her parents' beautiful home. The invitations went out and the preparations were made, but as the day grew closer, rain appeared in the forecast.

Leon and I huddled under the umbrella as the rain pattered, but my nervousness for my dear friend quickly subsided when I saw the outdoor scene she'd prepared. Although the flagstone patio wasn't dry, a huge white canopy helped shield it from the rain, and the fall colors were vibrant, set against the green grass surrounding the wedding altar. Sprinkles of rain persisted, but nothing could dampen the joy we all felt for McKenna and Steven. Leon and I were overtaken by the love of God for this couple we'd been praying for. We had been waiting for this moment for a long time, and it felt like our own kids were getting married.

"Despite our months of planning," McKenna told me, "God had a better story. The rain and the wind came. Our wedding and reception venue changed seventy-two hours before the wedding, but that wouldn't ruin our day. We were excited to be before our family, friends, and God to declare our love and commitment to each other. This day was what we patiently waited four and a half years for."

Not only does God want to be a part of your relationship, but He also wants to be a part of the wedding. That, in brief, is one of the main points of this book. You get to do this with Jesus.

As much as we try to plan every detail of our weddings, the unforeseen often happens, yet that is what makes weddings so exciting. I once heard about a wedding coordinator who forgot to order the bouquet and told the bride just before she walked down the aisle. At the last wedding I attended, I left to pick up the bridal party's bouquets a few minutes before the ceremony because they had forgotten all about them and I was the only one available who knew where they were. At my wedding, they forgot to include the beautiful centerpiece that went in the cake, as well as the pretty serving knife that had been decorated especially for the occasion. They also gave us some very interesting drink during communion that wasn't grape juice . . . or wine. The photographer had to leave early for another wedding. The unexpected happens—but the important thing to remember is that when you get married, if you've invited God to be an intimate part of your relationship and the wedding itself, He is with you in a special way and He doesn't make mistakes. Embrace the craziness of your wedding day and enjoy it! Sometimes the preparations can be so stressful that everyone just needs to relax and realize that even though it's one of the most important days of your life, it really is just a day. The real prize is the journey of staying married forever.

Creating Family Culture

When you marry another person, you become a member of their family and that person becomes a member of yours. You are in each other's space, and you get to unearth the smallest intricate details about the other person. You find out if they're messy in the bathroom, in the kitchen, in the garage, in the shower. Do they remember to put the toothpaste cap back on? Are they a towel dropper, or are they really strict about cleanliness? You get to experience bad breath in the morning, fighting for covers, snoring, laughing, secret times, adventures, and memories you will cherish forever.

But the blending doesn't stop there. A deeper type of blending happens when you start a family. Two people create an atmosphere when they live together, and that atmosphere shifts when they have children. I think of this idea as family culture. A year and four months after Leon and I married, I moved with him to the United States. For me, this started the process of assimilation into a new culture. Adjusting to the absence of my family and friends was hard for me. I knew some English, but having to listen and try to speak English all day long was a challenge. Knowing I needed to make new friends, I became involved in a church and reached out to Leon's family.

Not long after coming to America, we got pregnant with our first child. We were very excited but a little surprised and nervous as I was still adjusting to my new life in the States. Leon and I realized God didn't forget what we had talked about before we were married; we had decided to wait two years after our wedding to start having children, and we had our beautiful son just six months after our second wedding anniversary. Because of my Ecuadorian heritage and our unique cultural backgrounds, Leon and I were intentional about creating a certain culture in our home. He fell in love with my family, my culture, and me. He loved the warmth, love, and affection my family showered on him. I also fell in love with Leon's personality, his ideas, his loving heart, and his family. He and I shared faith and the desire to get involved with church, grow with other couples, and raise our children in a certain manner. From the beginning we wanted to create a warm atmosphere in the home. I wanted to bring the best of my husband's culture and the best of mine into our marriage. For instance, in Ecuador everybody greets you with a hug and a kiss; Leon and I were intentional and taught our children to embrace people if they were open to it. Our children also learned Spanish, which we spoke in our home.

Another trait Leon and I wanted to include in our family culture is what I call *God's culture* or Christian living. Jesus described it in Matthew 22:37–40:

> *"'Love the Lord your God with all your heart and with all your soul and with all your mind.' This is the first and greatest commandment. And the second is like it: 'Love your neighbor as yourself.' All the Law and the Prophets hang on these two commandments."*

God gives us a biblical plan for making family relationships work—and then He gives us the power to follow that plan in relationship with Him. *"I have come that they may have life, and have it to the full"* (John 10:10).

Every family is unique. There's no parenting plan that will guarantee a healthy and happy family, but here are some basic principles that will help you create an excellent family culture. The goal is to generate an atmosphere where each member can grow spiritually, emotionally, and relationally. Creating a mission statement as a couple and writing a vision for the future are good ways to begin thinking about creating a family culture. Matthew 22:37–40 and John 10:10 highlight several areas at the heart of God's culture:

- Love God and each other. Make the teachings of Jesus the center and foundation of your home. Love means thinking about the interests of each person in your family and their growth and fulfillment as individuals. It means putting yourself second, after the needs of your spouse and family. In humility recognize you are nothing without God. Give Him credit for your personal accomplishments, while encouraging your family members in their gifts.

- Love yourself and your identity in Christ. The more you personally and intimately know God, the more you will see God's Spirit in you. See yourself the way God sees you. It's when you know how much God loves you that you can love God, others, and yourself. Loving yourself also means guarding your heart, for you are the temple of the Holy Spirit.

- Remember God is a God of miracles. Nothing is impossible with Jesus. God is always ready to heal you physically and emotionally. I cannot count the abundant miracles I, personally, have encountered throughout my married life—with Leon, my kids, and our family and friends. The more you expect miracles, the more you will see them. You won't be disappointed when you trust God to do miracles on your behalf. Some things may take a little while, but if they are in God's will, they will happen. Even the littlest things in life are miracles.

- Be present. Children will typically interpret your presence as a sign of caring and connectedness, so to have a great family life, it's crucial for you to spend quality time with them. Your job as a parent is a calling from God. Aside from your relationship with the Lord and building a strong marriage, raising children is the most important aspect of your life. Your influence on your children will be your greatest legacy. Be available to talk with them, attend their events, and cheer them on. Tell them how much you love them and how precious they are to you and to God. Nothing can make up for your absence.

- Practice open communication and acceptance. Forgiveness is not simply one option of many; there will be conflicts and misunderstandings in the home, which means each member needs to practice repentance before God and learn how to forgive others. Realize you're in the process of becoming more like Jesus and you and your spouse are a team, united in His love and purpose.

- Practice spiritual growth. Make your relationship with God through Christ your top priority. Pray for and with your children in a regular family devotional time and talk about God often. Prayer should be a centerpiece of your family time. Some say the family who prays together stays together, and that has been the golden rule in our household. Our kids have learned God works on their behalf when they pray.

- Understand that worship is a twenty-four-seven attitude. Everything you do is unto God and can bring Him honor. From watching television to playing on your computer to falling asleep at night, understand that God delights in you and watches over you. Sing and praise Him as much as possible and listen to good music that inspires your walk with Him.

- Fellowship every chance you get. Gathering with friends at church or over a meal, having a family movie night, building family traditions, going on vacations—these activities are all part of having a healthy family. Work at togetherness. Have fun and laugh a lot.

- Demonstrate love through your warmth and encouragement. Shame-based parenting, which is performance oriented and approval focused, causes children to think they aren't loved or valued. Help your children and spouse feel more secure by showing warmth and encouragement. Say, "I love you," often and give them plenty of physical affection like hugs, kisses, and back rubs. Develop expectations for them that are realistic, and at the same time help them understand their dreams can come true. With God all things are possible! Encourage them to pursue their areas of interest and become the people God wants them to become.

- Instill healthy morals and values in your kids. The decisions your kids make today could affect them for the rest of their lives. Talk openly and honestly with them about sex, alcohol, and drugs from a young age through their teen years. Answer their questions in age-appropriate ways, and encourage them to commit to a lifestyle of purity.

- Practice healthy stewardship and make sound financial decisions. Follow a budget that allows you to live within your means, avoid debt, tithe and give in other generous ways, and save regularly. Modeling these healthy financial practices will teach your kids practical and spiritual lessons.

- Have a servant's heart. Serve at home, work at your church, and help out in the community. Serve because it teaches you to give. Start in small ways and make time to bless others. Sometimes just a big smile can do wonders for another person's soul.

Discussion Questions:

1. Why is it important to talk about married life before the wedding?

2. What does "becoming one" with your spouse actually mean?

3. What type of family life did you have growing up? Describe the type of family life you would like to have.

4. How will you create family culture?

Prayer:

Dear heavenly Father,

I come to You in the name of Jesus to ask You to help me be one with You first. I want to know You and spend time getting to know Your heart. Please teach me how to put the needs of my future spouse ahead of my own needs. Please protect that person and help us to be united.

IV

BUILDING YOUR LIFE TOGETHER

He replied, "Because you have so little faith. Truly I tell you, if you have faith as small as a mustard seed, you can say to this mountain, 'Move from here to there,' and it will move. Nothing will be impossible for you."
— Matthew 17:20

Long, satisfying marriages aren't just found in fiction. They are possible the way all things with God are possible. You can have the amazing marriage you hope for through continual learning, good communication, prayer, sacrifice, and letting the Holy Spirit lead you.

There will be times when marriage feels like work, but the work is worth it as you truly become the one.

Chapter
13

A PLEASANT SACRIFICE
How to Make Your Marriage Successful

When I use the word *sacrifice*, what's the first image or word that flashes into your mind? Maybe it's a cross. Maybe you think of your parents and a selfless act they did for you. You may think of the words *friend*, *parent*, or *spouse* and how that person put your needs before their own. Perhaps you have sacrificed for someone and it wasn't even noticed.

The idea of sacrifice can fill us with a sense of wonder and gratitude, but for many of us, giving up what we want is not our first impulse. Laying down our rights for someone else is easier said than done. But it is for the sake of something *better* that we are called to make sacrifices in relationships and marriage.

If you're in a long-term relationship or perhaps already married, you know what it's like to make small sacrifices daily. It's the small details of life that make a big difference. Marriage is not a fifty-fifty relationship; each of us is called to give 100 percent. But how are we supposed to get to the point where we are willing to sacrifice for our significant others—not just once or twice but repeatedly? How do we learn to lay our lives down for our spouses?

When I am having trouble being a servant, I try to take a moment and consider the great sacrifice Jesus made for me on the cross. He endured the most painful death imaginable. He carried every sin committed by every human in the past, present, and future, and He was separated from the presence of His Father until the Holy Spirit resurrected Him victoriously. He did it for us, knowing this would bring us back to the heart of Father God. He did it out of love for us. No one pushed Him to do it. Jesus *chose* to die. That is the ultimate sacrifice.

Making the Investment

A wedding band serves as a reminder that a marriage takes constant effort. Rings symbolize eternity with no beginning and no end. As important as it is to become the one and find the right spouse, once you marry, both of you will share the responsibility of making your marriage work. Having a great relationship with your spouse will require a mental and emotional investment, so be committed to the process. Marriage is the union of two imperfect people—two sinners saved by the grace of God—who need His help to succeed in the second most important decision of their lives.

Lessons Learned

At the beginning of my marriage with Leon, it seemed easy to compromise and make personal sacrifices. Maybe we just didn't have many problems, but it seemed we agreed on almost everything. As the years went by, however, Leon and I started disagreeing on more topics, such as parenting, home improvements, church styles, and social commitments. We found a safe place in knowing that God is in control and, simply put, He doesn't want us to be mad at each other. Sacrifice in marriage is the desire to give the best of yourself so you can see the best of the other person.

When I first got married, I knew part of my marriage commitment involved loving my husband with all my heart, even to the point of setting aside some of my own goals and desires. A compromise I made at the beginning of our marriage was embracing America as my home. At first Leon and I considered living in Ecuador and he tried to find a job there, but as we prayed and asked God, I knew in my heart He wanted us in the United States. This was not easy for me. Leaving my family, friends, church, career, Ecuadorian food, language, and culture was a sacrifice, but I did it for love. Leon understood this was difficult for me and, as a result, was always willing and eager to visit my family in Ecuador.

Marriage is full of sacrifices like this. Out of love we need to think of our spouses first. The compromises we make may include spending less time with friends, taking on new responsibilities or chores, watching an action-adventure instead of a romantic comedy, feeding the baby at two in the morning, or moving to another country or state. Another sacrifice we make in marriage is choosing to actively listen instead of talk. Most people want to be heard and understood but struggle to listen attentively. If we're honest, many of us are thinking about what we want to say while our spouses are talking. Some sacrifices seem easy at the beginning of a relationship and others are harder. Couples will have to collaborate when deciding who to visit over the holidays, which car to purchase, or how to decorate a room. One thing is certain: The longer a couple is together, the more sacrifices they will make.

I think of the words from John 15:13 when I face a hard choice in my marriage: *"Greater love has no one than this: to lay down one's life for one's friends."* Although most of us won't be called to give up our lives for our spouses literally, we are called to think of our spouses' needs before our own. Making sacrifices is an important part of maturing in a marriage relationship.

Start Building

You could buy a hundred different books about how to build a great marriage, and each book would give you a slightly different answer. The truth is, growing your marriage cannot be whittled down to a formula or doing life a certain way. For each couple the keys to success are a bit different.

Building a successful life together with your partner involves starting with the blueprint for successful living, which is the Bible. In *The Surprising Secrets of Highly Happy Marriages*, Shaunti Feldhahn states, "Highly happy couples tend to put God at the center of their marriage and focus on Him, rather than on their marriage or spouse, for fulfillment and happiness."[1] You can't put God in the center of your marriage without making His Word your foundation. God's Word has always been the living, fresh wind of the Holy Spirit telling Leon and me what to do. His Word has reminded us to forgive, to be humble, to defer to the other, to love unconditionally, to refrain from unfaithfulness, to pray without ceasing, to be compassionate with each other, to serve and encourage each other, and so much more. The Bible has absolutely everything you need. It gives life and will encourage you to embrace your marriage covenant daily. One of Jesus' names is the Word, and the more we know Him, the more we understand why this is true.

Another aspect of building your marriage is keeping the right perspective. Typically, couples view marriage as a union or a journey. If you call your spouse your "other half" or your "soul mate," you're probably thinking about the union you have with them, yet there will be times when you realize your relationship with this person you adore is a journey and it can be hard. In those moments, your attitude

---

1 Shaunti Feldhahn, *The Surprising Secrets of Highly Happy Marriages: The Little Things That Make a Big Difference* (Colorado Springs: Multnomah, 2013).

is closer to that of many wedding vows: "I take you, from this day forward, for better, for worse, for richer, for poorer," etc. Couples who view marriage only as a union tend to lose their footing when difficulties arise. In contrast, couples who view marriage as a journey can remember past conflicts without thinking less of their relationship. I believe both perspectives are crucial for a solid marriage relationship. Marriage is a journey, and at the same time, being unified with your mate is what will keep your marriage strong.[2]

From being quick to forgive to developing a friendship, from discussing financial priorities to going out on date nights, couples who are intentional about their relationship are more successful. Marriage partners thrive when they practice active listening and know how to communicate so each person in the relationship feels acknowledged, understood, and cared about. I think you will agree with many of the characteristics in the next section, and I challenge you to look for ways to integrate them into your marriage or relationship.

Characteristics of a Successful Marriage

This is not a complete list by any means, but these are key points to remember when you are building a healthy marriage:

- Sacrifice: Putting your spouse's needs before your own is a hallmark of a successful marriage.
- Prayer: Listening to God's voice and getting together for regular prayer times is crucial. Just as families who pray together stay together, so couples who pray together are closely knit with one another.
- Commitment: Having a personal and moral commitment to your spouse and family will contribute to your success in marriage.
- Common interests or goals: When a couple has similar goals, their lives align and they become a better team. Common goals could include children, work, travel, sports, helping in the community, and expanding God's Kingdom.
- Communication: Establishing an atmosphere of sharing opens up the lines of communication in a relationship.
- Trust: When you trust your spouse, you don't have to hide who you are or be self-protective. Relational happiness is the result.

2 Spike W.S. Lee and Norbert Schwarz, "Framing Love: When It Hurts to Think We Were Made for Each Other," *Journal of Experimental Social Psychology* 54 (September 2014): 61–67, http://www.sciencedirect.com/science/article/pii/S0022103114000493.

- Respect and honor: When partners feel a deep admiration for each other, their marriage is marked by respect. Respecting your spouse means you treat them with dignity and kindness, as you would a best friend.
- Forgiveness: You will have plenty of opportunities to apologize and make restitution in your marriage. A humble heart and an openness to ask for and receive forgiveness strengthen the marriage relationship.
- Financial priorities: Valuing family and marriage over the accumulation of material goods is a crucial characteristic of a successful marriage. Practice financial self-control and live within your means.
- Friendship and continual dating: Couples who have a strong friendship are happier in marriage and live longer. Not only do they love each other, but they also genuinely like each other as people. They enjoy hanging out together.
- Sexual desire: Having sex on a regular basis brings joy and satisfaction. Healthy sexual activity is a gift from God that deserves to be treasured and maintained. Every time you make love with your spouse, you are essentially recommitting to your marriage covenant.
- Laughter: Working hard at your marriage can be draining. You are here to thrive, not to strive; sometimes you need to take things seriously, but often you just have to let go and relax. Proverbs 17:22 says, *"A cheerful heart is good medicine, but a crushed spirit dries up the bones."* Laughter and a good sense of humor can bring happiness to your relationship.
- Acceptance and delight: Don't try to change your mate. Understand that only God can change a person. Accept your mate the way they are. Remember you're fearfully and wonderfully made.
- Faith: Certain factors will help you grow spiritually. These factors include committing to maintain an intimate relationship with the Lord, developing a sincere love for His Word, and helping in a local church or serving your community. Strong faith can help establish a stronger marriage. Fervent faith produces true humility, a servant's heart, and unconditional love.

Overcoming Challenges

We were driving home from a local restaurant on a beautiful sunny afternoon in Ecuador. Our stomachs were full and our hearts were happily in love. Leon and I had been married for six months, and we were enjoying an extended honeymoon when the car decided to make things more interesting. A tire blew and the vehicle swerved.

As Leon pulled to the side of the road, I could see he was upset.

"We better change the tire," I offered.

Leon looked at me in frustration.

"Maybe we should call for help," I added.

He wrapped his hands around the steering wheel. "Honey, I'll take care of it." Opening his door, he stepped out from the vehicle and started assessing the damaged tire. When I climbed out of the car, I said to him, "Let's call someone to fix it."

Leon just shook his head. "Honey, I can fix it."

"Are you sure?" I said, moving closer.

Leon jokingly tried to kick my rear end, and I moved fast so he didn't even touch me. I felt a mixture of anger and embarrassment at his childish gesture, and I was suddenly keenly aware of my surroundings and hoped no one I knew could see us.

"I said I can fix it!" Leon told me.

While he pulled the spare from the trunk and began to change the popped tire, an uncomfortable silence settled between us. I kept thinking about how he had treated me, trying to kick me like that. I hadn't taken his gesture as a joke. It reminded me of my parents' many arguments and how my father, on many occasions, had treated my mother in a similar fashion.

Leon got back into the car and slammed the door. "Fixed!"

Neither of us said a word on the way home. A wall of anger and sadness had risen between us, with me on one side and Leon on the other. We were emotionally stuck.

When we walked into the entryway of our apartment, all the frustration, disappointment, and sadness overwhelmed me. "If you ever do that again," I erupted, "I will just divorce you." My heart was broken as I thought about how Leon had treated me.

Words spoken in anger can be intensely damaging. Most of the time, we don't fully mean them, but they can create divisions between a husband and wife. Leon was surprised to hear me say something so final. He knew I wasn't the type of person who would be flippant about marriage. When I married him, in my heart I knew it was going to be a forever commitment. It took time, but later I realized my words had come from my wounds. I used to hear my parents use the word *divorce* all the time.

Leon apologized, and his response to me showed great wisdom and understanding. It was just what I needed to hear. "I am committed to you for the rest of my life," he said. "I was really joking when I tried to kick your rear end and never would have meant to touch you in an offensive way."

I realized he was trying to protect me by taking care of the problem himself, and I should have allowed him to take care of it. By challenging his solution, I wasn't honoring him. Instead, I should have encouraged him. On that day we committed never to use the word *divorce* again, and we have kept this promise.

Many couples start marriage strong, as Leon and I did. We knew we had the blessing of God and our parents, and we were totally in love and committed to each other. Right after the wedding, everything tends to seem sweet and fuzzy and rose colored. But what happens when you are tested? Becoming the one by preparing to be a gift to your future spouse is very important because your heart in this matter will determine your future. Even after marriage you continue working on being the one for your partner, the one who will bless them for the rest of their life. It may not feel easy sometimes, but with God's help even the most difficult circumstances can help you be united. Leon and I have chosen—and will always choose—God, each other, and the covenant we've made with Him. When a couple doesn't know how to do this, their marriage will be that much harder. Unwanted circumstances, misunderstandings, and conflict are a part of life, but how you learn to deal with them and treat each other in the moments when these events surface is the key to building a good, healthy, and understanding marriage. It has to do more with how you recover from a situation than the painful situation itself. It also has to do with learning more ways you can help your spouse deal with their insecurities and cooperate with the emotional healing God is doing in both of you.

Here are a few things you should never do in your marriage. These are the "don'ts" that can help you build and maintain a strong, healthy relationship with your spouse:

- Don't use the word *divorce*. If it comes to your mind, ask God to replace it with a prayer of unity and intimacy for your marriage.

- Don't allow yourself to look at another man or woman in a lustful, unfaithful way. Remember temptation is different than actually falling into sin. If you are tempted, replace those thoughts by running away from the temptation. Do not entertain those thoughts, but think of how God sees you and your spouse.
- Don't put your spouse down with diminishing and disrespectful adjectives. Choose good words even when you are upset.
- Don't allow physical and emotional abuse in your relationship. If there's even a small sign of it, ask other married people for help, converse with your spouse in a healthy and loving way, and potentially seek counseling. Learn what "healthy" looks like in a marriage as you observe and talk to couples who have marriages you would like to emulate.

As good as they are in a dating relationship, healthy boundaries are even more important in a marriage. This is what God's Word calls self-control, which is a fruit of living in God's Spirit. In marriage we will need all the fruits of the Spirit:

> *But the fruit of the Spirit is love, joy, peace, forbearance, kindness, goodness, faithfulness, gentleness and self-control. Against such things there is no law.*
> — *Galatians 5:22–23*

Keep on Building

If you listen to God's voice and face the challenges in your marriage with trust in Him, you will find success. Go over the following points and start incorporating them into your relationship:

1. Focus on Encouragement

Ask yourself, "How can I make my spouse happy today? How can I let my spouse know I truly delight in them?" Take the time to sit down with your spouse, have a heart-to-heart talk, and actively listen. Encouragement might involve a back rub, making love, shopping, or a heartfelt apology when necessary. Remember that after a seedling sprouts, it needs to grow in rich soil. You replenish that rich soil by how you treat your spouse. When Leon was trying to change the flat tire, I unconsciously doubted his ability and let him know he didn't have what it took. Instead, I should have said something like, "I'm sure you can do this, honey. You're a stud!" Small things like that can change the whole course of your day and, eventually, your life together. Words of affirmation and thankfulness for what your spouse means and does for you can break any confusion in your relationship.

Remember what God says about you and your spouse and reiterate these things to your spouse. Say things like, "You are kind, gentle, and compassionate. I can tell you are becoming more like Jesus. You have been cleansed by the blood of Jesus. You are beautiful and wonderfully made. I honor you and I love you. You are worthy of my respect."

Verbalize your gratitude for the things your spouse does. Sometimes it can be easy to start taking these things for granted because they are "normal" things you do for each other. Every time I go to a restaurant with Leon, I make a point to thank him for the meal, and when I return from a shopping trip, I say something like, "Thank you for working hard so I'm able to buy all these great things." In the same way, Leon thanks me for the many things I do for him, the kids, and others. Every time your spouse does something for you or your home, make sure you express your gratitude. Create these great habits at the beginning of your relationship, and you will reap their fruit for the rest of your life.

2. Establish a Rich Environment

Build your marriage by getting connected with other couples and family members in a church, marriage group, or Bible study. Spend time with other couples doing your favorite activities. A new marriage requires mentoring, regular communication, and quality time. Work on love, trust, intimacy, and commitment, which are the pillars of marriage. Grow deep together and cultivate your relationship intentionally. Read books about marriage, go on dates, and see a marriage mentor. Challenges are handled better when couples work together.

3. Challenges Are Opportunities

See challenges as opportunities for growth. If you have a sense that something isn't going well, find help immediately. Reach out to trusted friends or mentors for prayer, counseling, and coaching. Don't allow bad patterns of behavior to exist between you. In moments when I feel disconnected, upset, or discouraged because of my behavior or my husband's, I try to see the challenge as an opportunity for the Lord to teach us a life lesson. As you can imagine, God has taught us many wonderful lessons through our twenty-seven years of marriage. His Spirit is our biggest encourager, comforter, teacher, and daily companion.

4. Have Hope

No matter how difficult your relationship may feel at times, never, ever give up hope. When I ask divorced couples what caused them to make the decision to separate, their responses usually involve losing hope. "There was nothing else to do. I've tried everything and given so many opportunities for change, and nothing happened."

Remember God is the One who gives hope. As long as you cling to Him and ask for help, there is always going to be a way. Engage your will with the belief the Holy Spirit will always provide in every area of your marriage.

A House Full of Treasure

> *By wisdom a house is built,*
> *and through understanding it is established;*
> *through knowledge its rooms are filled*
> *with rare and beautiful treasures.*
> — *Proverbs 24:3*

When couples get married, they believe their marriages will work. No one goes to their wedding ceremony thinking, *This relationship will never last.* At the beginning of our marriage, Leon and I discovered that if we established our marriage on biblical principles, God would produce treasure in our lives. When I married him, I knew in my heart he was a man of high integrity. I do my best to show him I value him and he is a treasure to me. From the day I met him and saw his concern and love for people, I had insight into the type of person he is and who he would become. Neither of us is perfect, but Leon is an amazing man who is deeply committed to our relationship.

One way I know my husband treasures me is when he greets me after a long day at work. We enjoy a long hug and a sweet kiss. He is also openly affectionate with me in front of friends and family.

"How's my beautiful wife?" he says. Sometimes he calls me *bunny*, and in the mornings he always makes time to pray for me.

You will become a treasure to the person you wed. God knows you are a blessing and will complement the person you marry. As you delight in Him, He will give you the desires of your heart.

What's Your Love Language?

The Five Love Languages by Gary Chapman is a must-read. The idea of love languages is simple—people have different ways of receiving and expressing love. After thirty years as a marriage and family counselor, Chapman heard hundreds of couples describe their issues and he began to see patterns. "I realized I was hearing the same stories over and over again," he says.

Chapman sat down and read through more than a decade's worth of notes, and he realized what couples really want from each other falls into five distinct categories:

1. Words of affirmation: compliments or words of encouragement
2. Quality time: their partner's undivided attention
3. Receiving gifts: symbols of love like flowers or chocolates
4. Acts of service: setting the table, walking the dog, or doing other small jobs
5. Physical touch: having sex, holding hands, kissing[3]

When I say Leon speaks my love language, what I mean is that he is aware I need his undivided attention and his touch. For women, physical touch and compliments go a long way, but more than anything, I've seen that most women love spending quality time with their spouses. Generally speaking, the primary love language of men is physical touch, which usually translates to sex. Many men also love words of appreciation or affirmation. They need to hear they are honored, respected, and admired and that they have what it takes. In addition, men like to be heard, just as women do, which I would include in the quality-time category. Hearing each other has to do with honoring each other's hearts, showing care, and expressing delight in each other. (We'll discuss this topic in greater depth in chapter 14.) Study your future spouse and determine what their love language is.

3 Gary Chapman, *The Five Love Languages: The Secret to Love That Lasts* (Chicago: Northfield Publishing, 2014).

The Power of the Armor of God

For our struggle is not against flesh and blood, but against the rulers, against the authorities, against the powers of this dark world and against the spiritual forces of evil in the heavenly realms.
— Ephesians 6:12

Everywhere we turn these days, we face battles. Life in this sinful world is full of struggles that test our faith in God. From illness and financial crises to broken relationships and the loss of hopes and dreams, life can feel like a war. On a regular basis, most people struggle with body image, lust, guilt, doubt, depression, pride, and how to keep spiritually fresh. What battles do you currently face? Do you feel like you're winning?

The battle between good and evil is everywhere we look, and all too often, married couples don't know what to do when they feel triggered—when something bothers them. Unfortunately, the marriage relationship can seem like a battleground, too. When we have conflicts in marriage, we have a tendency to end up fighting against our spouses, but there is a better way.

In the Book of Ephesians, Paul highlights several qualities and actions you can use as protection in battle. These are called the armor of God. When you are facing a spiritual battle, consider praying and declaring these words:

- Belt of truth: "Lord, show me the truth about who You are. Help me understand the plans You have for me."
- Breastplate of righteousness: "Thank You for showing me the truth about myself—that on my own I could never be good enough, but through Jesus I am righteous."
- Sandals of peace: "Thank You for the peace You give me when I trust and follow You."
- Shield of faith: "Thank You for helping me have faith in You. I will live by faith."
- Helmet of salvation: "I receive Your promise of salvation for today's battles and those I will face in the future."
- Sword of the Spirit (the Word of God): "Thank You for the Scriptures. Please show me which verses will cut through the deceptions I face today."

Leon and I can get agitated with one another at times, but we have learned not to use absolute words such as *never* or *always*. We try not to say sentences like these:

"You never listen to me."
"You always work late."
"Whenever we talk, it's always about your issues."
"You asked me how much we should spend on this gift, and then you added a hundred dollars. Why can't you ever respect what I say?"

Criticism leads to defensiveness, which typically results in more quarreling or someone shutting down emotionally and not talking. A sense of heaviness rushes in between us, so thick I can feel it in the air. In some cases, I feel the Lord is trying to bring us together and help us resolve an issue. At other times I sense a spiritual attack, and I call this the spirit of dissension. When this happens I stop, pray, and put on the armor of God by inviting the Lord into the conversation. Warring against this spirit of dissension requires spiritual reflection, a humble attitude, and active listening. Learning to communicate effectively when there is tension takes some practice, but it is well worth the effort. It's important not to get triggered (deeply bothered) by external factors; instead, be aware of why you are having such intense feelings. Simple "I" statements are a good place to start:

"You never listen to me" can be replaced with "I'm not feeling heard."
"You always work late" can be replaced with "I feel abandoned."
"Whenever we talk, it's always about your issues" can be replaced with "Sometimes I don't feel like you're hearing my heart."
"Why can't you respect what I say?" can be replaced with "I don't feel respected when my opinions aren't honored."

Fight the Good Fight

And I answered the king, "If it pleases the king and if your servant has found favor in his sight, let him send me to the city in Judah where my ancestors are buried so that I can rebuild it."
— Nehemiah 2:5

You get to choose. You can fight for your marriage, not against your spouse. This perspective changes everything and is a key to building a successful marriage. It's important to realize you and your significant other are not enemies. When conflicts arise, many people think of their spouses as the enemy and resentment begins to build, but if you plan to have a successful relationship, at some point you will have to fight for it! Marriage—really, all relationships—is full of opportunities where you have to fight against the enemy and build the relationship at the same time.

A biblical story that illustrates this concept is found in the Book of Nehemiah. A Jew in exile, Nehemiah was an official in the Persian court of King Artaxerxes I, near the Tigris River in modern-day Iran. Nehemiah served as the king's cupbearer, which put him in a position to speak to the king and request favors. After hearing about the destruction and plunder of Judah, Nehemiah asked the king's permission to go to Jerusalem and rebuild the city. In return, he was given letters from the king for both safe passage and permission to obtain timber for the project from the king's forest. God clearly had a plan, and it was to use His willing and faithful servant Nehemiah.

Nehemiah returned to Jerusalem in 445 B.C., surveyed the damage, and began work on rebuilding. He enlisted the help of the people to repair the breaches in the wall and urged them to set up guards to defend against the constant threats of those who opposed them, including the armies of Samaria, the Ammonites, and the Ashdodites. The hurried work of repairing and rebuilding Jerusalem's wall and gates took just fifty-two days.

Despite the dangers they encountered, Nehemiah was able to rebuild the wall for the following reasons:

1. He was determined to complete the project with God's help. *"Unless the Lord builds the house, the builders labor in vain. Unless the Lord watches over the city, the guards stand watch in vain"* (Psalm 127:1).
2. He and the people were ready to defend Jerusalem even in the midst of construction. Nehemiah's workers had a sword in one hand and a tool in the other (Nehemiah 4:17).
3. Nehemiah understood he could complete this project only with the help of those who shared his vision for rebuilding the wall of Jerusalem.
4. He understood he was involved in a spiritual fight. No matter what he encountered, he knew God was going to win.

On many levels, marriage requires Nehemiah's perspective. He knew rebuilding the wall of Jerusalem was a worthy endeavor, despite the challenges. When a relationship becomes strained, married couples need to understand and believe that putting effort into the marriage is necessary, productive, and worthwhile. We must fight the lie that the marriage isn't worth it. Nehemiah learned that great things are accomplished with a divine perspective and with community. Marriage follows this same principle. Unless we have the right mindset, are willing to learn, and are involved in a community of believers, we will never receive the encouragement and mentoring we need to build the marriage.

You need to be prepared to put time and effort into building your marriage, resisting the temptation to give up. Remember the fight is not against your spouse. The enemy wants to ruin your marriage. Don't allow him to divide you. God is calling you to raise your sword and defend your marriage.

> *You need to be prepared to put time and effort into building your marriage, resisting the temptation to give up. Remember the fight is not against your spouse. The enemy wants to ruin your marriage. Don't allow him to divide you. God is calling you to raise your sword and defend your marriage.*

The Path to Success

How do you measure success in your marriage? My understanding of what a successful marriage looks like has gone through a metamorphosis over time. In the first years of my marriage, I wanted everything to be perfect. If Leon and I had a conflict, I thought it meant we'd somehow failed as a couple. I realize now that conflicts will happen. It was a hard lesson to learn, but I discovered the couples who are willing to work at resolving pressing issues and are intent on growing closer are the ones who find true intimacy.

One practice that has revolutionized our marriage is connecting with other couples and coaching them through their struggles. Couples who are willing to open up and talk about their problems end up enjoying more intimacy, no matter how poorly their marriages are doing. Often couples want to share only the good things that are happening in their marriages or declare their marriages are doing "just fine." Marriage can be great, but we need to acknowledge problems when they occur. I've found that not opening up about marriage problems can create emotional distance within the marriage.

If you want your marriage to grow, you will need to become part of a group where relationship coaching is practiced or have friends who welcome and model healthy vulnerability. Friends, coaches, or mentors who provide a place where you can bring your deepest concerns and prayer requests as a couple are crucial for marriage success. These conversations are not about complaining or emphasizing the weaknesses you see in your spouse, but they focus on meeting challenges you encounter as a married couple head on. The more you focus on learning with a humble heart, the better results you will see as you share with your marriage coaches. In addition, sharing about your struggles can be a positive force because your coaches hold you accountable, and it teaches you to communicate more effectively.

> *If you want your marriage to grow, you will need to become part of a group where relationship coaching is practiced or have friends who welcome and model healthy vulnerability. Friends, coaches, or mentors who provide a place where you can bring your deepest concerns and prayer requests as a couple are crucial for marriage success.*

Arnold and Shelly

A couple I'll refer to as Arnold and Shelly had challenges from the beginning of their marriage. Both brought painful traumas from their childhoods into the relationship. Shelly was molested as a child, and this experience left her unable to engage emotionally with her first husband.

"I was holding my own heart hostage because of the childhood wounds of molestation," she told me. "I had a locked heart and, as a result, withheld intimacy from those around me. No one was going to protect me. I was going to do it myself out of a fear of rejection."

However, Shelly knew she needed love, so she pushed through the pain and married Arnold, her second husband. They got involved in a local church by leading Bible studies and regularly attending services. For a time they were able to blend their lives together, but Shelly couldn't trust her husband. This inability to trust him, as well as her decision to withhold physical and emotional intimacy from him, sabotaged the relationship. Then disaster struck. Shelly began to believe the lie that her relationship was doomed, and failure turned to paranoia. She ended up having a nervous breakdown and found herself in a mental institution.

"We hid our pain as a couple. No one was aware of the pain we were in," she says.

Meanwhile, Arnold was dealing with his own issues. He wanted his own children and to be in control, and he believed he deserved more. Compounding the problem, he had a pornography addiction, which he considered a personal issue; he didn't realize how it was affecting his marriage.

As Shelly recovered and began to deal with her fear of rejection, Arnold slipped further into despair and addiction. When the pressure became too great for him, he served Shelly with divorce papers, which left her feeling rejected, unwanted, and filled with self-hatred. She felt she wasn't good wife material. But the Lord was at work. He gave Shelly Ezekiel 36:35 and with it a new hope: *This land that was laid waste has become like the garden of Eden; the cities that were lying in ruins, desolate and destroyed, are now fortified and inhabited.*

Shelly told me, "He used that verse to expose all the lies I believed about myself and how to get off the road of condemnation. I surrendered and cried out. The Lord used divorce papers to get my attention."

Arnold and Shelly decided to try one more marriage seminar—and the Lord rescued their marriage. Arnold describes it this way: "The Lord rescued us from the cliff of divorce and repaired the hole in each of our hearts. When we saw that other people struggled and that it wasn't just us, we felt relief. Coupled with that, we realized that we could get help with our marriage and the emotional healing we both needed."

Arnold and Shelly are now leaders in a marriage group and mentor couples who are struggling with relationship issues. They have learned to focus on intimacy. "Our goal is to understand each other's hearts," Arnold says. "When situations arise that make it difficult to engage emotionally, we ask the Lord for guidance and then reach out to friends for support and encouragement."

When a husband and wife are determined to let God help them, this is an act of surrender. They are surrendering their marriage to Him, which allows them to work things out. It also fills them with hope, and in any marriage, holding on to hope is what will keep the couple going. Two committed, surrendered hearts will find comfort in God, and they will be able to learn from Him and other people what will help them overcome any situation.

Discussion Questions:

1. What do you see as the characteristics of a successful marriage?

2. What are some specific ways you can maintain intimacy in your marriage?

3. Do you have a positive perspective on marriage?

4. Do you have any fears or negative beliefs (lies) regarding marriage?

5. How will you fight for your marriage?

Prayer:

Heavenly Father,

I come to You in the name of Jesus to ask You to give me Your mindset about marriage. I want to think like You. Please do the same for my future spouse. I ask Your Spirit to give us the right tools and weapons so we can have the marriage You intend us to have.

Chapter
14

COMMUNICATION AND CONFLICT

How to Recognize What Your Spouse Is Really Saying

Does the thought of conflict scare you?

Conflict in a relationship doesn't always mean what most people think. It does not, for example, mean the relationship is doomed to fail, because conflict can lead to resolution and result in genuine communication and understanding.

Most couples need to go further than simply learning how to be effective communicators. They need to be willing to cherish and respect each other before the talking can begin. Once their hearts are active, they can engage each other in conversation, genuinely listen, and empathize. This is what the Bible calls delighting in each other. Engaged couples need to learn to hear each other's hearts, which lays a foundation for delight.

When there is no delight and respect in a relationship, arguments pop up like weeds and partners don't feel heard. A spouse who is ignored feels misunderstood and uncared for. Good communication is an art, and using scripts (preplanned patterns of conversation) or active listening tools is essential. Both men and women need this kind of understanding in order to feel valued, honored, and cherished. When we lay down what we think we deserve and how we think we should be treated, we receive an amazing measure of joy:

> *Do nothing out of selfish ambition or vain conceit. Rather, in humility value others above yourselves, not looking to your own interests but each of you to the interests of the others. In your relationships with one another, have the same mindset as Christ Jesus.*
> — *Philippians 2:3–5*

Relationship expert Chris Hogan asks an important question that helps make understanding relationships and communication fairly simple:

What is the one thing we cannot fail to do to have a successful relationship? It's a conversation! If you take all the meaningful conversations out of a relationship, what do you have left? Nothing! Conversations where people are able to accurately interpret one another and feel seen, heard, understood, cared for, and appreciated lead to greater intimacy and connection. Relationships are satisfying and successful when people know others are willing to show up meaningfully.[1]

True communication occurs when both people are able to speak and be heard. Another relationship expert, Dr. Terri L. Orbuch, talks about the importance of mutual communication: "The happy couples from my long term study of marriage all said that good communication skills were what kept them together and thriving. This means not only asking your partner what he or she needs, but telling your partner what you need."[2] Learning to express what you feel, need, and want in a healthy, communicative way is vital. Be assertive while maintaining kindness.

Good communication is key to a lasting and successful relationship, but most couples I know have conflict and, at one level or another, struggle to communicate. For many years my husband and I thought that not having conflict was one of the best things we could do. When we did have conflict, Leon would reassure me and express we were both on a learning curve.

"Don't worry, honey—we are both learning. You're just a baby wife."

I tend to be the kind of person who likes to resolve problems quickly, whereas my husband's style is to avoid certain conflicts and put hard discussions off until later. Once we discovered that conflicts were inevitable, we were able to work at effectively resolving disagreements through active listening and genuine communication. We had to learn when to be humble, when to defer, and when to accept we were wrong. Conflict can bring problems into the light and help couples face their issues instead of denying them.

Communication is about empowering your spouse with the awareness that you delight in them, which means listening and showing a keen interest in their life. When

1 For more information on this topic, check out *Noble Moments: Relationship Matters*, a DVD from Chris Hogan and Noble Call Institute Inc. Visit www.noblecall.org.
2 Terri L. Orbuch, *5 Simple Steps to Take Your Marriage from Good to Great* (Austin, TX: River Grove Books, 2015).

you delight in your spouse, they feel cherished and valued, heard and understood.

Developing Conversation Skills

In many cases, a wife wants her husband to sit down and listen, not just with his ears but with his heart. As women, we desire a level of communication where someone can completely appreciate our emotions, feelings, and points of view. Husbands, meanwhile, typically want to reason something to completion, maybe even give a lecture on the topic. The goal is to fix the problem. In this kind of situation, a wife can start to feel like she's talking to a wall. The husband sees his advice isn't being accepted, so he starts to believe the wife isn't interested in his opinions and therefore he is not being respected. This miscommunication can escalate to the point where couples don't even try to share their feelings and thoughts with one another anymore—when all they needed to do was learn to communicate in a different manner.

If you've ever had a problem with communication in a relationship, don't feel isolated or discouraged because it happens to everyone. Above all, don't begin to think that communicating with your spouse or partner is a lost cause.

When two people are willing to understand an issue from each other's point of view, they are at the starting line for authentic communication. As we learn how to actively listen to our spouses, we help them express their feelings and process whatever issue is bothering them. What does active listening look like? Here is an example:

Step 1: The couple shares facts and information.
"Did you have a rough day?"

Step 2: The couple shares personal ideas, dreams, or beliefs.
"Why was your day so bad? What happened?"

Step 3: The couple shares how they're feeling. Feelings are great indicators of something much deeper than what surfaced in the conflict. Each person should be patient and comforting toward the other's feelings.
"I'm sorry! How did that make you feel when your boss yelled at you?"

Step 4: The couple shares secrets, fears, or failures.

"What I hear you saying is that you didn't respond to the yelling because of fear. What were you afraid of?"

Step 5: The couple shares needs and insights.
"What do you think you should have said?"

Step 6: The couple prays together.
"May I pray with you about this?"[3]

Some partners expect their spouses to go from Step 1 (talking about facts and details) to Step 4 (talking about intimate topics) instantly. But that isn't what happens! When you sense your partner is struggling, be patient and ask them questions through every level of communication. Don't add your opinion unless it's asked for. Take the statements you want to express and turn them into questions. Keep in mind that most men process internally and most women process verbally, so look for opportunities to become an active listener.

Recognizing the Deeper Issue

My husband is hypersensitive about nagging. Before we got married, we had a conversation in which he begged me never to nag him.

"I know this couple where the wife can't stop nagging her husband," he said. "I feel sorry for him. Please promise me you won't nag me."

I honestly didn't even know what *nagging* was in Spanish, but Leon did his best to explain to me the horrid effects of repeatedly reminding your husband to do something. When I understood what he was saying, I pledged to do my best not to be a nagging wife. After years of marriage, let me tell you—that is easier said than done. Reminders have to happen in a marriage from time to time. I try to be careful in this area of my life, but sometimes I find myself slipping. Thankfully, we don't talk like this about my husband's love of sports anymore, but here's a glimpse of how our conversations used to go:

Picture a beautiful evening in March. Dinner is made and the kids are working on their homework. The smell of chicken and vegetables is wafting through the air. When I hear the car door swing shut outside, I know Leon is home.

3 This is based on a connecting conversation model from Chris Hogan and Noble Call Institute Inc. Visit www.noblecall.org for more information.

We greet each other and Leon sniffs the air. "What's cooking? It smells so good!"

"It's your favorite, chicken divan," I say with pride, looking forward to a peaceful, relaxing family dinner.

But instead, Leon announces, "Warriors are on tonight," and walks into the family room to flip on the television. "And the Giants are playing, too!"

My plans for the night start to slide off the table like a casserole dish. "Oh, no! Are you watching the game again tonight? You just got home and we all want to eat."

"Honey, I just want to watch a bit of the game. We talked about this."

"Can you come to the table for dinner, please?"

We all sit down at the table, but Leon fills his plate, gets up, and watches a bit of the game while he eats. The kids are shooting glances at me.

"Honey, are you coming back to eat with us?" I yell into the living room.

"I just want to relax after a long day," he replies.

"Well, it's kind of late and we want to eat together. We've been waiting for you to get home so we could be together. Can you please turn off the television?"

"Let's compromise," he suggests. "We can all eat while we watch the game."

"I feel like baseball is your only priority. Can you please turn it off?"

"Honey, I'm just gonna watch an inning or two before the Warriors play."

"Leon Roat! Be reasonable. Why can't we share a meal together?"

"Honey, you're nagging me again. I just want to have fun and relax after a long day. There's nothing wrong with that."

I groan and pick at my food with my fork. "Okay, just this once," I say on the outside, but inside I'm thinking, *I can't believe he prefers to spend time watching that stupid game instead of connecting with his family. Next time he can make his own meal.*

There's some communication going on here, and not all of it is good! Leon is tired and is growing annoyed with me because he feels I'm trying to control him. He wants to feel free to relax in any way he desires—why would his wife want to take that pleasure away from him? I am beginning to feel ignored, which leads me to feel abandoned and let down. It seems to me like the whole family is being robbed of a perfect evening, and the only one who gets what he wants is Leon.

In this sort of situation, both people need to be heard and understood. The Warriors are my favorite team and I love watching my husband enjoy sports, but both of us know that family time is more important. The key for us in this conversation was allowing one person to express their thoughts without nagging.

We didn't have to agree with each other; we just needed to listen. Since that evening, we have decided watching some games is okay but not at the cost of family time. My issue was deeper than whether or not to watch sports—it was about having quality time with the family.

Like many couples, Leon and I have different styles of communication. He came from a home where challenges were rarely faced, and his parents didn't talk about pressing issues. His father, in most cases, would retreat when there was something "delicate" that needed to be discussed. I, on the other hand, came from a home with lots of fighting. My parents both dug into their own perspectives, trying to prove they were in the right. Differences in communication style are common with most couples. When there are differences, a couple should come together and decide to make changes in how they communicate so both partners feel heard, understood, and valued.

How to Have a Great Conversation

If you follow these practices in your conversations, you will be amazed at the positive changes you see in your relationships:

1. Set aside time to talk. This communicates you are willing to engage and connect.
2. Provide a safe place for the conversation, where your significant other feels welcome.
3. Remember how God sees you and your spouse. Many times conflicts escalate into intense and unhealthy arguments because couples forget their true identity.
4. Practice actively listening during conversations. Make sure you have invited the Holy Spirit to be part of your potentially difficult conversation by starting with prayer.
5. Be thankful for at least one thing at the beginning of a deep conversation and let the other person know what it is.
6. Determine who is going to be the speaker and the listener. Frustration comes from two people trying to talk at the same time.
7. Don't talk when you feel hungry, angry, or tired. If you are sensing tension, take a break from the conversation and set a time to pick it up again later.
8. Use the conversation techniques mentioned in this chapter when big issues arise.

9. Practice acceptance and encouragement before offering a challenge. The listener's job is the most important because they are asking the questions.
10. Switch roles so both parties feel heard, understood, and cared for.

The rest of this chapter is a series of "couple stories." As you read the following conversations, try to put yourself into each situation and look at it circumspectly. How could you improve your active listening skills? What could you say to help your spouse or loved one feel heard and understood, even if you disagree with them? Think about how to bring up pressing issues in a non-confrontational way with your spouse. As always, pray and ask for God's help in becoming a better communicator.

Canceled Plans

Sally and Bob struggled in the area of communication for years. Sally felt her husband "listened" to her but didn't hear her heart.

"What's the matter, honey?" Bob asked.

Sally put the phone down and stared out the window. "He's too busy to talk."

"Did you invite Jon over again?"

"What do you mean again?" Sally replied sarcastically.

"I simply mean that you've asked him to come over a lot," Bob replied, shaking his head. "Our son is a busy man."

"I just can't seem to get through to the kids. Every time I call one of them up and invite them over, they're busy. Too busy to spend some time with their parents."

"Remember this is about Jon. Don't generalize to all the children."

Sally glared at Bob. "I'm not generalizing! You haven't heard a word I said."

"I heard every word. Let's get back to the problem. What was his excuse this time?"

"You don't even love him."

Bob clenched his jaw. "Sally, what's the problem?"

"Okay! He said he's busy this week and he can't make it tonight for dinner. He doesn't want to even talk on the phone. Why doesn't he like us?" Sally hung her head.

"Something important must have come up. That's all." Bob rubbed his chin. "Call him back and invite him over next week. It's no big deal. Don't be so emotional."

"It seems like all we ever do is argue when there are tough topics to discuss. You're not listening." The tears began to flow.

"I'm listening—I heard every word you said. I'm standing in front of you." Bob looked at her. "Why are you crying?"

Sally put her hands over her face and cried harder.

Bob rolled his eyes. "You have my attention now. What's the big deal, anyway? He can come next week. We will see Jon then."

"Never mind. I don't like talking when you have that tone."

"I'm listening. You always say I don't listen. I get tired of it."

"I feel like you're going through the motions."

Bob finally threw his hands in the air and muttered, "Women!"

This kind of back-and-forth is unfortunately common in households. One person is in pain and the other doesn't understand why, or they don't see the pain at all. Sally is torn up because of the rejection she thinks she's receiving from her son. The issue has less to do with Jon coming over for dinner and more to do with the pain of rejection. She feels alone. On top of everything, she believes she's a poor parent and, somehow, it is her fault Jon won't come over.

Bob, meanwhile, is willing to talk to Sally about the issue, but he isn't actively listening. He tends to make statements more than ask questions, and he wants to solve what he believes is the problem—that Jon can't make it tonight—but that isn't Sally's real concern. She already feels rejected, so her conversation with her husband just makes her feel worse. In other words, Sally has pain in her heart that needs healing, but her husband is not cooperating with that healing. In situations like this, each person needs to understand how to connect with the other even when they are feeling emotional, down, frustrated, lonely, rejected, abandoned, etc. As each spouse learns to listen to the other's heart, the conversation brings comfort and healing to wounded places.

Through good communication tools, this couple has since learned to listen to each other. The next time they found themselves in an emotionally charged conversation, they used conversation tools to help them communicate. Bob was able to pause and ask, "How can I hear you better? I want to understand you and make sure you feel that I care about your feelings and your needs."

Sally was able to thank him for understanding her and meeting her in a place of brokenness. "I'm sorry I overreacted in our first conversation. Now that I feel heard by you and that you are understanding me, it's your turn to bring something, and I really want to listen and care for your heart."

This is the way couples learn to take turns and care for the deep places in their hearts. By actively listening, they put themselves in the other person's shoes so the person feels cared for. Ultimately, this leads to both spouses feeling delight in each other.

A Bad Day at Work

When you are actively listening, you help the speaker feel heard. Nonverbal cues—such as nods, smiles, appropriate eye contact, leaning toward the listener, and so forth—help the speaker feel comfortable enough to continue sharing with you.

Verbal cues used by an active listener often include statements such as:

- "Mm-hmm."
- "I see."
- "How strange."
- "Tell me more."
- "Am I hearing you right?"
- "Can you please repeat that? I'm not really getting it."
- "Am I understanding you correctly?"

Here's an example of what actively listening can look like. After a difficult day at the office, Ben comes home and begins to take out his frustrations on his wife.

"Hi, babe. What's for dinner?"
"I haven't started dinner yet," Sandra replies. "I thought we'd cook together."
"But it's your turn tonight."
Hearing the tension in his voice, Sandra doesn't say a word. Instead, she pours Ben a glass of juice and hands him a platter of veggies to snack on. As he eats, she asks, "Did you have a tough day at work?"
"Heck, yeah!"
Sandra makes eye contact with him. "Is your boss riding you again?"
"How'd you guess?"
"It seems like he's got it in for you," she says, nodding. "How does that make you feel?"
"Every day I show up and try to finish the projects he assigns, but he never

gives me any feedback about my performance."

"Does that make you feel angry?"

"Really angry. I wish I could work for another manager, but I'm afraid that's not possible."

"Tell me more."

By leading him to tell her more and actively listening to his heart, Sandra is not only able to sidestep a potential fight, but she is also able to help her husband feel heard and supported in a difficult situation.

Bringing Up Pressing Issues

Money is a common area of conflict for couples. To this day, Leon jokes about my spending habits. On one occasion about sixteen years ago, my father was coming to visit and I wanted to buy some new furniture. The couches we had were old and out of style, and someone had given them to us, but Leon wouldn't have it. At that time in our lives, he could only think of saving money. The idea of spending money on home improvements seemed like a waste to him. As a financial advisor, he doesn't think many things are necessary unless you plan and save for them. All day long he helps his clients plan for their financial future, which usually involves investments and saving. Obviously, these things are good, but at the time he wasn't open to the possibility that we had the money to spend. Disagreeing with Leon about money is like disrespecting him. Our conversation went something like this:

"Have you thought about the home improvements I mentioned?" I asked.

"Honey," Leon said, "the house looks fine the way it is."

"I think we should repaint a few bedrooms. The rooms are in need of a fresh coat of paint, but what we really need is new furniture."

"Your father isn't going to even notice."

"I'd also like to upgrade the guest room with some new carpet. That's where my dad will be staying when he comes."

"New carpet? First you wanted to paint and now you want to carpet. What's next? A new kitchen?"

"That's not a bad idea," I teased him and smiled.

"You're right—it's a terrible idea!" Leon scowled. "Spend, spend! That's all you want to do. You don't need to impress him, honey. The house is fine."

"It's embarrassing. I want to get a bid soon. And honestly, it's not about impressing my dad. You know I don't care about that. I just want it to look pretty because I live here and I see it all the time."

"Stop nagging me about this," Leon bellowed. "Let's talk about it later."

I was frustrated at Leon's resistance and knew we needed an outside perspective to help walk us through this money issue. So I made an appointment with a counselor, and after our first and only counseling session, Leon and I agreed to set aside one particular account for home improvements. He opened up and understood that it was okay for me to make our home look beautiful. In fact, with frugality in mind, he decided to forgo counseling and spend the money on home improvements instead. I thank God for our past arguments about money because they've allowed us to start to use money in a more balanced way. These days my husband and I can find closeness and intimacy as we talk about finances. We might disagree sometimes, but we put it before God, knowing He is always in control and things will work out the way He intends.

When you know a conversation is likely going to produce conflict, it is best to approach it with a conversation plan already in place. The purpose of a scripted conversation is to uncover the deeper issue. Does she feel alone? Does he feel rejected and controlled?

One way to actively listen to your partner is to develop a list of questions and follow those questions until your partner feels heard and understood. Consider the following steps and try to incorporate them into your conversations with your partner. Keep in mind that the first step is always to invite the Lord into your conversation.[4]

1. Define the issue. Listen deeply to what your spouse is saying and ask leading questions so you can better understand what's going on. These are fairly simple questions designed to help your spouse open up. They could sound something like this:

    •   "What happened today?"
    •   "I can see you're upset. Is there anything you want to talk about?"

2. Clarify the core issue. Dig a little deeper and ask questions that reveal the core issue.

---

4 Certain conversations in this chapter are based on the communication tools presented by Chris Hogan. For more information, visit www.noblecall.org.

- "What was the worst part of this experience?"
- "How did this make you feel?"

3. Describe the effects. Find out how this situation is affecting your spouse.

  - "Does this make you feel angry?" (Or frustrated, ashamed, embarrassed, etc.)
  - "What are you feeling?"
  - "How is this making you act?"

4. Clarify future results. Step back and consider the future with your spouse.

  - "What do you think will happen?"
  - "What are you going to do about it?"

5. Determine your role in the problem. Listen to what your spouse is saying and don't react, even if you feel an accusation is unjustified. Find out what your spouse needs.

  - "What is the best way I could help you right now?"
  - "How have my actions been hurting you?"
  - "How could I help you with this in the future?"

6. Characterize the ideal outcome. Your spouse is like the other half of your heart. Find out what they need so you can help them thrive.

  - "What is the best possible outcome in this situation?"
  - "What are you hoping will happen?"
  - "What can I do to make this better?"

7. Pledge to act. Let your spouse know you've heard them and will do something about what they've said.

  - "I will work on this."
  - "I believe in you."
  - "I trust you."

8. Pray together. Always end with prayer. The two of you are going through life together, and spending time together in prayer is one of the more important things you can do as a couple. See what God shows your heart, and allow the Lord to bring you to a place of repentance if necessary.

Be careful about the timing of potentially difficult conversations. When your partner comes home after a hard day, it's probably not a good idea to bring up a pressing money issue. Talking about politics right before bed could result in one person falling asleep in the middle of the conversation or both people jumping into a fight. It takes time for most people to share their deep emotions, so don't expect your mate to plunge right into the details when you ask them what is wrong. Meaningful conversations take time and effort, and they require a lot of mental energy. Good listeners must work to develop trust, and trust is easier to establish when you pick the right time for a conversation.

Out All Weekend

Many couples struggle with hurt feelings and the inability to overcome past pain. Although the argument concerns a current issue, the real problem is usually something deeper. For example, let's say a husband has fallen into the trap of mistaken priorities. He has arranged his days and weeks in such a way that his wife does not feel valued; instead, his work, friends, or hobbies get the majority of his time. Consequently, the wife starts to feel ignored and maybe even abandoned, but when she tries to talk to him about it, it comes off in an aggressive way. The husband feels like the wife is trying to control him when she says, "You never spend time with me," or, "We used to do everything together, and now you don't want me around."

Again, the real problem is not that he has his own friends or is committed to his job. The real problem is how these things are making her feel.

Sonny and Claire are one such couple. Sonny has made plans for the weekend, and Claire is concerned that she isn't a priority in her husband's life. Their conversation doesn't start well, but Sonny has been practicing actively listening to his wife, and he has a "script" of questions he's working from.

"You never spend time with me on the weekends," Claire says. "You're always out with your buddies. Frankly, I can't stand your friend John! He always calls here and acts like he owns your time. You should be at home on the weekends doing chores like me. I always end up doing all the work around here while you play."

Instead of getting heated, Sonny replies, "I can hear that you're upset. What I hear you saying is that I never spend time with you on the weekends. I go out with my friends. John calls here and acts like he owns my time. You want me home doing chores with you on the weekends. Am I hearing you right?"

Claire nods. "You heard what I said, but you still don't know how I feel. You're not listening."

"Is there anything else? What's the most important issue?"

"Really, I like John. He's annoying, but what really bothers me is you just leave on the weekend."

"It bothers you that I just leave on the weekend."

Claire nods again.

"How is this affecting you?"

"I feel abandoned," she replies as she tears up.

Sonny puts his hand on her shoulder. "So when I leave on the weekends, you feel abandoned. Is that right?"

Claire nods.

Sonny then asks an important question that helps put difficult conversations in perspective: "What will happen if nothing changes?" This is a simple question that can help clarify more difficult ones.

"You're gonna be living with a very sad and angry woman!"

"So if nothing changes, you're going to be sad and angry. Is that right?"

Claire puts her hands on her hips and looks into Sonny's eyes. "And you know what happens when I get sad."

Yes, Sonny does know. And he does not want this.

"No loving, baby!"

He gulps. He has a pretty good sense of the situation now and how she's feeling, but he asks her to be specific about the key issue that is driving the problem. "What is my role in all of this?"

"Your role is that you never even let me know you're leaving. I don't have any notice."

"Okay, my role is that I don't prepare you when I hang out with the guys."

Claire smiles. "Really, I don't mind that you spend time with your friends, but I need some notice."

"Okay. What would be the ideal way to handle this issue?"

"Like I said, it's okay if you hang out with your friends. Just let me know a few days before if you're making plans on the weekend. That way I'm not stuck at home."

"Cool." Sonny nods. "I'll let you know a few days ahead of time when I want to hang out with the guys. I can do that. No problem."

Then he asks her if they can pray about it, because he knows that both of them want God involved in every aspect of their lives, even in discussions like this one. He's pretty sure he's done a good job with his listening skills when she puts her arms around him and makes a suggestion that does not have anything to do with sadness.

What's Behind Your Addiction?

Whenever root issues are not addressed in a conversation, pray and try to understand what's going on. Healing needs to take place, but it is vital not to challenge your spouse if they aren't ready to hear it.

Carrie wanted to talk to her fiancé, Donnie, about his smoking addiction, but she was afraid of how he'd react. She knew he was smoking less than he was, but it was still a problem, and—more important—he'd started trying to hide his habit from her rather than face a confrontation. One afternoon she decided to bring up the issue.

"I have an issue I think we need to talk about," she began.
Immediately, his walls went up. He folded his arms and shook his head. "Let me guess—smoking."
She nodded. "Yes, that's right. We need to talk about it."
But Donnie didn't want to talk about it. "I'm well aware of my problem. Believe me. And it's my problem."
"You don't smoke as much as you used to, but you're still smoking. I know you've tried several times to stop."
"You really want to talk about this, I can see." Realizing the confrontation was upon him whether he wanted it to be or not, Donnie asked, "So is there anything else?"
"This is the only issue, but there are other parts that make it problematic—like you sneaking around to smoke or lying about it."
Donnie could understand what she was saying. Even though he didn't want to

have this conversation, he decided to practice the active listening skills they'd been talking about in marriage counseling. Both of them worked off a script of questions as the conversation moved forward.

"So what I hear you saying is that I don't smoke as much, but it's still a problem. Not only that, I've started to try and hide my habit from you. Is that it?" Donnie slumped in his chair. "You don't like the smoking or the lying?" Folding her arms, Carrie answered, "You got that right."

"I can see that this is affecting you. Tell me how?"

"Well, it affects our relationship," she replied. "I would hate to make the decision to marry you, and then you die and I suffer. You know how much I hate it. It's really by God's grace that I have been able to let it go. I used to contemplate if I could go through with this relationship. I wondered if I could marry you. I never thought I would be with someone who smoked. I was raised without my real dad, and my mom would apologize and say, 'I am sorry I made a bad decision when choosing your dad, but when you get older, you make a better choice than I did.' So if I choose to marry you, knowing that you smoke, and we have kids and you die, then I have chosen to put them in a bad situation. I'm not trying to discount your efforts because you're doing much better than before."

"So you are afraid of me dying?" Donnie said.

"Yes. You keep smoking, so that tells me there is something about it that you are attracted to—like maybe there is something deep down that needs to be addressed. I don't know, but you haven't been able to stop completely and that says something. I think I have biblical backing to how I feel because the Bible says that our bodies are His temple. Doing anything to harm our bodies goes against God. When I try to bring it up to you, you don't react positively, and I don't even feel like I can talk about it. It gets so awkward so fast and I shut down."

Donnie took a deep breath. "Okay, so you are saying you are being affected by my smoking because if we have kids and I die, then you don't want the kids to be without a father. And we can't talk about it?"

Carrie nodded. "Yes, but even if I don't have kids, I don't want to make that choice to be with you and then you die and I am all alone."

"I get it," Donnie said. He then asked the question that can change everything, offering clarity and perspective: "What will the future be like if nothing changes?"

"You might die," Carrie replies, her eyes beginning to tear up.

Donnie fought back the emotion, too. "And you want to grow old with me?"

234

"Yes, I do."

He asked the next question from their script: "What's my responsibility for all of this?"

"Well, you continue to smoke, so I guess that's your part."

"Okay, so you're saying that me continuing to smoke is how I'm contributing to the issue?"

"That's right," Carrie replied.

"What do you see as your responsibility for this issue?"

"Hmm . . . that's a very good question. I guess my responsibility would be to pray for you. That seems to be all I can do. I don't even feel like we're able to have a conversation about it right now, but then I feel bad about being angry with you for smoking when I don't even remember to pray for you. I think prayer is the only thing I can do. That and speaking kindly to you."

"You're very good at that. At saying nice things. I appreciate your kind words."

"Thanks," Carrie said, reaching out to touch him.

"What does the preferable future look like to you? What would the future be like if this issue was resolved?"

"You stop smoking and we grow old together," Carrie said with finality.

"Okay, yes, I would like that, too. What is the most powerful thing we can agree to ask God for?"

"Maybe we should just stop and pray right now," Carrie offered. "That way, we will know."

After they prayed together, Donnie looked into Carrie's eyes. "I've got to know. What's the one thing we cannot fail to do? How am I gonna beat this?"

"Maybe you need some help, Donnie," she replied. "People with addictions beat their problems by partnering with people who've faced similar problems. Maybe that's what we need to do."

Donnie nodded. "That might work. I think I could live with that."

Whether you're married or just starting a relationship, focus on becoming a good listener. Hear and understand each other's hearts through good communication tools and the desire to connect with your spouse. Be compassionate, give each other the benefit of the doubt, and think the best of one another.

Gary Smalley in his book *The DNA of Relationships* defines the core issue of marital conflict as fear, which causes a "fear dance" or relational crisis.[5] Conflict doesn't have to be a negative mark in a relationship because it's an opportunity for

5 Gary Smalley, *The DNA of Relationships* (Carol Stream, IL: Tyndale House Publishers, 2004).

growth. Start by getting rid of the fear, because the sooner you understand your spouse is not the problem, the sooner the healing can start.

Good communication tools are important to get to the core problem. Arguments usually arise when two people have competing needs, but a good conversationalist learns to put their needs behind the needs of their partner; they know how to die to self. As James 1:19 states, *"My dear brothers and sisters, take note of this: Everyone should be quick to listen, slow to speak and slow to become angry."*

If you're about to address a difficult topic, it's a good idea to start the conversation with prayer, purposefully inviting the Holy Spirit into the talk. This can keep couples from name calling, blaming, and saying dishonoring things. Always remember to show respect and honor. *"Be devoted to one another in love. Honor one another above yourselves"* (Romans 12:10). Getting to the core problem is challenging and takes time, but if you can figure out why your spouse is responding the way they are, you will be much more able to communicate well.

No matter what the conflict is, the goal of any healthy conversation is to show the delight you have for your spouse. Due to outside frustrations, personal triggers, and the need for emotional healing, couples can forget how to put the other person first and instead find themselves focusing the conversation on them. Leon and I have fallen into this trap several times, but thankfully, we've been able to learn good communication tools that have helped us recover well. We've learned how to reduce arguments to their lowest level (the core issue) and delight in each other to the highest level. Whenever an argument starts, we both are prompt to recognize it is due to our own fears. This helps us understand that the other person, if they're willing to die to self and just listen, will help the speaker get to a better place. We continue practicing how to communicate and remind each other that the more we practice good tools of communication, the better conflict-resolution conversations we will have. Learning better ways to communicate is not an option in marriage; it is a necessity.

Discussion Questions:

1. How do you resolve conflict?

2. Why is it important to have good communication tools?

3. Why is it important to be an active listener? Explain.

4. What is the goal of good communication?

5. What is your personal script for conflict? Write it down.

Prayer:

Heavenly Father,

Please teach me to be a great communicator. Help me to be a good listener. Teach me how to hear Your voice better so I can hear my future spouse better, too. Bless me with a wise tongue so I can bring healing to my spouse.

Chapter
15

THE FAVOR OF GOD

How Your Marriage Can Lead to a Lasting Legacy

He who finds a wife finds what is good
and receives favor from the Lord.
— Proverbs 18:22

Last summer Leon and I traveled to Ecuador to visit my family and friends, and we found some time to go walking together, just the two of us. One afternoon we walked to the mall, and he left me at the hair salon for a few minutes. The stylist and I started talking, and I mentioned I had been married for twenty-six years. She immediately said, "Wow! That is love." I suppose longevity means love to many. During our conversation, Leon returned with a big smoothie for the two of us to share, and the stylist later told me, "I can see your love for each other by the way he looks at you and how you respond to him."

I am touched whenever people tell me they can see our love. I am blessed when my family and friends tell us we're a good example for them. But more than anything, I love when my kids and Leon have that satisfied look in their eyes that comes from feeling secure, loved, and content because they have seen the favor of God in our home. It all starts at home. That is where we truly know if we are loved, respected, and honored. That is the place where we experience true intimacy with God and each other.

I define *favor* as living in the knowledge of God's great delight and love for us. It is the tangible evidence that we have the approval of the Lord. No more do we struggle with whether or not we're good enough or if we "deserve" something. Before Jesus' sacrifice for us, nothing was good enough, and we weren't capable of having the complete assurance of freedom from sin; it was not yet "finished," like Jesus said. But now we come from a place of victory, knowing Jesus conquered death, sin, and the enemy when He died on our behalf and rose victoriously from the grave. Many of us have mistakenly thought we aren't good enough for God, or no matter what we do, we can never have His approval. But something amazing happens when we discover the truth that God delights in us freely, with all His love, and not because of anything we did or didn't do. When we accept the truth of His unconditional love, God sees Jesus in us, and we are able to receive freely the inheritance of His favor in our lives.

Proverbs 18:22 says he who finds a wife finds what is good and receives favor from the Lord. Does that mean God has given Leon favor in his life through me? Is that really possible? What an incredible thought! Favor starts at home. This is more than a physical house; it is your place of dwelling. If you wish, you can choose to dwell in the best place of all—the shelter of the Most High and under the shadow of the Almighty (Psalm 91). This concept of "home" is the foundation of marriage. When your house has been built by Him and in Him, you never have to labor in vain (Psalm 127:1). You're still in the process of growing and maturing, as all of us are, but you can learn to live in the favor of your heavenly Father's love.

The more you recognize and acknowledge His loving presence, the more aware you'll be of His favor over you. The more you look for His face and learn to love His Word, the more you'll live in His favor. Jeremiah 29:13 says, *"You will seek me and find me when you seek me with all your heart."* When you find God, you find His loving favor, which Psalm 5:12 describes as a shield: *"Surely, Lord, you bless the righteous; you surround them with your favor as with a shield."* With the Lord's favor in marriage, you can do things you couldn't accomplish by yourself, like forgive, love unconditionally, and consider the needs of your spouse before your own. Just the act of getting married reveals God's favor. Marriage in itself is God's favor over you, allowing you to share in a healthy relationship, start a family, and experience a sense of purpose in your life.

Leon and I have learned that His goodness and mercy will follow us every day of our lives and we will dwell in the house of the Lord forever (Psalm 23:6). This is our continual prayer for our family and the ones we've had the privilege of meeting and mentoring. It is our prayer for you as you read this book.

Favor in Marriage

During the early years of my marriage with Leon, the Lord taught us about His favor. We chose to live in Ecuador following our honeymoon so I could finish my thesis and get my degree. We had a little apartment not far from my parents. Leon had to find a job in my country because in addition to our living expenses, we also had to pay the mortgage on the house we owned in America. He worked as a tutor and secured a job as a financial mathematics professor at a university, but it still wasn't enough to cover our monthly expenses. However, shortly after Leon started his job at the university, I was able to take a part-time job at a law firm in Ecuador, which provided enough money for us to cover the rest of our expenses.

We knew God was calling us back to America so Leon could continue his dream of pursuing a career in financial advising. Three days after I got my doctorate in law, we made the move. Although America had more opportunities for Leon's chosen career, he didn't find a job for quite a while, and we lived with his parents for about eight months. It felt great to have a network of family members so close to us, but we wanted to have our own place. When Leon started a job as a financial planner, we were able to move into the house we already owned. We lived on a very tight budget during those first years and repeatedly learned that happiness and contentment come from relationships, especially our relationship with Jesus. Leon was barely making enough money for our mortgage payment and a few expenses, but we felt confident we were in God's will and chose to give the Lord 10 percent of our income. Tithing, or giving 10 percent of your income to a church, may seem unnecessary to some people, but it is actually a matter of great joy. Leon and I felt the Lord was showing us His favor, and in return we wanted to show Him how grateful we were.

When I became pregnant with our son, Christian, our home began to feel more financial pressure. Leon and I decided I should stay home and care for our son instead of pursuing a career. I didn't have my parents with me, and I just couldn't leave my Christian in childcare. Leon worked long hours, but when he came home to be with us, he was always a loving husband and dad. Not long afterward, we purchased and moved into a bigger house that was close to foreclosure, and this was a gift from Heaven. We had the room we needed to raise more children, host Bible studies and gatherings, and provide space for my family when they came to visit us from Ecuador.

A couple of years later, I became pregnant with our beloved Amy, who was born premature at thirty-four weeks. In the middle of my labor, the doctors told us her lungs weren't fully developed and rushed us to an emergency delivery room. We had to deal with the fear caused by their words, but we prayed and managed to set it aside. To our relief, Amy thrived, and again we knew God was faithful to us.

While pregnant with our precious child Jessica, I was diagnosed with detached placenta and was hospitalized for a week. When I returned home, I had to lie in bed for two months, but God did another miracle and blessed us with Jessica a few months later.

During each crisis in those early years of our marriage, God's protection was over us. Although we struggled financially for a long time, through hard work Leon built a business and provided for his family. I also saw God's favor in the generosity we encountered when my parents and Leon's parents came alongside us to support our decisions. And the biggest blessing of all: The Lord gave us healthy, loving, godly children.

God's favor is a constant force in my life, and Psalm 23 has been one of my life Scriptures. Psalm 23:6 was the first verse I memorized when I became a born-again believer and the one I have felt every day of my life: *"Surely your goodness and love will follow me all the days of my life, and I will dwell in the house of the Lord forever."* Whether I'm facing a tough circumstance or the opportunity to watch my children thrive, I see it as a gift from God. This is the favor of our loving God over our marriage. His kind, protective, and generous arms are always around us.

From Favor to Legacy

It is exciting to watch as the Lord brings two people together for the holy union of marriage. Equally exciting is the knowledge that His favor rests on the relationship and can lead to a lasting legacy. Marriage is the intertwining of two souls, two lives, two dreams, and two families. We were created for a relationship where our need for emotional and spiritual connection can be met. The marriage relationship exists to bring glory to God, and when God is glorified in a marriage, there is favor. As we grow in our marriages, treat our spouses in a godly manner, and develop Christlike character, God is delighted and His favor rests over us. This is the beginning of a legacy that impacts not only us as a couple but our children and friends as well. What a wonderful experience to be around people who exhibit the favor of God.

> *As we grow in our marriages, treat our spouses in a godly manner, and develop Christlike character, God is delighted and His favor rests over us.*

The sooner we understand that God favors us and He's given us everything necessary to live blessed lives, the sooner we can start building a legacy through our marriages. Many think a legacy is something we give our children, such as financial gifts or tips on living, but a legacy is much broader than these things. A couple's legacy reaches further than their own family and the message is much deeper than an inheritance or advice. Anyone who comes in contact with that couple can be the recipient of their legacy.

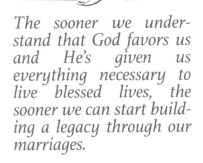

The sooner we understand that God favors us and He's given us everything necessary to live blessed lives, the sooner we can start building a legacy through our marriages.

My grandparents left me with great memories of a long and fervent marriage filled with love for their children and grandchildren. They were honorable, generous people. My grandma was a woman of prayer who loved the Lord, and to me, that is her greatest legacy. When it is time for you to go be with Jesus, what do you want people to say about you at your memorial service? What are you known for among your friends and family? These questions can help you focus and understand what legacy is all about. They offer insight regarding your perceptions of legacy and where your priorities lie.

Building a Legacy

Recently, I had the privilege of talking with Pastor Dick Bernal of Jubilee Christian Center. When you meet Pastor Dick, it's hard not to think of the word *legacy*. He founded Jubilee Christian Center with his wife, Carla, after they graduated from Rhema Bible Training Center in 1980. More than three decades later, Dick continues pastoring, writing, and serving as a missionary in various places around the globe.

As Dick told me his story, I was struck by his humility and the great legacy he is creating with his wife. Dick and Carla met the day after Christmas in 1974 at a bar in Fremont, California. He had recently divorced and was lonely, while she was out with her sister looking for a place to chat. When Carla and her sister entered the bar, Dick went over to meet them and after much persistence convinced Carla to dance with him. He invited her out the next evening and she accepted. The next night over Chinese food, the Holy Spirit spoke to Carla and told her she was going to marry Dick. She had her doubts about the relationship, since Dick wasn't a Christian, but they continued to date. They fell in love, got married, and soon Carla was pregnant.

But she wanted more. She would often pray for Dick's salvation, not wanting to raise their child in a non-Christian home, and sometimes she would talk to Dick about the Lord.

"I wasn't a bad person, but I was just lost," Dick told me. "I might drink or cuss too much, but I thought I was okay. I wasn't stealing or hurting anyone. But Carla let me know that I wasn't going to Heaven because I wasn't born again. At first it offended me when she said this. I said to her, 'People like you are going to Heaven and people like me aren't because we aren't born again?' But it was true."

Dick's spiritual journey started on December 21, 1976, ten days after his daughter Sarah was born. Carla was still in the hospital due to blood loss, and it looked like she was going to die.

"This is when I got serious about talking to the Lord," Dick told me. "'Don't let my wife die,' I said to God. 'I have a ten-day-old little girl.'"

Every journey must begin somewhere, and God met Dick Bernal in those life-and-death moments in the hospital. While he was crying out for his wife's life, Carla was having an intense encounter with Jesus.

"You can't come to Heaven because I have something for you and Dick to do," He told her.

This critical moment for both Carla and Dick would change their lives forever. No doubt, it was Carla's comments about God and the intense desire to see his wife healed that brought Dick to his knees in prayer that night. He came to Christ two months later at a Christian Missionary Alliance church, and forty-one years later, he is the pastor of the largest non-denominational church in San José, a family man, and a grandfather.

"Our kids have been raised in church all their lives," he told me. "We made life fun with ski trips and camping. Even to this day with grandkids, we make sure that our interpretation of the Christian life is joy, happiness, peace, love, and lots of laughter—forgiveness when there are problems and working things out. We try to make sure that Jesus is in the middle of the conversation. That's why all my kids are here serving. Our kids know we're not perfect. We're transparent and I think that attracts them. We never force things on them."

Relationships Matter

Relationship is an important aspect of leaving a legacy. Our lives are the product of relationships. If people encourage us when we're young and speak into our lives when we encounter challenges, we gain confidence and find success. But if our childhood is filled with confrontations, and those around us tell us we'll never amount to anything, our chances of success diminish. If our parents treated us with hostility, we tend to carry similar behaviors into our adult relationships. Relationships matter. As we grow up and become adults, we bring all our relationship experiences with us into the marriage. Dr. Gary Smalley starts the first chapter of *The DNA of Relationships* with these words: "Life is relationships; the rest is just details."

My friends Carl and Susan Orthlieb are all about building relationships. They believe that empowering and equipping people to strengthen their relationships is one of the greatest legacies a couple can leave behind. They have seen their own marriage transformed in recent years, so naturally they want others to experience the same joy and fulfillment. For Carl and Susan, leaving a legacy means becoming more relatable with each other and then passing those skills to other couples through mentoring and coaching.

To understand why they are so passionate about relationships, we just need to look at the beginning of their relationship. They met at the University of Waterloo around 1985. After graduating in 1986 and getting their first full-time jobs, Carl rented a place from Susan's dad while Susan lived with her parents nearby. Although Carl and Susan were dating, her parents were unaware of their relationship and constantly fought with her. Her father in particular would yell at her and force her to do things his way, and Susan was desperate to find an escape from her family turmoil. Carl came to the rescue. She would often call him and say, "They're at it again. Please get me out of this house!"

Carl and Susan dated for some time and then decided they were ready to take their relationship to the next level: They moved in together.

"It was great because Susan was with me all the time," Carl told me. "I was captivated by her and felt a false satisfaction as a man for saving her from her family. She was different than anyone I'd ever met. She was vibrant, full of energy, and fun to be with. I knew I had something special. Falling in love was easy. To me, deciding on whether you want to spend a lifetime together was scary. I thought that if you want to get married, you had to be good roommates and friends. It seemed logical to me to move in together first. Looking back, I realize I wasn't protecting Susan. Living with her and not committing to marriage only fed her insecurities. Getting married would have been the right thing to do, but I had a lot of doubts."

Susan explained, "I needed to get out of my house and I had no way to do it on my own. It was wonderful to play house but it was a means to an end. Carl was my ticket out. My parents were unaware, and so I felt that we were living a lie. At the same time, although I was a Christian, I condemned the church for its hypocrisy and I had stopped attending what I called 'organized religion.' I knew for sure that I didn't want a relationship like my parents had, so I gladly enabled Carl to rescue me. I wanted him to win me over and let me know that I was worth it. Unfortunately, I didn't have a father who called out my identity—that is, he didn't speak to my true potential and challenge, support, and encourage me in a loving and understanding way. He was all about my grades and achievement and not about the person I was becoming. With my mother, she could not stand up to my father and she didn't demonstrate what it meant to nurture nor instilled a sense of value in me. Naturally I wanted to escape."

In 1987 Carl declared his love for Susan. He had a special wedding ring made and proposed, though not without hesitation. Susan was relieved to accept. It was a sweet time for them as a couple, despite the struggles they were dealing with as individuals. In 1988, two years after they moved in together, Carl and Susan married, but they both brought serious emotional issues and dysfunction into their marriage.

They learned to push through the tough moments and blend their lives together. They worked hard and achieved professional success, had two beautiful children, and experienced a measure of happiness, but their relationship was lacking. Both found it difficult to tend to each other's emotional needs. Carl was unable to hear

Susan's heart because he had no internal framework for dealing with her dysfunction and emotional outbursts. Susan, meanwhile, continued to struggle with expressing her feelings and was frustrated by Carl's lack of empathy. Her frustrations turned into rage and Carl retreated further. This cycle caused her to build a well of deep bitterness, and her outbursts grew more frequent and took longer and longer to cool down. Things started to spiral downward.

"The first sixteen years of our marriage was like a roller coaster of heated discussions, spiteful words, blame, tearful apologies, regret, and torment," Carl told me. "Susan was angry and aggressive, and I was withdrawn and passive. On the inside we were both dying."

But the Lord was at work in their lives, and change waited on the horizon. During those difficult years, Susan found comfort in Bible study groups. "Digging into the Bible for the first time as an adult changed my life. I started going to a women's group with a friend and started doing my own observation, interpretation, and application of Scripture. I did two to three years of study. Because Carl saw me grow as a Christian and began to see the impact on my life, he was curious. I was just sharing the delight I had for God's Word. Carl and I also started going to a local church at that time. The turning point for me was that I finally understood the spiritual legacy that my parents had deposited in me through a program called Cleansing Stream,[1] and I asked the Lord to break it and replace it with something new. The rage that I felt was evicted. The children noticed the difference immediately. I continued to grow spiritually."

Carl's turning point came when he went to a conference called Zero to Hero.[2] In 2008 he started to understand how God wanted him to become a spiritual leader for his family. As he sought to do this, he slowly realized how he could care for Susan and her emotional needs. Previously, he had avoided tough conversations, but through working with Chris Hogan, the founder of Noble Call Institute Inc., he began to understand how to actively listen, truly understand his wife's heart, and lead her with spiritual authority.

Carl and Susan both learned how to build their relationship one conversation at a time.

---

1 Visit www.cleansingstream.org for more information.
2 Visit www.noblecall.org/conferences for more information.

"We learned a safe framework for hearing each other's heart, dealing with emotions, and developing greater intimacy," Carl said.

Twenty-eight years after their marriage, Carl and Susan find themselves leading Relate 20/20,[3] teaching workshops, training leaders, and coaching relationships. They're dedicated to changing lives by revealing, restoring, and reviving relationships in the greater San José, California, area.

"Our ministry was born out of a desire to give away the tools and methods we benefited from the most," Susan told me. "It's our positive experience with them that allows us to credibly proclaim our testimony and give hope to others."

Leaving a Legacy

How can you build a legacy for your friends, family, and community?

We know the importance of God's favor, which naturally leads to legacy. We also know legacy is about relationships and how a person affects the people around them by the life they live. So with these things in mind, here are several ways you can leave a godly legacy as a marriage partner and one day as a parent. Ponder the following principles as you consider your legacy:

- Keep your marriage covenant. Your family will never be stronger than the covenant that established it. Your marriage covenant sets your relationship with your spouse and children apart.
- Pray with and for your spouse. If you can adopt only one new habit in your marriage right now, start praying together every day. It is a simple act of love. Daily prayer will keep you from building walls between each other.
- Embrace suffering as a couple. It's so important that a husband and wife bear one another's burdens. Stand together, looking to God to sustain and guide you.
- Use words to edify your spouse. Proverbs 18:21 warns that death and life are in the power of the tongue, while James 3:8 declares, *"No human being can tame the tongue. It is a restless evil, full of deadly poison."* Choose to build your spouse up with your words, not tear them down.
- Pursue a relationship with each of your children. Rules without relationships make children angry. That's why Paul admonished fathers in Ephesians

---

3 Visit www.relate2020.com for more information.

6:4, *"Do not exasperate your children; instead, bring them up in the training and instruction of the Lord."*

- Call your children to a spiritual mission. Give them a vision for the world by making them a part of your work in the church and community. Around the dinner table, share stories of what God is doing. Take them with you on mission trips and teach them it's always better to give than to receive.

The Powerful Legacy of Marriage

When I came to live in the United States nearly thirty years ago, many of the people I met didn't know where my little country of Ecuador was. A few church people asked, "Isn't it the country where the five missionaries were killed by savage Indians?"

"Yes," I replied. "It is."

The story of Jim and Elisabeth Elliot means a lot to me because it is personal. For most Americans, this is a story of selfless love and sacrifice in a distant land, but there is very little distance for me. My heart has cherished their lives and their work in the jungle of my country since the first time I heard their story. Though we could admire many different things about their story, I want to highlight how it was their marriage that made their work impactful.

Jim and Elisabeth met at Wheaton College during her sophomore year. It was 1947, and Jim later wrote his parents, "I met a tall, lean girl, far from beautiful, but with a queer personality-drive that interests me."[4] The more Jim and Elisabeth talked, the more she noticed he was what she'd been hoping for in a husband. She writes, "He loved to sing hymns, and he knew dozens by heart. He loved to read poetry, loved to read it aloud. He was a real man, strong, broad chested, unaffected, friendly, and—I thought—very handsome. He loved God. That was the supreme dynamic of his life. Nothing else mattered much by comparison."[5]

The two of them became good friends. In her book *Passion and Purity*, Elisabeth writes about how she fell in love with Jim and he declared his love for her. They both prayed about their feelings, but their story didn't follow the typical path of two young people in love. Because Jim's heart was for God first and to do His work in remote

---

4 Elisabeth Elliot, *Through Gates of Splendor* (Carol Stream, IL: Tyndale Momentum, 1981), 17.
5 Elisabeth Elliot, *Passion and Purity: Learning to Bring Your Love Life Under Christ's Control* (Grand Rapids, MI: Revell, 2013), 35.

places where he knew it was better to be single, he told Elisabeth that even though she was the only one he could marry, they couldn't do it. Elisabeth describes the passion of her heart and how agonizing it was to give up the man of her dreams, but she found comfort in knowing that God had a perfect purpose. So she learned to wait.

Jim was called to take the Gospel to an unreached people group, the Aucas (Ow-cahz), who live in the eastern jungle of my country between the Napo and Curaray Rivers. The Aucas, now called the Waodani (Wah-o-dah-nee), were known to kill all outsiders, but Jim was focused on his calling. He told Elisabeth she had to learn Quichua (an indigenous language), which she did. Years passed before he proposed, and she lived in a different missionary station for quite a while until God confirmed it was the right time for them. They married in Quito, Ecuador, the city where I was born.[6]

The unity in their marriage as they pursued God's calling astounds me. Not every couple is called to give their lives for the lost in a literal sense, yet we know there is no greater love than when someone gives his life away for his friends (John 15:13). Almost three years of jungle ministry and hours of planning and praying led Jim and the Operation Auca missionary team to a pivotal moment. They set up camp near the Aucas' territory to make direct contact with them. After several days two Auca women walked out of the jungle. Jim and Pete excitedly jumped in the river and waded over to them, but as they got closer, they realized something was amiss. These women did not appear friendly. A terrifying cry erupted behind Jim and Pete, and they saw a group of Auca warriors with their spears raised.

Jim had a gun with him, but he never used it. Each of the missionaries in their group had promised not to kill an Auca who didn't know Jesus, even if it meant saving himself from death. Every missionary on the team died that day: Ed McCully, Roger Youderian, Nate Saint, Pete Fleming, and Jim Elliot.

If the story ended here, it would still be a remarkable history proclaiming the glory of God as seen in sacrifice. But the story didn't end here. A legacy waited. In a decision that would be unimaginable to most people, the wives and children of the murdered missionaries decided to continue the effort to reach the Auca people. And they were successful. Less than two years later, Elisabeth Elliot, her young daughter, and Rachel Saint (Nate's sister) moved into the Auca

---

6 Elliot, *Gates.*

village itself and helped care for them. They forged a friendship that continues to transform lives. Many Aucas have come to know Jesus, and they are now considered a friendly tribe. Missionaries, including Nate Saint's son and his family, still live among the Aucas today.

What a legacy! No one was able to reach this tribe in my country until these five missionaries and their wives came along and willingly gave away their lives because of their great love for God and for a people who didn't know Him. No one took their lives from them; they gave them as an offering of love.

This story is important for every couple to understand because it reveals what the power of marriage is like. God brings people together in marriage to impact those around them and leave a legacy on the earth. All of us are "missionaries" wherever we are. We are called to bring the good news of Jesus and manifest His love. Your marriage is part of this calling to spread the Gospel. You can ask God what kind of impact He wants your marriage to have. Many couples forget there is a bigger calling than just to stay together and make it through life. This bigger calling is to be aware of Christ in you, the hope of glory. Through a powerful marriage, you can touch other people by sharing the love and good news of Jesus everywhere you go. You are a light that carries His light.

"You are the light of the world. A town built on a hill cannot be hidden. Neither do people light a lamp and put it under a bowl. Instead they put it on its stand, and it gives light to everyone in the house."
— *Matthew 5:14–15*

Discussion Questions:

1. What does favor mean to you? In your own words, how does God show people His favor?

2. Share a story where you clearly saw God's favor in your life.

3. Have you thought about the kind of legacy you want to leave behind? Describe it.

4. What is the greatest legacy a person could have?

Prayer:

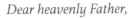

Dear heavenly Father,

Please show me Your favor. Thank You for Your great love, mercy, and protection. Teach me how to pray for the legacy You want me to have, and show my future spouse and me what Your mission is for us as a couple. Show us how to love You with all our hearts, minds, and strength. Help us to know how to love others. Give us a pure love and help us to live out a legacy of love.

Chapter
16

THE POWER OF TRANSFORMATION

How God Can Use Your Marriage to Impact the World

You have the opportunity to impact the world through your marriage.

As you've read this book, I hope you've come to understand more about marriage, preparing yourself for your wedding day and, if applicable right now, growing together with your partner. The ceremony is only the beginning of a life-changing journey. As you move past the wedding and into everyday family life, understand the Lord has great things in store for you. Transformation is the greatest purpose of your marriage. When we allow God to transform us as people, we naturally grow in our marriages, which is a huge benefit, yet the transformation doesn't stop there. The Lord then uses our marriages to transform those around us. Couples who are dedicated to growing their marriages can impact the lives of friends and even acquaintances. When we have willing hearts and a unity of purpose, the Holy Spirit can empower us to help others transform.

Whether you are engaged, married, or single, the process of transformation can start now. Do you want to be spiritually transformed, allowing God to transform your marriage so you can help others transform their lives?

One transformational couple is Vinicio and Melania García. They have been married for just five short years, but their hearts are committed to loving God, each other, and the lost. Their transformational moment came when they'd been married for less than a year. Focused on God's purposes in Ecuador, they were working with a juvenile hall ministry and bringing women out of sex trafficking and prostitution. On the outside Vinicio and Melania were enjoying a vibrant marriage and effective ministry, but they were struggling with communication and compatibility issues. They'd fallen in love with each other and with their mission, but they were having a hard time getting along.

"We were both thirty years old, and we each had such a different way of thinking and doing things. We were opposites in a lot of ways. That first year was tough. It's crazy to say, but we felt like giving up and divorcing," Vinicio told me. One afternoon they sat and talked about the state of their marriage, and both of them felt led to seek the Lord in prayer, surrendering their hopes and struggles to Him. Out of the deepest parts of their hearts, they asked the Lord for help, and He revealed to them how to move past their differences and follow a new path based on unconditional love. He gave them two verses from 1 Corinthians 13:

> *If I have the gift of prophecy and can fathom all mysteries and all knowledge, and if I have a faith that can move mountains, but do not have love, I am nothing. If I give all I possess to the poor and give over my body to hardship that I may boast, but do not have love, I gain nothing.*
> — *1 Corinthians 13:2–3*

That afternoon they discovered a new love that doesn't give up and isn't selfish. They sensed God telling them true love is about sacrifice. As He deposited within them a revelation about how to love each other in a way they never had, their lives and marriage were transformed. Equipped with a deeper understanding of God's love, they began to understand how to change and strengthen the vision of their ministry and reach the lost more effectively.

When the Lord gave them an unconditional love for each other, their transformation began to affect the lives of the people around them. Melania became the director and founder of Casa Mis Sueños, a nonprofit foundation that seeks restoration, education, and empowerment of youth and women at risk in Quito. Vinicio serves as the communications director, and he is also in charge of worship for the foundation.

"Our mission is to do what Jesus would do," Vinicio says. "Love genuinely and be the voice of those that can't speak with freedom. We are an option to a generation that has gotten completely degenerated."

God began to expand their work in Quito. They are now in charge of seven different projects and have forty trained volunteers who support the poor. One particular project takes women off the streets and trains them for jobs.

Along with the power of the Holy Spirit, our willingness is the key to transformation. When the Holy Spirit empowers us and directs our steps, doors begin to open and His Kingdom expands. Transformation starts in you and through you and continues when you get married. As you let God be the center and foundation of your marriage, it impacts the world around you.

A Willing Heart

Author and evangelist Dr. Ed Silvoso knows about transformation. He is the founder of Harvest Evangelism and also Transform Our World Network, the objective of which is to end worldwide poverty. In his book

> *Transformation starts in you and through you and continues when you get married. As you let God be the center and foundation of your marriage, it impacts the world around you.*

Transformation: Change the Marketplace and You Change the World, he writes:

> Something extraordinary is going on all over the world. Ordinary people are doing extraordinary things that are radically transforming schools, companies, prisons, cities, and even nations. Today millions of men and women are walking out their call to full-time ministry in the marketplace.

Ed goes on to describe how transformation takes place: "This is the real transformation taking place in real time as the result of a singular discovery: that God passionately cares—not just for people but also for the marketplace and for cities and nations."[1]

To understand how Ed came to this conclusion and experienced transformation himself, we need to take a look at his spiritual journey and his relationship with his wife. Growing up in Argentina, Ed received the Lord when he was thirteen years old. He was the first and only born-again Christian high schooler in a city of a hundred twenty thousand. In spite of small victories and leading many people to Christ, Ed begged God for revival. He longed to see mass conversions. His question was, "Why not, Lord? Why not here in Argentina?"

Not long after Ed graduated from high school, he was drafted into the army. From there he went into hospital administration, and during his second year at this job, he married Ruth. In his book *Women: God's Secret Weapon*, he writes, "She touched my heart like nothing else ever had. I knew a river of love existed, but I

---

1 Ed Silvoso, *Transformation: Change the Marketplace and You Change the World* (Grand Rapids, MI: Chosen Books, 2010).

was totally unaware of how powerful it was until it invaded my soul. That day my life changed forever."[2]

Their courtship is a sweet story that began when Ed was still a teenager. In his own words, he made a deal with God. "I told Him that I did not want to date a series of girls to find out which one I should marry. Instead, I was determined to wait for Him to tell me when the right one came along. It was not easy, but I kept my promise."

God honored his heart, and a couple of years later, a friend showed Ed a picture of a family with several girls in it. Ed felt the Lord saying that the girl in the lower right corner was the one for him. Ed reached for a magnifying glass and, looking at the girl more carefully, told God He had excellent taste.

At the same time Ed was looking at a picture of Ruth, Ruth was handed a picture of Ed's youth group. In the same way, she heard God say to her, "The tall guy in the black leather jacket—he is the one I have for you."

They met in Ed's hometown at a church meeting Ruth attended when her family stopped on their way to her sister's wedding in Buenos Aires. The way Ed tells it, he was so excited to meet her that he tripped right in front of her on their first visit. That was the first day of a long courtship that resulted in their marriage.

As much as he enjoyed his job as a hospital administrator, his greatest joy came after work when he would rush home, eat a quick dinner, and drive with Ruth to evangelistic meetings. They both relished the experience of sharing their faith with non-Christians. Their passion and longing for God's Kingdom to come in their city was so strong that they eventually left their professions and went into full-time ministry. In the 1970s they started doing street evangelism. Later they shared the Gospel message through radio and eventually pioneered the first Argentinian Christian television program.

Then much to their shock, Ed was diagnosed with an incurable disease called myasthenia gravis, which is similar to Lou Gehrig's disease. The doctors at Stanford Medical Center in Palo Alto, California, gave Ed a maximum of two years to live.

2 Ed Silvoso, *Women: God's Secret Weapon: God's Inspiring Message to Women of Power, Purpose and Destiny* (Grand Rapids, MI: Chosen Books, 2010).

"My muscles were weakening, my speech was slurred, and I suffered from double-vision and shortness of breath," Ed said. During his treatment, he took forty-two pills every day and had cortisone and chemotherapy treatments. Once or twice a week he was hooked to a machine that performed a plasmapheresis, a process in which his plasma was separated from the cells. The most discouraging fact to accept was that none of these procedures was capable of providing a cure. They were done to keep Ed alive.

Through this experience God taught Ed many powerful lessons about transformation. One lesson was that two are stronger than one. Ed didn't face the illness alone; Ruth not only encouraged him with words and lots of prayer, but she assisted him with the daily treatments. The Lord also taught Ed about faith. The vision for Argentina's salvation wouldn't leave Ed's heart. God placed within him a deep desire to see revival in his country. Although Ed was weak physically, he and Ruth pushed forward with their dream to reach Argentina with the Gospel. On August 30, 1980, Harvest Evangelism was officially and legally born, and in 1983 they dedicated a retreat center in Ed's native city of San Nicolás. They challenged the pastors and leaders of the surrounding areas to reach each one of the 109 unchurched towns with the Gospel.

Meanwhile, Ed's health only worsened. Although the combination of prayer and medical treatment had stretched the initial prognosis from two to four years, he was barely hanging on.

The spiritual darkness over Argentina began to lift. Several revival meetings were held and reports of mass conversions surfaced. In Mar Del Plata close to ninety thousand decisions for Christ were reported, and in San Justo almost seventy thousand people publicly repeated the sinner's prayer. From then on, decisions for Christ began to come in like a flood. As Argentina started to turn to the Lord, Ed's symptoms became milder and his need for medication became less. Pastors and leaders within Argentina began to ask for his training.

"All of a sudden, our dreams, modestly started at the retreat center in San Nicolás, began to materialize on a national scale," Ed said. "Requests for help began to come in from all over the nation." He called their model for transformation prayer evangelism; it's a lifestyle of Christian witness based on Jesus' teaching to His disciples in Luke 10:1–9. Ed says that *prayer evangelism* starts by "talking to God about our neighbors before we talk to our neighbors about God."

One of my biggest takeaways from Ed's story is how faithful he and his wife are as a couple. Their marriage has always been solid. Through the good moments and the bad, Ruth supported her husband and contributed to the revival in Argentina, and the impact of their work is amazing to me. Imagine seeing a whole city lifted out of spiritual darkness. Ed's books, teachings, and mentorship have impacted people, churches, and nations all over the world. In addition, his testimony about being healed from myasthenia gravis has inspired thousands. Ed and Ruth are also passionate about each other and family. As Ruth says in her book *Food, Family & Fun,* "The Lord brought us together for a marriage made in heaven."[3] They have four daughters—Karina, Marilyn, Evelyn, and Jesica, who are all happily married—and twelve beautiful grandchildren.

When I look deeper into Ed and Ruth's story, I see a happily married couple God has empowered to do great things. At one level it is the strength of their marriage that has made their impact on the world possible. God uses their daily love and commitment to Him and each other to bring not just a transformational teaching to many people and nations but a lifestyle that is focused on God and growing His Kingdom.

Living a Transformational Life Every Day

Another transformational couple is Dave and Sue Thompson. Dave is Ed's right-hand man and works as the senior vice president at Harvest Evangelism. Dave and Sue joined Ed and Ruth from the United States to become Harvest Evangelism's first overseas missionaries in 1984. The Thompsons were instrumental in leading the revival in Resistencia, Argentina, in the late 1980s, and today in their mission to transform the globe, they give assistance and guidance to leaders of more than three hundred developing cities and nations. They are a transformational couple because of how they've demonstrated the principles of prayer evangelism. As Dave puts it, "We believe the plan of God is precisely to use marriages and families to change the world."

The Thompsons are not only effective missionaries, but they also value family. They have been married for fifty years and have four children and ten grandchildren. Dave and Sue understand that God can use their marriage and their example of effective parenting in reaching others for Christ. When I asked

---

3 Ruth Palau Silvoso, *Food, Family & Fun: A Glimpse into Our Family's Table, Traditions & Travels* (Santa Clara, CA: Transform Our World, 2016).

them about their love story, they told me they were very young when they first met. Sue was just eleven years old. Dave says that Sue, "the girl from Randolph, New York," was always on his mind after meeting her for the first time at summer camp. They were fifteen when they attended a regional Youth for Christ camp, and Dave made sure he caught her just before she stepped on the bus for the ride home. That was when they agreed to send each other Christmas cards. They started corresponding back and forth until he visited her on her sixteenth birthday with a nice bottle of perfume as a gift. They managed to see each other once a month, and sometimes he had to get up and take the train at 4:30 a.m. to visit her. They courted for several years and spent time in the presence of family and peers. When they were about to go to college, Dave heard God say to him, "Don't you dare let that girl out of your sight." He gladly obeyed and they both went to Moody Bible Institute, where their relationship deepened.

Dave told me, "I began asking her if she would marry me. She kept putting me off with non-committal answers. Still, I kept posing the question, knowing that she was not ready to agree."

One day in the fall of 1964, Dave posed the question again, and Sue's reply totally took him off guard: "Yes, I will marry you!"

Dave blinked, gulped, and looked at her wide eyed. He blurted, "Wow! What do I do now?"

To which she calmly replied, "I don't know, my love. You'll have to figure that one out."

They married a week after their college graduation and set themselves on the lifelong journey to "figure it out." Dave told me, "In 1985 the Lord took us and our little clan of four kids to Argentina as the first missionaries with Dr. Ed Silvoso and Harvest Evangelism. That move took a lot of prayer, and soon we were 'figuring it out' in a different language! Prayer became the main event, and soon we discovered it was the foundational component of all things transformational. Our first assignment was to identify and pray for all the towns and villages within a hundred-mile radius of San Nicolás that had not yet been evangelized. There were 109 of those towns. It did not take long before those towns began to receive the Gospel."

Dave described the subsequent revival this way: "Once empowered by seeing these answers to prayer, we did not shy away from leading our team to Resistencia—a city of 400,000 people and less than 6000 believers attending 70 congregations on a given Sunday. We began to apply prayer—in fact, we called it 'prayer evangelism'—talking to God about our neighbors before we talk to our neighbors about God. We literally filled the city with prayer by enlisting families to pray for their 'barrios' right where they lived. It was amazing! It was like the spiritual climate over the city began to change for the better, which was exactly what was happening. The Lord's power and presence were being put on display throughout the city by means of prayer."

According to Dave, revival is still taking place in Argentina. "Today, by the grace of God, there are over 100,000 believers in the city and over 500 congregations. One congregation alone has over 12,000 members. The pastor was a young leader during the days we were directing 'Plan Resistencia.' Not only has there been a spiritual change, there has been a physical renaissance taking place over the years as righteousness, joy, and peace have come in increasing waves to the city. Resistencia became the launching pad for transformation in cities and regions around the globe, because it put transformation on display as being doable. Can we take credit for it? By no means. Many others were involved. Could it have happened without us? We don't know. All we know is that what took place took place with us on the playing field. And if God can use the Thompson family, God can use your family!"

God has used transformational couples throughout history, many of them going unnoticed to our eyes, but they had a powerful effect on the world. God is calling married couples to get in tune with what He wants to do through them. As you become the one, understand you and your spouse are powerful. And if you are willing, God can use you to change the world.

Marriage was the first institution God set up on the earth. He wanted to empower Adam and Eve to have a marriage that would allow their future generations to enjoy a peaceful, loving world in which everyone lived in personal communion with God Almighty. When sin entered the world through their disobedience, God provided a plan to get all of us back to that personal communion with Him. He sent His Son, Jesus, to die for our sins and resurrect in victory so we could have what God wanted for us in the first place. Out of all the different points in the universe, God chose this planet to be humanity's dwelling place, and He plans for it to go back to what He always desired it to be—a peaceful and loving earth where He is welcome to live among us. The apostle Paul says in Romans 8:19 that all creation waits in eager expectation for the children of God to be revealed.

The Holy Spirit is the transformational force that empowers us as individuals and couples to live the kind of lives God intends. It is only through the Holy Spirit that we can be transformational couples who bring the changes God's creation waits for. This is why we pray for revival and for souls to come to Christ; this is why we recognize that life can be different through Him. I am convinced that creation's growing pains (Romans 8:22) will stop when God's glory is revealed through married couples who go back to the place God intended for us—a place of authority in which our relationship with Him is so evident that present and future generations are blessed as we allow the Holy Spirit to do His loving and powerful work in and through us. Through strong, powerful, godly marriages, this world can once again become a good dwelling place. Therefore, it is vital we let the Holy Spirit prepare us before marriage and work through our marriages. We are called to be the source of change in this world that so desperately needs to know there is a loving God with great plans for His people.

True Transformation

Many think the greatest blessing in life is to find the right person and get married, and yes, there is some truth in that thought. However, a year or two after marriage we find our goals beginning to shift, and we start thinking the greatest blessing is to remain happy in marriage. We love our spouses, are loved by our spouses, have wonderful children, live good lives. Those things, too, are a part of what God wants for us. The Lord is a generous and loving Father, and He wants His children to be happy. Yet the journey of becoming the one is about something greater than our own goals. It's about a life of loving God and loving others with a pure love only His Spirit can give us. That is a transformational marriage and the heart of what the Lord wants for us.

"God's Kingdom on earth as it is in Heaven" is the prayer of every believer. If we receive His Kingdom when we ask Him to be our Lord and Savior, it follows that we get to share it with others. This is how a loving couple becomes co-laborers with Christ. It starts by becoming the one, continues as you build your marriage and start a family, and is complete when you see transformed lives around you.

May God bless you on this powerful journey of becoming the one.

Discussion Questions:

1. In your own words, what does it mean to be spiritually transformed?

2. Is spiritual transformation something you value in your life? If it is, how are you seeking spiritual transformation?

3. Which story in this chapter appealed to you the most and why?

4. How is God transforming you?

Prayer:

Dear heavenly Father,

You are the transformational power I need. Holy Spirit, please transform me to be more and more like Christ. Give me unconditional love so I can love You back and love others the way You want me to. Help me to be a person who loves You with all my heart, soul, and might. Please guide my future spouse in the same path of love so when we get married, You can use us to transform others and expand Your Kingdom.

Appendix

Finding Your True Identity

If you want to know who you are, you need to know what God says about you in His Word.

As Chris Hogan of Noble Call Institute Inc. teaches, every human being has four basic needs: safety, security, sufficiency, and significance. When these four core needs are met by God, we are on the path to having a truly noble identity.

The following chart is used with permission from Noble Call Institute Inc. and Relate 20/20. They provide a format in which you can discover your true identity statement based on God's Word. The process involves writing the meaning of your first and middle names, your rhema verse (a verse you feel God has been speaking to you), your life verse, and the name of a person you admire in Scripture. Your true identity statement reflects how each of the four core needs is met through God.

You finish your statement with what you would like to be known for—the legacy you want to leave behind, as well as the gifts God has given you to bless others.

Safety - Finished Work in Christ: MERCY

I find *safety* knowing *(circle one verse that speaks to your heart)*:

John 1:12   I am God's child.

John 15:15   I am Christ's friend.

Romans 5:1   I have been justified.

1 Corinthians 6:17   I am one with the Lord.

1 Corinthians 6:20   I have been bought with a price and belong to God.

1 Corinthians 12:27   I am a member of Christ's body.

Ephesians 1:1   I am a saint.

Ephesians 1:5   I have been adopted as God's child.

Ephesians 2:18   I have direct access to God through the Holy Spirit.

Colossians 1:14   I have been redeemed and forgiven of all my sins.

Colossians 2:10   I am complete in Christ.

Security - Who I Am in Christ: TRUTH

I find *security* knowing *(circle one verse that speaks to your heart)*:

Romans 8:1–2   I am free from condemnation.

Romans 8:28   I am assured that all things work together for good.

Romans 8:33–34   I am free from any condemning charges against me.

Romans 8:35   I cannot be separated from the love of God.

2 Corinthians 1:21–22   I have been established, anointed, and sealed by God.

Colossians 3:3   I am hidden with Christ in God.

Philippians 1:6   I am confident God will perfect what He has begun.

Philippians 3:20   I am a citizen of Heaven.

2 Timothy 1:7   I have been given power, love, and a sound mind.

Hebrews 4:16   I can find grace and mercy in time of need.

1 John 5:18   I am born of God and the evil one cannot touch me.

With permission from Noble Call Institute Inc. (www.noblecall.org) and Relate 20/20 (www.relate2020.com).

Meaning of My First Name & Verse:

Certain Christian name books give you the meaning of your name and include a Scripture verse to support it. Write both below.

Meaning of My Middle Name & Verse:

Who I Admire Most in the Bible and Why
(What qualities do you admire about them?)

With permission from Noble Call Institute Inc. (www.noblecall.org) and Relate 20/20 (www.relate2020.com).

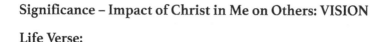

Significance – Impact of Christ in Me on Others: VISION

Life Verse:

Rhema Verse
(a verse the Holy Spirit has recently spoken directly into your heart):

I find *significance* knowing *(circle one verse that speaks to your heart):*

Matthew 5:13–14	I am the salt and light of the earth.
John 15:1,5	I am a branch of the true vine, a channel of life.
John 15:16	I have been chosen and appointed to bear fruit.
Acts 1:8	I am a personal witness of Christ.
1 Corinthians 3:16	I am God's temple.
2 Corinthians 5:17–20	I am a minister of reconciliation.
2 Corinthians 6:1	I am God's co-worker.
Ephesians 2:6	I am seated with Christ in the heavenly realm.
Ephesians 2:10	I am God's workmanship.
Ephesians 3:12	I may approach God with freedom and confidence.

Funeral Statement
(what you would like others to say about you):

With permission from Noble Call Institute Inc. (www.noblecall.org) and Relate 20/20 (www.relate2020.com).

Sufficiency – Power of Christ Through Me: STRENGTH

My God-given Gifts, Talents, and Strengths

Romans 12:6–8 (NASB): Since we have gifts that differ according to the grace given to us, each of us is to exercise them accordingly: if prophecy, according to the proportion of his faith; if service, in his serving; or he who teaches, in his teaching; or he who exhorts, in his exhortation; he who gives, with liberality; he who leads, with diligence; he who shows mercy, with cheerfulness.

1 Corinthians 12:8–11 (NASB): For to one is given the word of wisdom through the Spirit, and to another the word of knowledge according to the same Spirit; to another faith by the same Spirit, and to another gifts of healing by the one Spirit, and to another the effecting of miracles, and to another prophecy, and to another the distinguishing of spirits, to another various kinds of tongues, and to another the interpretation of tongues. But one and the same Spirit works all these things, distributing to each one individually just as He wills.

I find *sufficiency* knowing   *(circle one verse that speaks to your heart):*

Luke 22:32   I can strengthen others through my failures.

Romans 8:37   I am more than a conqueror through Christ.

2 Corinthians 3:5   I am competent in Christ.

2 Corinthians 12:9   I am sufficient through Christ.

2 Corinthians 12:9   His strength is made perfect in my weakness.

Philippians 4:13   I can do all things through Christ.

1 John 4:4   Greater is He who is in us.

With permission from Noble Call Institute Inc. (www.noblecall.org) and Relate 20/20 (www.relate2020.com).

Finding your True Identity Statement

Write a short paragraph by combining the statements you completed in the chart. Begin with the first statement in the Safety section ("I find safety knowing _____"). When you are finished, speak your identity statement out loud as a prayer to God and renew your mind concerning who you are in Christ.

Here is an example of a true identity statement written according to this format:

Name: Leon Albert

I'm courageous, bold as a lion, and a righteous man of honor. I'm safe in the knowledge that God loves me unconditionally, and I am secure in knowing that all that is in the world is His and under His control. I find significance knowing that when I do something well, it is a reflection of my dedication to the Lord. I know deep in my heart that God is providing all that I need for life, love, and happiness. Just like Joseph, I am persistent, optimistic, and determined to recover all. I trust the Lord in that all the plans He has for me are good, and He will always deliver me.

I am smart, wise, discerning, and a man of integrity devoted to the Lord. I understand that all things work together for good for me because I love God and am called according to His purpose. I trust the Lord my God with all my heart and lean not on my own understanding. As I acknowledge Him in all my ways, He makes my paths straight. I am kind, generous, fun, loving, and always willing to help a friend in need. I am a loving husband and father, pursuing God's character as a model for my family. Everything I do in life shows that I love God with all my heart, and I proclaim His goodness and love to all those I encounter and rejoice in their coming to know Him. I am a practical leader and friendly teacher, generous, merciful, and witty, and I demonstrate those gifts in dealing with people and their finances.

For more information about how to write your true identity statement, visit noblecall.org or relate20/20.com. They can answer your questions, and they also offer workshops covering this material.

With permission from Noble Call Institute Inc. (www.noblecall.org) and Relate 20/20 (www.relate2020.com).

Bibliography

Chapter 2

Cohn, D'vera. *"Love and Marriage."* Pew Research Center: February 13, 2013. http://www.pewsocialtrends.org/2013/02/13/love-and-marriage.

Silk, Danny. *Keep Your Love On*. Redding, CA: Red Arrow Publishing, 2013.

Chapter 3

Busby, Dean M., Carroll, Jason S., and Willoughby, Brian J. "Compatibility or Restraint? The Effects of Sexual Timing on Marriage Relationships." *Journal of Family Psychology* 24, no. 6 (December 2010): 766–774. http://psycnet.apa.org/doiLanding?doi=10.1037%2Fa0021690.

Centers for Disease Control and Prevention. "Sexual Risk Behaviors: HIV, STD, & Teen Pregnancy Prevention." Accessed August 28, 2017. https://www.cdc.gov/healthyyouth/sexualbehaviors.

Donovan, Chuck. "A Marshall Plan for Marriage: Rebuilding Our Shattered Homes." The Heritage Foundation: June 10, 2011. http://www.heritage.org/marriage-and-family/commentary/marshall-plan-marriage-rebuilding-our-shattered-homes.

Feldhahn, Shaunti. *The Good News About Marriage: Debunking Discouraging Myths About Marriage and Divorce*. Colorado Springs: Multnomah, 2014.

The Henry J. Kaiser Family Foundation. "Sexual Health of Adolescents and Young Adults in the United States." August 20, 2014. www.kff.org/womens-health-policy/fact-sheet/sexual-health-of-adolescents-and-young-adults-in-the-united-states.

Jay, Meg. "The Downside of Cohabiting Before Marriage." *New York Times*: April 14, 2012. http://www.nytimes.com/2012/04/15/opinion/sunday/the-downside-of-cohabiting-before-marriage.html.

Jozkowski, Kristen. "How Often Do We Think About Sex?...Results from a New Study." Kinsey Confidential: January 12, 2012. https://kinseyconfidential.org/sexresults-study.

Rhoades, Galena K., and Stanley, Scott M. "Before 'I Do.'" The National Marriage Project at the University of Virginia. Accessed August 28, 2017. http://before-i-do.org.

Rhoades, Galena K., Stanley, Scott M., and Markman, Howard J. "Working with Cohabitation in Relationship Education and Therapy." *Journal of Couple & Relationship Therapy* 8, no. 2 (May 2009): 95–112. https://www.ncbi.nlm.nih.gov/pmc/articles/PMC2897720.

Pew Research Center. "The Decline of Marriage and Rise of New Families." November 18, 2010. http://www.pewsocialtrends.org/2010/11/18/the-decline-of-marriage-and-rise-of-new-families/2/#ii-overview.

Waite, Linda J., and Gallagher, Maggie. *The Case for Marriage: Why Married People Are Happier, Healthier, and Better Off Financially*. New York: Broadway Books, 2002.

Chapter 4

Canelos, Cristian. "La Situación de la Mujer en la Iglesia del Siglo XXI." In *Biblia, Teología y Ministerios en Contextos*, edited by Ángel Manzo. Guayaquil, Ecuador: Publicaciones Seminario Bíblico Alianza del Ecuador, 2016.

Rainey, Dennis, and Rainey, Barbara. *Starting Your Marriage Right: What You Need to Know in the Early Years to Make It Last a Lifetime*. Nashville: Thomas Nelson, 2006.

Chapter 5

Vallotton, Kris, and Vallotton, Jason. *Moral Revolution: The Naked Truth About Sexual Purity*. Grand Rapids, MI: Chosen Books, 2012.

Chapter 7

Chen, Zhansheng, Williams, Kipling D., Fitness, Julie, and Newton, Nicola C. "When Hurt Will Not Heal: Exploring the Capacity to Relive Social and Physical Pain." Psychological Science 19, no. 8 (August 2008): 789–795. https://www.researchgate.net/publication/23282492_When_Hurt_Will_Not_Heal_Exploring_the_Capacity_to_Relive_Social_and_Physical_Pain.

Hegstrom, Paul. "Wounds." Life Skills International. http://www.lifeskillsintl.org/Articles/Words_from_Paul/Wounds.html.

Jantz, Gregory L., and McMurray, Ann. *Healing the Scars of Emotional Abuse.* Grand Rapids, MI: Revel, 2009.

Chapter 8

Locke, John. *An Essay Concerning Human Understanding*, 1689.

Chapter 9

Augsburger, David. *Sustaining Love*. Ventura, CA: Regal Books, 1988.

Costa Jr., Paul T., Terracciano, Antonio, and McCrae, Robert R. "Gender Differences in Personality Traits Across Cultures: Robust and Surprising Findings." *Journal of Personality and Social Psychology* 81, no. 2 (2001): 322–331. http://www.cin.ufpe.br/~ssj/Genderdifferences%20in%20personality%20traits%20across%20cultures%20Robust%20andsurprising%20findings.pdf.

Gungor, Mark. "Laugh Your Way to a Better Marriage" (lecture). https://vimeo.com/77545336.

Hybels, Bill, and Hybels, Lynne. *Fit to Be Tied: Making Marriage Last a Lifetime.* Grand Rapids, MI: Zondervan, 1993.

Murphy, Caryle. "Interfaith Marriage Is Common in U.S., Particularly Among the Recently Wed." Pew Research Center. June 2, 2015. http://www.pewresearch.org/fact-tank/2015/06/02/interfaith-marriage.

Orbuch, Terri L. "What Keeps Marriages Together? It Depends on Your Gender!" *Hitched*. http://www.hitchedmag.com/article.php?id=1703.

Chapter 10

Edwards, Scott. "Love and the Brain." On the Brain: *The Harvard Mahoney Neuroscience Institute Letter*. Accessed August 28, 2017. http://neuro.hms.harvard.edu/harvard-mahoney-neuroscience-institute/brain-newsletter/and-brain-series/love-and-brain.

Larson, Jeffry H. *The Great Marriage Tune-Up Book: A Proven Program for Evaluating and Renewing Your Relationship*. San Francisco: Jossey-Bass, 2002.

Sexual Assault Support Centre of Waterloo Region. "Signs of Healthy/Unhealthy Boundaries – Blueprint for a New Life Style." Accessed August 28, 2017. http://www.sascwr.org/files/www/resources_pdfs/incest/Signs_of_healthyunhealthy_boundaries.pdf.

Chapter 12

Silk, Danny. *Keep Your Love On*. Redding, CA: Red Arrow Publishing, 2013.

Chapter 13

Chapman, Gary. *The Five Love Languages: The Secret to Love That Lasts*. Chicago: Northfield Publishing, 2014.

Feldhahn, Shaunti. *The Surprising Secrets of Highly Happy Marriages: The Little Things That Make a Big Difference*. Colorado Springs: Multnomah, 2013.

Lee, Spike W.S., and Schwarz, Norbert. "Framing Love: When It Hurts to Think We Were Made for Each Other." *Journal of Experimental Social Psychology* 54 (September 2014): 61–67. http://www.sciencedirect.com/science/article/pii/S0022103114000493.

Chapter 14

Orbuch, Terri L. *5 Simple Steps to Take Your Marriage from Good to Great*. Austin, TX: River Grove Books, 2015.

Smalley, Gary. *The DNA of Relationships*. Carol Stream, IL: Tyndale House Publishers, 2004.

Chapter 15

Elliot, Elisabeth. *Passion and Purity: Learning to Bring Your Love Life Under Christ's Control*. Grand Rapids, MI: Revell, 2013.

Elliot, Elisabeth. *Through Gates of Splendor*. Carol Stream, IL: Tyndale Momentum, 1981.

Chapter 16

Silvoso, Ed. *Transformation: Change the Marketplace and You Change the World*. Grand Rapids, MI: Chosen Books, 2010.

Silvoso, Ed. *Women: God's Secret Weapon: God's Inspiring Message to Women of Power, Purpose and Destiny*. Grand Rapids, MI: Chosen Books, 2010.

Silvoso, Ruth Palau. *Food, Family & Fun: A Glimpse into Our Family's Table, Traditions & Travels*. Santa Clara, CA: Transform Our World, 2016.

Made in USA - Kendallville, IN
46382_9780692972113
02.09.2023 1320